EDWARD BULWER-LYTTON

ALLAN CONRAD CHRISTENSEN

Edward Bulwer-Lytton

The Fiction of New Regions

Long since, in searching for
new regions in the Art to
which I am a servant, it
seemed to me that they might
be found lying far, and rarely
trodden, beyond that range
of conventional morality, in
which Novelist after Nov-
elist had entrenched himself.

THE UNIVERSITY OF GEORGIA PRESS
ATHENS

Library of Congress Catalog Card Number: 74–27550
International Standard Book Number: 0–8203–0387–9

The University of Georgia Press, Athens 30602

Set in 11 on 14 pt. Monticello type
Printed in the United States of America

Til minne om

Mor

som tok imot innbydelsen

"Kom til mig, alle I som strever og har
tungt å bære, og jeg vil gi eder hvile!"

Contents

Preface

The fiction of Bulwer is not, according to the generally prevailing critical view, fairly judged by purely literary standards. Critics who apply such standards "do Bulwer injustice," maintains Michael Sadleir in his uncompleted biography of 1931, "by doing him more than justice. They ignore one element in his novel-writing which was seldom wholly absent . . .—the opportunist element of giving the public what it wanted." Indeed few recent critics of Bulwer have ignored this allegedly fundamental aspect of his craftsmanship. Ernest Baker emphasizes the "alert opportunism" and the "versatility" that enabled him to heed "the beck and call of opinion and the popular whims and fancies." Bulwer's experimentation with so many varieties of fiction has thus redounded to his dishonor: "Unlike the great novelists," says Walter Allen, "who have usually been concerned with the examination and exploration of the moral implications of, in Conrad's phrase, 'a few simple ideas,' and have accordingly been content to plough a single furrow, narrow but also deep, Lytton pursued at least four very different lines of fiction. His was an ambitious, restless talent, but that of the popularizer rather than that of the creator." From such an impression it has naturally followed that Bulwer's fiction can remain interesting to us only as an accurate historical index or reflector of the tastes of the last century. While tending not to find any special significance in his career as a whole, critics have studied individual novels in terms of their relationship to various popular schools—in particular, the silver-fork, apprenticeship, Newgate, historical, colonial, occult, and satirically utopian types of fiction.

Without wishing to deny the historical usefulness of such studies, I find it nevertheless fortunate that at least a few voices have raised objections to the prevailing view of Bulwer as opportunistic popularizer. Michael Lloyd, for example, has discovered—though he dislikes the result—that even the popular *Last Days of Pompeii* may have issued from its author's loyalty to a very personal theory of ideal art. In a few intriguing pages Jack Lindsay seems to go further as he emphasizes the degree to which Bulwer has caught his inspiration from deeply private and practically demonic sources. Above other Victorians, hints Lindsay, Bulwer may have inherited the aesthetic theories of the great Romantics and have committed himself to the sort of inward-looking vision characteristic of the French Symbolists. Joseph I. Fradin then appears to validate some of Lindsay's notions: his impressive analysis of *A Strange Story* reveals Bulwer locating reality within the human psyche while attempting valiantly to attack the insidiousness of philosophical materialism. A fascinating and still more erudite monograph by Robert Lee Wolff extends the analysis to other novels as well and demonstrates the surprising learnedness and adventurousness of Bulwer's explorations into esoteric and occult traditions. So devoted was Bulwer to his private studies and speculations that one can, as Edwin M. Eigner has in fact argued, characterize only three of his novels as principally directed toward the vulgar public. Only in the three Caxton novels, believes Eigner, did he sacrifice some of the integrity of his own aesthetic theories and philosophical ideas; otherwise his novels tended to set rather than to follow fashions.

This book represents an effort—primarily implicit—to enlarge upon the insights of these last critics and to establish a view of Bulwer as dedicated artist rather than facile opportunist. For even in his own day the fiction of Bulwer seems to have made its appeal not only to the vast novel-reading public but also to other writers and intellectuals who respected Bulwer's noble commitment to his calling. Such figures as Goethe, Carlyle, Mill, Harriet Martineau, Macaulay, Dickens, Poe, and Arnold all paid tribute at various times to the serious artistry and intellectual vigor they discerned beneath the surface of his works. The seemingly self-conscious mannerisms of that surface tended, to be sure, to displease them, and these mannerisms have probably been chiefly responsible for Bulwer's declining reputation. Yet as Conrad has suggested in a passage often quoted from *The Nigger of the Narcissus*, Bulwer's "polished and so curiously insincere sentences" and "elegant verbiage" cannot fully stifle the mysterious power and vitality of his underlying vision. One may even perceive some evidence of that continuing vitality in the fact that Bulwer "somehow . . . managed to appropriate more space . . . than was intended" in Ernest Baker's unsympathetic summary of his career.

Bulwer repays study, I believe, when one forgives him—as one now tends to varying patronizing degrees to forgive other Victorians—for the tendency toward a bombastic rhetoric. What Baker terms the "immense amount of word-spinning," "so-called 'metaphysics,'" and "discursive casuistry" may not, in fact, be quite so bombastic or gratuitous as impatient readers have assumed. Nor are what Allen refers to as Bulwer's attempts "at a bastard poetry" so illegitimate after all. For close to the heart of the novels and romances does lie a genuinely metaphysical conception, and Bulwer's vision is, as Lindsay implies, an authentically and fundamentally poetic one. Without really meaning, then, to suggest approval of Bulwer's often inflated prose style, I wish in the ensuing chapters to overlook the mannerisms and to concentrate on the metaphysics and poetics of the overall fictional structure. To belabor once more the point that Bulwer's style has its flaws has in any case become unnecessary.

At the significant heart of the novels lies a conception of the lasting verities of human life. Bulwer always attempted, as the preface to the first edition of *Pompeii* states it, "a just representation of the human passions and the human heart, whose elements in all ages are the same." Embodying those elements in forms that are to varying degrees allegorical or archetypal, the novels constitute symbolic treatments of what Bulwer considered the ideal or what we might term the mythic dimensions of man's earthly experience. As he thereby sought constantly to treat "the development of the

secret man," he also believed he was creating his own spiritual autobiography, which might, as a symbolic biography of Man, remain
valid for all times. Like Devereux, the supposed autobiographer of
his fourth novel, he even expected succeeding centuries to appreciate him more fully than his own age. So far was he from wanting
merely to placate "the popular whims and fancies" of the transient
moment. (Even the "popular" Caxton novels, as I shall have occasion to argue, fit into this pattern and do not evince the sacrifice
of aesthetic integrity that Eigner has seen in them.)

When approached in terms of their underlying mythic conception, the individual works may thus seem to be far more artistically
and intellectually stimulating than most criticism has indicated.
Still more significant, though, may be the degree to which the individual novels and romances help to inform each other as the portions of a coherent, unified oeuvre. For the often-noted versatility
and variousness of Bulwer's forays into different types of fiction are
to some extent more apparent than real; each stage carries forward
the development of the same "secret man." Throughout all his experimentation he was seeking, in Conrad's words, better forms in
which to render dramatically the same "few simple ideas," and he
was actually ploughing, as Allen believes the great novelist must,
his own "single furrow, narrow but also deep."

Not that Bulwer belongs in the ranks of the very great novelists:
although some of his novels—notably *Zanoni* and *What Will He
Do with It?*—are extraordinarily impressive and successful, he
never did find a form entirely adequate to his "few simple ideas."
Indeed his own awareness of the discrepancy between his underlying conceptions and the awkwardnesses that marred what he
called his "execution" always caused him to chafe. Yet beyond most
less-than-great artists Bulwer seems to demand assessment on the
basis of the grandeur of his unrealized intentions. His critical pronouncements keep urging the need to overlook the details and
blemishes of the visible portions of a work in the effort to intuit the

grandly simple idea in the artist's mind. And while evidently taking, like Browning's Rabbi Ben Ezra, comfort in "What [he] aspired to be, / And was not," he has managed to communicate more than an inkling of what those high aspirations were. Above all he has communicated both the intense vitality of his belief in the lasting value of his own inner life and something of the nature of the invisible conflicts wherein he discerned the ideal pattern of any human identity.

These remarks suggest that I am trying to rehabilitate Bulwer less as the historically interesting Victorian than as the man whose essential humanity the oeuvre may finally convey. I wish, however, to do both because an appreciation of the quality of Bulwer's individual humanity may help in a more profound sense than has been realized to suggest the humanity of his generation. Even when feeling himself most alienated, he was deeply involved in his age. The way in which his Romantic idealism sought, for example, to assimilate Benthamism and later reacted against Darwinian and Marxist theories enables us to understand the complicated Victorian zeitgeist more completely. And the parallels between the development of his own secret man and those of poets such as Tennyson may indicate how the specifically poetic sensibility becomes relevant to the Victorian novel more generally. Yet the principal historical lesson of Bulwer's career may concern the irreconcilable hostility of an increasingly materialistic and empirical age to the individual committed to the integrity and vitality of ideals. For such an inheritor of the Romantic faith as Bulwer, no comfortable or opportunistic concession to the aesthetic "whims and fancies" or to the intellectual vagaries of the day was ultimately possible. The apparent reconciliation suggested by the Caxton novels in the 1850's proved to be simply the prelude to his recognition that the artist could not after all find his aesthetic fulfillment or the man his salvation amidst the materials of Victorian England. Or put more starkly, the case of Bulwer contributes its share to the definition of the crisis that still seems to be threatening the human spirit with extinction.

Despite the obvious relevance of Bulwer's essentially lonely quest to those of other Victorians, though, I have reserved for my afterword the effort to develop the connections in explicit detail. My primary purpose remains that of demonstrating the coherence of the fictional works of Bulwer in terms of the particular aesthetic theories and ideas that underlie them. In the interests of concision I have also attempted to keep the retailing of biographical and other historical facts to the minimum. The important features of the story of Bulwer's life are, I believe, sufficiently familiar. The facts are in any event readily available in the standard two-volume biography of 1913 by his grandson, in Sadleir's account of the early life, and in the grandson's useful, brief summary of 1948. Robert Blake and Sibylla Jane Flower have recently published short biographical sketches, and the latter is also preparing a new official biography.

My avoidance of the somewhat cumbersome appellation "Bulwer-Lytton" throughout the text of this study is in accord with an increasing tendency among Victorian scholars. For most of his life—the first forty years in fact—the man bore the simple surname "Bulwer." He was then "Bulwer-Lytton" for about twenty-two years and "Lord Lytton" for about seven.

I wish to acknowledge generous grants from the University of California Humanities Institute and from other university funds in support of my research. In response to my requests for advice, Jerome H. Buckley and my colleagues Ada Nisbet and Ronald E. Freeman have graciously offered many valuable suggestions. To G. B. Tennyson go heartfelt thanks not only for his careful reading of my manuscript at various stages of its development but also for the constant generosity of his help and encouragement. I am gratefully indebted to Edwin M. Eigner for an evaluation of this study as well as for permission to read the manuscript of his important, forthcoming book on "the metaphysical novel." Finally I should like to pay tribute to the memory of Pamela, Countess of Lytton, a most lovely and humane woman, who some years ago first kindled my interest in Edward Bulwer and his remarkable family.

A.C.C.

Rome

A Note on Citations and Editions

For the sake of brevity, references in the notes to works listed in the bibliography do not include all the standard bibliographical information. Where practicable, I have cited works—even in the first reference to them—by giving simply the name of the author or editor (or the title in the case of most of Bulwer's own works). In each case, I believe, sufficient information is conveyed to enable the reader easily to find the work in the bibliography.

Bulwer's various essays are not conveniently available in any standard edition. For passages taken from *The Student* or *Caxtoniana* I have cited the first collected editions of those essays (1835 and 1863 respectively), but in addition to page references my notes include the title of the relevant essay so that readers may locate them in other editions too. References to essays not belonging to these two collections are to the periodical in which the particular essay first appeared. Most of these uncollected essays, it will be found, were published in the *New Monthly Magazine* between 1830 and 1833, although the most important of them, "On Art in Fiction," first appeared in the *Monthly Chronicle* in 1838. In the case of *England and the English*, first published in 1833, I have used the edition of 1970 by Standish Meacham.

All references to *Pelham* are to the recent edition by Jerome J. McGann, who preserves the arrangement into three volumes and reprints with certain modifications the text of the second (1828) edition of that novel. For all of Bulwer's other novels and romances, my references are to the New Knebworth Edition. Like all of the important editions of Bulwer, however, this one is difficult to find, and so my citations do *not* give page numbers; my numbers refer instead to the part (or to the book or to the volume, depending upon how the particular novel is subdivided) and / or to the chapter.

Since my references to the novels and romances are given parenthetically in the text, I have also made use of a system of abbreviations to designate the title of the work in question. The following table indicates the abbreviations and, as a matter of convenience, gives the date of the first edition of each novel:

F	*Falkland*	1827
Pe	*Pelham; or, The Adventures of a Gentleman*	1828
Di	*The Disowned*	1828
De	*Devereux: A Tale*	1829
PC	*Paul Clifford*	1830
EA	*Eugene Aram: A Tale*	1832
G	*Godolphin: A Novel*	1833
Po	*The Last Days of Pompeii*	1834
R	*Rienzi; or, The Last of the Tribunes*	1835
EM	*Ernest Maltravers*	1837
A	*Alice; or, The Mysteries*	1838
NM	*Night and Morning*	1841
Z	*Zanoni*	1842
B	*The Last of the Barons*	1843
L	*Lucretia; or, The Children of Night*	1846
H	*Harold, The Last of the Saxon Kings*	1848
C	*The Caxtons: A Family Picture*	1849
MN	*My Novel, by Pisistratus Caxton; or, Varieties in English Life*	1853
W	*What Will He Do with It? by Pisistratus Caxton*	1858
SS	*A Strange Story*	1862
CR	*The Coming Race*	1871
Pa	*The Parisians*	1873
KC	*Kenelm Chillingly: His Adventures and Opinions*	1873

CHAPTER I

The Author's Temperament

The author's talent, no doubt, Guy Darrell once had—the
author's temperament never. What is the author's temperament? Too long a task to define. But without it a man may
write a clever book, an useful book, a book that may live a
year, ten years, fifty years. He will not stand out to distant
ages a representative of the age that rather lived in him than
he in it.

What Will He Do with It?

If Edward Bulwer has stood out to the ages, it has been as a writer
possessed of the "talent" rather than the "temperament" of the
author. Yet no writer has desired more strenuously than Bulwer to
give proof of his author's temperament. Designing his books to
be more than simply clever or useful, he has appealed to a posterity
existing well beyond the fifty years allotted to the merely talented
Victorian. His works have derived, as he wrote in his unfinished
autobiography, from "a conviction that [his] life had been entrusted
with a mission to the hearts of beings unborn, and that in the long
chain of thought connecting age with age [his] own being would
hereafter be recognised as a visible link."[1]

Although Bulwer's link is far less visible now than he had hoped,
his works still convey the fervor of his devotion to the author's
calling, and here if anywhere does lie the value of his often very
experimental novels. The longing to communicate across temporal
barriers informs the structural and thematic elements. His concern
for the symbolic and timeless level of human experience has led
him to create works of fiction that do not conform to the prevailing,
realistic modes of his age. Beyond his usefulness as a talented reflection of the age, Bulwer is therefore engaging as a Victorian who
has aspired to escape the confining times. And while he was by no

means alone in that aspiration, he has dramatized his rebellion—as well as his attempts at reconciliation—with his own particularizing and even touching passion.

The belief that enduring art issues from its author's intense consciousness of his own particularity provides one of the bases of Bulwer's aesthetic theory. The passage I have quoted from *What Will He Do with It?* continues:

The author's temperament is that which makes him an integral, earnest, original unity, distinct from all before and all that may succeed him. And, as a father of the church has said, that the consciousness of individual being is the sign of immortality, not granted to the inferior creatures—so it is in this individual temperament one and indivisible, and in the intense conviction of it, more than in all the works it may throw off, that the author becomes immortal. Nay, his works may perish, like those of Orpheus or Pythagoras; but he himself, in his name, in the footprint of his being, remains, like Orpheus or Pythagoras, undestroyed, indestructible. (W 8:1)

A means toward the larger goal of immortality, the work of art itself serves a curiously transient or incidental function in Bulwer's scheme. That scheme, as this chapter will consider it, involves several stages. The first stages concern the author's understanding of his individual being and the way in which he strives to communicate aspects of it in his fiction. The later stages involve the reader, who should, Bulwer believes, approach the novel in a certain way in order to receive the author's communication. The author's utterly particular awareness of "individual being" may finally prove, however, to have been incommunicable. What the work of art conveys, then, is not the actual quality of the authorial temperament, but rather a persuasion that some "intense conviction" of it has inspired the creative process. As the author's name on the title page will thereby seem to become the "footprint" of a totally unique personality, the work will preserve and immortalize at least the idea of identity.

Indeed art creates and sustains a whole myth of identity, and

Bulwer seems to have valued individual works primarily as adumbrations of this myth. Like "the long chain of thought," the general myth derives from the particularity of its links but subordinates them to the task of forging the unity of the race across the centuries.

As the myth may imply, Bulwer usually analyzed an identity first with respect to its "integral, earnest, original" individuality and then in terms of its likeness to all other human identities. In his own case—to begin with the "temperament" from which his fiction has issued—the "two lives" appear to have been especially contradictory, and it will be useful to consider each in turn.

He has envisaged the utterly particular aspect of himself in the imagery of certain Edenic landscapes and hieratic figures. As if they constituted the very essence of his identity, the same "cherished and revered images" of pastoral settings with their various "bright" and "shadowy" inhabitants haunted him throughout his life. "Fancy is a life itself" that went in his case beyond "mere reveries or castle-building." Sometimes he even had the sensation that he could retreat within himself and do without the entire external creation: "Our imagination, kept rigidly from the world, is the Eden in which we walk with God. . . . We learn thus to make our dreams and thoughts our companion, our beloved, our Egeria. We acquire the doctrine of self-dependence,—self suffices to self. In our sleep from the passions of the world, God makes an Eve to us from our own breasts."[2]

This hermetic Eden also refers to the identity that Bulwer hoped he would possess fully beyond the tomb. He had first begun to reflect about the meaning of his intense inner life in 1810 when his scholarly grandfather Lytton had died. The old man had evidently stored enormous quantities of important thoughts and impressions within himself, and the disturbed child had wondered about the present location of the "remote regions and dim recesses of that silent world in which [his grandfather had] lived unseen." Fearing the passage of that "Elfin Land" into oblivion, he had spent hours sifting through his grandfather's books to discover possible signs of it. "Pray, mamma," he had asked at this period too, "are you not sometimes overcome by the sense of your own identity?" And so, as he wrote many years later, the regions "behind the portals of the grave" and the mystery of human identity had continued to fascinate him: "Hour upon hour, day upon day, do I sit alone amidst the books; still, as then, absorbed in the desire to know. Still, the question that perplexed the infant occupies the man: still, in that sense of identity which comprises the perception of all things living, and with which, were it perishable, all things would perish, I find the same mystery, and receive from it the same revelation."[3]

Far beyond all other events, as his son has indicated, Bulwer's love affair at Ealing molded his sense of the Eden within and caused him to associate it with zones beyond the grave. He fancied during the summer of 1820 that he had indeed found his Eve. Each day along the lovely Brent, he met "the only being in the world," in a phrase from *Falkland*, "whoever possessed the secret and spell of my nature." But the mysterious girl suddenly disappeared one day —removed by her father and harried into a ruinous marriage—and "melancholy became an essential part of my being. . . . I attained to the power of concentrating the sources of joy and sorrow in myself."[4] Three years later she wrote him that she was dying for the sake of their love and summoned him to her grave in the Lake District. (He obeyed her summons a few months after the death of Byron, with whom he had also "wound and wrapt" his youth— "burying in his grave a poetry of existence that can never be restored.")[5]

His true allegiance henceforth belonged to the regions from which he was cut off save in memory and imagination. This world thus remained interesting to him only insofar as it could continue to offer him platonic intimations of an immortality beyond "the Ebon gate." Especially in country reminiscent of the rural greenery along the Brent or of the lake at Ullswater would he look for signs of "the strange land that knoweth neither season nor labour": "I look upon the leaves, and the grass, and the water," the dying student of his early *Conversations* remarks, "with a sentiment that is scarcely mournful: and yet I know not what all else it may be called, for it is deep, grave, and passionate, though scarcely sad. I desire, as I look on those . . . to know . . . whether they have no likeness, no archetype in the world in which my future home is to be cast." And in old age, Bulwer would be looking in such settings with renewed earnestness for "hints of the invisible eternal future"—"go[ing] back with strange fondness to all that is fresh in the earliest dawn of youth."[6]

While certain actual landscapes could thus convey hints of the realm that haunted his inner awareness, no one "human or earth-born" could correspond to the being for whom he chiefly longed. His absolutely imperious "besoin d'être aimé," as he would always consider it, ever drove him to seek a sympathetic woman. But since he dreamed egotistically of "a wholly congenial spirit—an echo of the heart—a counterpart of self," his quest kept ending in disappointment or calamity. He became disastrously involved, for example, with Lady Caroline Lamb upon his return from the Lake District. Their amazing affair, depicted repeatedly and obsessively in his unpublished fictional fragments, also led indirectly to the lifelong torture of his marriage to her protégée, Rosina Wheeler. Over and over again, he believed, the events of his life demonstrated that "there is no chimera vainer than the hope that one human heart shall find sympathy in another" (Po 4:2). Surprisingly personal and bitter in its context within *The Last Days of Pompeii*, the conclusive statement resembles innumerable others scattered throughout his letters, essays, and novels.[7]

Bulwer may have taken a grim satisfaction, though, in the fact that he could not find the sympathy he required in this world. The impossibility of his yearning continually strengthened his "intense conviction" of immortality and individuality. While "no natures are made wholly alike," perhaps he more than most men lacked his sympathetic double on earth. Estranged from the earthly sphere,

[5]

he treasured the memories, the desires, and the phantoms that hinted at the buried, but timeless world to which all the "poetry of existence" had departed.

Yet Bulwer did, of course, live a very full life in the temporal sphere, and this other aspect of his personality often concerned him as fully as the Eden within. Occasionally his involvement in the realm of time and mortality also acquired a certain desperation, for that egoistic "doctrine of self-dependence" did sometimes fail him: "What we are alone hath flesh and blood," he stated when reflecting in 1848 upon the seeming discontinuity of his career: "what we have been, like what we shall be, is an idea; and no more! An idea how dim and impalpable! This our sense of identity, this 'I' of ours, which is the single thread that continues from first to last—single thread that binds flowers changed every day, and withered every night—how thin and meagre is it of itself!"[8]

As if to manufacture an external continuity that might conceal the meagerness of the thread within, Bulwer contrived a role for himself and enacted it rather faithfully. He was for many years frankly the dandy, and references to the world's stage may seem in this phase to replace those to the idyllic, interior landscapes. He emphasized the importance of *"the management of self"*: "the men of genius who have not disappointed the world in their externals . . . have always played a part, . . . they have measured out their conduct by device and artifice,—and have walked the paths of life in the garments of the stage." From the examples—sufficiently disparate, one would think—of Pythagoras, Diogenes, Louis XIV, Bolingbroke, Chatham, Napoleon, and Byron, he had learned that a certain *"charlatanerie"* might be as essential as the genius to success.[9]

Bulwer's public career nevertheless amounted to far more than the dandyism or charlatanerie that put off some of his contemporaries. His role, he often claimed, served a great purpose; in his mind that purpose was endowed with the aura of a mystique as fascinating in its way as that of his sacred landscapes. With an exaltation that may gradually become apparent, he had committed himself to the thrilling bustle and movement of modern times. The essays written at the outset of his career suggest that he and his generation had responded to a challenging new impression of the force of realities. "We awoke," he notes in *England and the English* of the period succeeding Byron's death, "from the morbid, the passionate, the dreaming, 'the moonlight and the dimness of the mind.' " The vicious and debilitating influence of egoistic values— and more especially of the aristocratic spirit, which he carefully dissected and found responsible for most of the national ills—was evidently waning: "The aristocratic gloom, the lordly misanthropy, that Byron represented, have perished amid the action, the vividness, the *life* of these times."[10]

The modern zeitgeist fascinated him primarily because it promised to unite men in sympathy with each other: "the great prevailing characteristic of the present intellectual spirit is one most encouraging to human hopes; it is Benevolence." While he associated his internal life with the egoistic longing for individuation, his external character thus derived from the altruistic instinct to go out of himself. Devotion to "the great mass of mankind" inspired him in particular to join what he considered the cooperative enterprise of the utilitarian movement. Although others might term it "low or selfish," Bulwer believed that utilitarianism actually inculcated "universal love." It demonstrated to individuals that their self-interest might require disinterestedness, and so in its larger tendencies—if not in some of its dangerous half-truths about human nature—it helped to subdue anarchic egoisms. To some extent taking Byron's place, Bentham impressed Bulwer as the embodiment of the type of nobility characteristic of the age: Bentham was a "pure concentration of benevolence" and "the most powerful advocate of the true interests of suffering humanity, who ever yet drew breath on English soil."[11]

The desire to feel that he was merging himself with a larger entity quite obviously influenced Bulwer's political career. When "the question of Reform came on," the intellectual spirit of the age "became *wholly* absorbed in . . . politics," and Bulwer entered Parliament as a Radical in 1831. He was eager to do his part, in the phrases of *England and the English*, "to unite . . . the people and the Government, to prevent that jealousy and antagonism of power which we behold at present, each resisting each to their common weakness, [and] to merge, in one word, both names in the name of state." Since Bentham had attained his greatest glory by creating his science of law ("equall[ing] the glory of the greatest scientific benefactors of the race"), Bulwer followed Benthamite principles especially in his career as legislator. Yet he always infused his utilitarianism with a certain emotional idealism. Like Coleridge and the German philosophers he had begun to study, he ascribed an organic life to the state and believed the individual might live most fully in terms of the national identity: "In a well-ordered constitution, a constitution in harmony with its subjects, each citizen confounds himself with the state; he is proud that he belongs to it; the genius of the whole people enters into his soul; he is not one man only, he is inspired by the mighty force of the community; he feels the dignity of the nation in himself, he beholds himself in the dignity of the nation."[12]

But perhaps the impulse to identify himself with "the mighty force of the community" figures most interestingly in Bulwer's conception of his literary duties. The modern writer, according to the student of the *Conversations*, "must have caught the mighty inspiration which is breathing throughout the awakened and watchful world. . . . He must address . . . the middle as well as the higher orders; he must find an audience in Manchester and Liverpool." And beyond that middle class audience, the writer must also make his works appealing to "the people at large": "when collectively considered," Bulwer maintained on the authority of Aristotle, "they are the best judges of music and of poetry." In his own age they particularly demanded novels, and Bulwer propounded some interesting, if not wholly convincing reasons for the suitability of the fictional form to the modern "commercial" sensibility. Even works like Disraeli's *Alroy*, which may seem to have issued from a vision of things practically inimical to prose, had now to take the shape of the novel.[13]

Bulwer did not, however, advocate any pandering to the popular tastes of the moment. In appealing to "the people at large," the author must imagine an abstraction far nobler than the frequently "contemptible" individuals who constituted the actual classes and interested groups of the particular times. Rather than following his readers, the author should try to lead them away from their jealousies, their antagonisms—in short, their individualities—and unite them too with the larger popular abstraction. As he sought to accomplish such a task, the author might also be seeking to enforce a collectivism that went beyond political boundaries. Bulwer seemed like Carlyle and others to respond to Goethe's notions about the possibilities for a *Weltliteratur* when he too proposed a grand, international union of authors. With "a universal combination of the creators of opinion" ranged against them, "Holy Alliances and secret Diets" would henceforth find themselves powerless. He even foresaw the ability of literature to redeem the world and establish the millenial reign of disinterested benevolence. Where political revolutionaries tended to produce anarchy, the organized press could diffuse the love that would bind society together in the new age: "The world hath had two Saviours—one divine, and one human; the first was the Founder of our religion, . . . the second is the might of the PRESS. By that, the Father of all safe revolutions, the author of all permanent reforms—by that, man will effect what the First ordained—the reign of peace, and the circulation of love among the great herd of man."[14]

The awakening to "the *life* of these times" came in this way to involve devotion to the noblest cause of all times—"the deep cause of the great family of Man!" And certain intimations of immortality thus came to give value not only to his private being but also to his public career. While his soul would regain its immortal home in another sphere, his public authorial personality would live in terms of its contributions to man's cause on earth. Bulwer's vision of a sort of earthly immortality has its characteristic imagery too. Where he typically protected the private phantoms within sheltered landscapes and "dim recesses" "kept rigidly from the world," the collectivist identity required boundless spaciousness for its habitation: "how vast and lovely is that field which it opens to our gaze!" he exclaims of the utilitarian enterprise: "It exalts our vision from the ills and disparities of the present time to the progress which the career of light shall make in the far future—it gives our hopes a resting-place amidst the ages that are to come—and bounding the prospects of Virtue to no petty limits of time or space, unites our momentary ambition with eternal objects."[15]

Much of Bulwer's language implies a conversion: he has awakened from "the moonlight and the dimness of the mind" in order to unite himself to "the career of light." His poem of 1824, "The Tale of a Dreamer," traces a spiritual movement which is in fact quite similar to that of Tennyson's *In Memoriam*. Intense private grief takes him to the tomb of his beloved where, eventually reborn, he renounces egoism and vows himself to the service of "Eternal freedom." (Bulwer would incidentally criticize Tennyson's *Poems*, 1833, for failing to exemplify just such a renunciation of egoism.) His friend Miss Landon, the writer known as L. E. L., who usually expresses his views in her essays in the *New Monthly Magazine*, also emphasizes the decisiveness of the change in him. Having entitled one of her own novels *Romance and Reality*, she finds it appropriate to contrast the "romance" of Bulwer's earliest works with the "reality" of the works beginning with *Pelham*.[16]

As I believe will become clear, however, Bulwer has not really experienced the definite conversion that he sees in the intellectual spirit of the nation as a whole. (Indeed, many Victorians were probably far less converted than they thought.) The conflicting egoistic and altruistic commitments remain to indicate the poles, and to a large extent the opposition continues to be one between the idea and the material as well. For while both commitments are to abstractions, altruism tends more fully than does egoism to involve him with the materials of earth.

The same awareness of dualities informs Bulwer's theories of the creative process. He indicates on the one hand that impulses arising from the private realm—"the *celata Venus* which dwells in the lonely heart"—drives a man in the first instance to authorship. Apparently not yet persuaded of his essential immortality, the youth in particular fears lest he die "with all the most lovely, the most spiritual part of [himself] untold!"[17] On the other hand, though, "the mighty inspiration which is breathing throughout the awakened . . . world," leads him to want his art to demonstrate his solidarity with "the great family of Man!" Bulwer therefore seems, as his theory of artistic creativity develops, to provide for the interdependence of the egoistic and altruistic instincts. He defines, particularly in *Zanoni* and in some of the *Caxtoniana* essays, his own rather interesting version of the Romantic imagination.

The egoistic element remains, in a sense, the primary one, for it governs the formation of the initial conception in what corresponds to Coleridge's primary imagination. This imaginative faculty goes to work on the impressions emanating from the external world, tyrannizing over them and forcing them into some accord with the purer images already existing in the artist's mind. Or it may be thought of as the process that revivifies and enriches mental tendencies and ideas that have been lying dormant. According to Bulwer's rather platonic epistemology, the mind can recognize the values of the external realm only insofar as the mind possesses corresponding values in itself: " 'We are conscious of excellence,' says some author, 'in proportion to the excellence within ourselves.' "[18] Through "an intense study" of the great art of the past, the artist acquires more and more consciously the "taste" or "feeling" for beauty he has already possessed unconsciously. He may even begin to observe all that is occurring outside himself as a means of dis-

covering himself more fully. To the painter nature becomes valuable for the "exquisite suggestions" it offers of "*the idea of beauty
in the painter's own mind*." Although "this idea is not inborn," the
predisposition or capacity to recognize it is (Z 2:9).

The work of art thus begins to take shape in the artist's "innermost mind." In a state of "reverie," he becomes aware of the "ever-
shifting panorama": "ideas float before us, magical, vague, half-
formed; apparitions of the thoughts that are to be born later into
the light, and run their course in the world of man." But before
they can come to birth, the artist must so meditate on them that they
coalesce around a particular, unifying "conception." This conception is "the soul of the idea which the love in my own heart renders
lovely to me." From it, all else follows, whether it be "a dramatic
plot, artistically planned, or . . . a narrative of which we have painted
on the retina of the mind the elementary colours and the skeleton
outlines."[19] The faithful translation of the ideal conception into
external form may then be all that really matters to the artist: "My
affection for my work," Bulwer remarks in the dedication of *Zanoni*,
"is rooted in the solemn and pure delight which it gave me to conceive and to perform. If I had graven it on the rocks of a desert, this
apparition of my own innermost mind, in its least-clouded moments,
would have been to me as dear."

As the secondary imagination guides the process of engraving
the apparition on the rocks—or the paper—the altruistic element
comes into play. The "enthusiasm of love," which represents, according to the introductory section of *Zanoni*, the noblest form of
imaginative energy, makes the artist long to reveal the intrinsic
value of his materials. "Art," as Bulwer defines it in an essay of
1838, "is that process by which we give to natural materials the
highest excellence they are capable of receiving." Far from imposing himself upon his materials, the artist may even find himself
submitting, through a sort of negative capability, to them. He can
create only what they already contain as their highest potentiality,
and in the service of that intuited potentiality, he may lose sight of

his own original preconception. Or the excellence in himself becomes simply a vehicle for bringing out their excellence, as Bulwer suggests with respect to oratory (an art form that seems to have fascinated him during his later years): "It was thus once very truthfully and very finely said by Mr. Pitt, in answer to the complimentary charge that his eloquence deceived and led away the assembly he addressed, 'Eloquence is in the assembly, not in the speaker'—meaning thereby that the speaker is effective in proportion as he gives utterance to the thought or the feeling which prevails in the assembly."[20]

In bringing out the eloquence or highest excellence implicit in his materials, however, Bulwer's artist does not exemplify negative capability in the usual sense. He surrenders in a highly selective way to his subject and does not leave his subject where he found it: "Nature is not to be copied, but *exalted*." As the artist obeys Bulwer's famous "idealising principle," he will furthermore astound observers with the degree of ideal beauty he has been able to intuit within the most unpromising of materials. Although he remains faithful to them, he will transform and redeem them—at times, nearly beyond recognition. In this way, as the narrator of *Zanoni* suggests in his anecdote of Guido Reni, the artist symbolizes and sustains "the perpetual struggle of Humanity to approach the Gods": "When asked where he got his models, Guido summoned a common porter from his calling, and drew from a mean original a head of surpassing beauty. It resembled the porter, but idealised the porter to the hero" (Z 2:9).[21]

Through the hero or saint, the artist has not only idealized the porter but embodied after all the apparition of his own innermost mind. The egoistic concern to remain faithful to a private vision and the altruistic desire to redeem the material world have somehow supported each other. And their reconciliation in the aesthetic process may also imply the theoretical possibility for reconciling the conflicting elements in life. As Schiller, whose poetry Bulwer translated in the early 1840's, had also recognized, each requires the other in order to fulfill its potential excellence. Bulwer remarks that Schiller's youthful quest for the pure ideal had given way to his more mature concern for "man's place and fate in creation" until in "Das Ideal und das Leben," "which constitutes the core of his last completest philosophy, the two existences unite in the crowning result of perfected art, life yielding the materials through which the Ideal accomplishes its archetypal form. From life the raw block is laboriously lifted out of the mine that embedded it, stroke by stroke sculptured into the shape which may clothe an idea, until the final touch of the chisel leaves the thought disengaged from the matter, and the block, hewn from Nature, takes from Art both its form and its soul."[22]

The imaginative reconciliation of opposites—whether in art or in life—is nevertheless a theoretical notion rather than a practical possibility during most of Bulwer's career. More characteristically, he complains of the discrepancy between the idea and the materials: "Writing, after all," he observes in the dedicatory epistle of *Devereux*, "is a cold and coarse interpreter of thought. How much of the imagination, how much of the intellect, evaporates and is lost while we seek to embody it in words! Man made language, and God the genius." And in the discussion of reverie in *Caxtoniana*, he muses at considerable and rather passionate length about the severe impoverishment and even profanation the conception must suffer in the course of its translation. The original image becomes "a miserable daguerreotype" or "caricature"; the "fairy gold" is reduced to "dry leaves." The redemptive idealizing principle evidently implies the simultaneous operation of a materializing principle whereby the artist degrades himself. One might even conclude that the author's altruistic instinct betrays the cause of his innermost being.

Yet that innermost aspect of the author's temperament never does quite evaporate; the work of art does continue in some fashion to demonstrate its existence. The debased caricatures can suggest, for example, the existence if not the gloriousness of their originals.

Since they alone can imply their first cause in the "imagination, kept rigidly from the world," these products of the secondary imagination still provide an essential link in the artist's communication with the ages. Bulwer therefore hopes that by appearing incomplete and inconclusive in themselves his own works will force the reader to muse about their hidden sources. Possessed of a tendency similar to what Pater calls *Anders-streben* in "The School of Giorgione," great works can "impress us with the feeling, that a vague but glorious 'SOMETHING' inspired or exalted the attempt, *and yet remains unexpressed.* The effect is like that of the spire, which, by insensibly tapering into heaven, owes its pathos and its sublimity to the secret thoughts with which that heaven is associated."[23]

It naturally follows that the recipient of the aesthetic communication should be most interested in what seems to lie invisibly beyond the spire-like shape. "One of my first tasks in studying a great author," remarks Bulwer's ambitious student, "[is to seek] proof that the writer *has* felt that vague something which carries us beyond the world." He has looked, in effect, for evidences of the immortal author's temperament. But since this temperament is intuited as an elusive "scent" about the work, Bulwer is not really advocating a simple or straightforward biographical criticism. While approaching literary works "as if they were meant to be autobiographies," he considers them autobiographies of that element in man that can scarcely be defined verbally. Understood in this way, the works can constitute "an appendix to [a writer's] biography far more valuable and explanatory than the text itself." In some cases the appendix may even tend to contradict the factual narrative of the man's life.[24]

Bulwer's method of gradually perceiving that "vague something" in fictional works deserves attention here, I believe, insofar as it indicates how he has wished his own novels to be read. Although, as he recognizes, authors often evaluate their works most inaccurately, his own critical theories do introduce certain con-

siderations that may help to make the study of his novels reward-
ing. Three stages in his critical approach, suggesting a process of
decoding or a movement from surface to the something beyond,
may be particularly significant. The reader should first appreciate
the author's conscious plan, then the "metaphysical" dimensions of
the work, and finally "the perfume from his genius; . . . by it he
unconsciously reveals himself."

"In regarding any work of art," the important essay of 1838
"On Art in Fiction" maintains, "we must first thoroughly acquaint
ourselves with the object that the artist had in view." Although the
author may sometimes need to explain his object in so many words,
it should be readily discernible in the organization of the work as
a whole. The need to evaluate a work in terms of its communication
of a sense of wholeness thus becomes one of the cardinal and most
reiterated of Bulwer's principles. If a work exhibits "symmetry of
the whole," a critic should indulgently overlook "blemishes in detail"; for this reason *Wilhelm Meister* succeeds—"ineffectual in
parts, the effect as a whole is wonderfully deep." (It is incidentally
noteworthy that Matthew Arnold, who also worries about the fragmentation of contemporary life, claims to have found Bulwer's concern for aesthetic wholeness especially helpful.) [25]

Already taking one beyond the superficial aspects or "blemishes"
of a novel, the quest for its wholeness comes to imply an impatience
with many of the "popular" elements of fiction. Bulwer refers dis-
paragingly to novelists who spend too much time on descriptions
of clothes, manners, or scenery, or on "antiquarian dissertations,"
or who crowd their "canvass" with unnecessary characters. His
interesting condemnation of Scott in this context may also help to
suggest the sort of positive wholeness of underlying conception he
wishes to find dominating a work:

Scott, with all his genius, was rather a great mechanist than a great
artist. His execution was infinitely superior to his conception. It may
be observed, indeed, that his conceptions are often singularly poor and
barren, compared with the vigour with which they are worked out. He

conceives a story with the design of telling it as well as he can, but is wholly insensible to the high and true aim of art, which is rather to consider for what object the story should be told. Scott never appears to say to himself, "Such a tale will throw a new light upon human passions, or add fresh stores to human wisdom: for that reason I select it." He seems rather to consider what picturesque effects it will produce, what striking scenes, what illustrations of mere manners. He regards the story with the eye of the *property man*, though he tells it with the fervour of the poet. . . . He had no grandeur of conception, for he had no strong desire to render palpable and immortal some definite and abstract truth.[26]

Scornful of "picturesque effects" and all that belongs merely to the "execution," Bulwer nevertheless continues to employ the terminology of painting to emphasize the "abstract" quality he always finds in a good conception. For the conception is perceived less as an "avowed moral" or message than as an aesthetic "design." Goethe, for example, has regarded "the vices or virtues of other men as the painter regards the colours which he mingles on his pallet—with passionless study of his own effects of light and shade." While still related to the author's desire to communicate certain notions about "human passions," the conception thus emerges in terms of the author's control of overall form. Bulwer goes beyond the observation of effective individual scenes and refers to the entire fictional "composition" when he speaks of the balancing of masses around a point of repose, the boldness of contrasts or the delicacy of line, coherence in the handling of lighting, and the use of "elementary" or "mixed" colors.[27]

Rather unexpectedly perhaps, the sense of an abstract formal design seems to have little to do with the story line, which Bulwer calls "the mechanism of external incidents." Quite apart from the clarity of an Aristotelian beginning, middle, and end, he looks for what might be called psychological unity of the dramatis personae. A good romantic, he invariably finds the characters in plays too, whether by Shakespeare or Byron, far more fascinating than the plots to which they are connected. And beyond his observation of the power of individual characters in themselves, he seeks the patterns that their psychological relationships establish. He wishes to interpret the characters as effectively juxtaposed mental tendencies. Thus a novel by his friend the Earl of Mulgrave is "delightful" because "the two heroes are the personifications of the negative and affirmative principles" (although Lord Mulgrave has made them "a little too antithetical"), while Disraeli's *Contarini Fleming* is like *Wilhelm Meister* "a delineation of abstract ideas. . . . Each character is a personification of certain trains of mind."[28]

Terming such characters "metaphysical creatures," Bulwer comes to believe that the "metaphysical" novel—which is "often allegorical and actual at the same time"—represents the *"noblest sphere"* of fiction. Although a metaphysical design may not always be "the object that the artist had in view," every good novel will possess a metaphysical dimension insofar as it deals with "the science of the human heart." The heart or "the soul" becomes the fundamental setting of the novel: beneath the visible colors on the novelist's canvas, one discovers the more abstract shapes that constitute "a painting of that internal world which in every age is the same" (Di, 1st ed., chap. 30). While diffused among the several characters, the various "trains of mind" in that composition should also help ultimately to show the warring elements within a single human psyche. The story would find its focus in terms of its dramatic definition of a *"compound"* character. Bulwer sets great store upon his notion of the compound personality that is fearfully caught among struggling emotions and instincts.[29]

Consideration of the metaphysical dimension, wherever it is possible, also tends to take the reader beyond the author's conscious, abstract conception and toward the more mysterious sources of the work. By "metaphysical" Bulwer means not only "psychological," as most critics have noticed, but more specifically "typical" or "archetypal." His long note to the 1853 edition of *Zanoni* defines his notion of "type" as a more complicated and subtler form of fiction than "allegory." Whereas "allegory is a personation of distinct and definite things," the "typical" story "takes the thought below the surface of the understanding to the deeper intelligence which the world rarely tasks. It is not sunlight on the water; it is a hymn chanted to the nymph who hearkens and awakes below." Indeed, that nymph figures within the hymn, for she and the other forms discovered in the depths are the archetypes that inhabit the human psyche. The lines and shapes of the novelist's design refer ultimately to his intuitions of their shadowy outlines and their dynamic conflicts and harmonies.

As Bulwer claims to have learned from Shakespeare and others, the conflicts within "that internal world" become most sublime and intense when focused in the mind of the criminal. In probing the mystery of evil, art enters the most awesome "recesses" and "caverns" of the human psyche, and so crime has always constituted one of the grandest subjects of literature. Although his contemporary critics have found in this aspect of his aesthetic theory and practice evidence of a "perverse" sympathy with evil, it would rather seem that, here especially, ethical categories become irrelevant. Archetypal forms suggestive of the demonic particularly fascinate Bulwer because they represent the energy in all men that lies beyond "conventional morality." The metaphysical novel, at least according to Bulwer's description in 1845 of his own fictional practice, thus conducts the reader to regions of awareness that it requires a certain daring to appreciate: "Long since, in searching for new regions in the Art to which I am a servant, it seemed to me that they might be found lying far, and rarely trodden, beyond that range of conventional morality in which Novelist after Novelist had entrenched himself—amongst those subtle recesses in the ethics of human life in which Truth and Falsehood dwell undisturbed and unseparated. The vast and dark Poetry around us—the Poetry of Modern Civilisation and Daily Existence, is shut out from us in much, by the shadowy giants of Prejudice and Fear. He who would arrive at the Fairy Land, must face the Phantoms."[30]

The Fairy Land guarded by the giants may recall the novelist's "lonely Ida" wherein the apparitions of innermost mind have given rise to his initial conception. Yet as an archetypal setting, the Fairy Land does not seem quite to manifest the intensely personal quality of the artist's inner awareness. The reader has, in any case, a further step to take in his efforts to appreciate the "vague something" to which the spire points.

The restless quest to perceive the wholeness of a novel is resolved in the awareness of a "latent coherence" that somehow exists as an element of order beyond all visible formal patterns: "On closing the work, we ought to feel that we have read a *whole*—that there is an harmonious unity in all the parts . . . and not only the mere isolated thoughts in the work, but the unity of the work itself, ought to leave its single and deep impression on the mind." The deep impression is also a profoundly moral awareness; in transcending "conventional morality," the metaphysical novel has "instruct[ed] not by the avowed moral but by the latent one." Although the reader cannot pinpoint the aspects of the novel that have conveyed the "typical and pervading moral," he nevertheless finds himself mysteriously "enriched" at the end. *Wilhelm Meister* thus figures once again as a fictional touchstone by virtue of its ultimate unity of effect. While "a wonderfully stupid novel" according to Bulwer's cynical Asmodeus (as according to Carlyle for that matter), it also resembles "a quiet stream that carries gold with it—the stream passes away insensibly, but the gold remains to tell where it has been." The specifically moral value of that gold is even more clear in the case of a novel by one Mr. Scargill. It leaves the reader's "soul insensibly smoothed, and, as it were, *Christianised* over. He will recollect the work, not in any detached passages, but as one which has made a gentle but no fleeting impression on his mind; it has soothed all his better feelings."[31] And in describing the "metaphysical" novels supposedly being composed by his own protagonists in the course of *My Novel* and *The Parisians*, Bulwer again emphasizes the mysteriously "etherealising" and "insensibly" soothing effect of these works as "wholes."

Such novels have led beyond the sound and fury of conflicts, the mysteries of evil, and the fearfulness of the demonic regions to a recognition of the fundamental beauty of the human spirit. Their latent morality derives from their authors' deep love for man. The reader of Scargill will have intuited "the presence of a quiet and deep love . . . through the whole book." And treating Shakespeare as a sort of novelist too, Bulwer observes that for all his fascination with crime, Shakespeare has conveyed his essential morality through his "strong sympathies with all that is human."[32] Sympathetic love unifies all the elements of the good novel just as sympathy constitutes, according to Bulwer's theory in his more occult phases, the magnetic force that binds the entire cosmos together.

Yet a certain inconsistency may enter Bulwer's theories at this stage. Supposedly it is the success of the formal design and the grandeur of the metaphysical conception that eventually lead the reader to apprehend that still more essential and cementing element—the presence of love. But the aesthetic values and the sympathetic love can apparently exist without reference to each other too. Thus Bulwer finds the love in Scott despite the absence of any all-informing, coherent, abstract, aesthetic conception: "There was in him," he remarks in his notice on the occasion of Scott's death, "a large and Catholic sympathy with all classes, all tempers, all conditions of men; and this it was that redeemed his noble works from the taint of party." On the other hand Goethe's works sometimes appear to have all the desirable aesthetic qualities but not the underlying love. Bulwer considers the "toryism" of Goethe's later years less excusable than Scott's, and as his early admiration cools, he complains that Goethe has escaped from the passions of life to the indifference of art. The famous Goethean "Equilibrium" and the serene, aesthetic tolerance of good and evil have not taken their being from an all-embracing sympathy. They conceal instead an unwillingness to experience the deep love that would fully engage the artist in the human condition.[33]

Goethe nevertheless remains "the greatest artist whoever lived,"[34] and the fact may indicate Bulwer's own unwillingness, in the final analysis, to treat sympathy "with all that is human" as the most essential and profound element in art. Beyond any altruism it must in fact be the secret egoism of the author's temperament that ultimately cements and sustains any great work. Having analyzed the formal, aesthetic qualities and in a sense rejected each one as unessential, Bulwer thus comes at last to "the sentiment of the work" which he associates with the very "heart of the author": "It is a pervading and indescribable harmony, in which the heart of the author himself seems silently to address our own. . . . The sentiment of a work is felt, not in its parts, but as a whole: It is undefinable and indefinite—it escapes while you seek to analyse it. Of all the qualities of fiction, the sentiment is that which we can least subject to the inquiries or codes of criticism. It emanates from the moral and predominant quality of the author,—the perfume from his genius; and by it he unconsciously reveals himself."[35]

So volatile and evanescent is the essential perfume that one can scarcely even distill it from a single work. To perceive the "undefinable and indefinite" quality that unifies the whole, one must look not just at one work but at an author's entire canon. Even then the reader may not be able to put his finger on the essential authorial presence: "Rarely indeed, if ever," Bulwer observes in the preface to *Pelham* of 1848, "can we detect the real likeness of an author of fiction in any single one of his creations. He may live in each of them, but only for the time. . . . He may have in himself a quality, here and there, in common with each, but others so widely opposite as to destroy all the resemblance you fancy for a moment you have discovered." So the works keep leading the eye insensibly beyond themselves to the something that "*yet remains unexpressed*": "The best part of beauty," according to the Baconian precept Bulwer repeats throughout his career, "is that which no picture can express." Still the reader has only the pictures—or the novels—to go on, and although he can hardly say how, their caricatures do manage to imply something of the apparitions of innermost mind behind themselves.

Whether or not one detects that implicit but volatile essence in Bulwer's own works, they are interesting as explicit treatments of the perennially problematic relationship between impalpable ideal presences and their imperfect material correspondences. For the notion of the "vague something" refers not only to what lies behind or outside the fictional framework but also, and less vaguely, to important structural and thematic elements within the work. As the titles of the following chapters are supposed to suggest, Bulwer's fiction explores several versions of the "new regions in . . . Art" that are invisible but extremely relevant to life in the daily world.

In accord with Bulwer's theories of the metaphysical novel, the various new regions refer primarily to the archetypal or mythic dimensions of the individual's efforts to work out his salvation. Most characteristically, Bulwer seems to develop his own versions of the neo-platonic–Wordsworthian myth whereby the soul has come to earth trailing clouds of glory. Since earthly life thus implies the ordeal of the soul, Bulwer's protagonists tend to discover higher meanings in the ordeal than does, say, Arnold's Empedocles (for whom "there is everything to be endured, nothing to be done"). Beyond simple endurance, they must seek out the figure of the anima in order to assure themselves of their essential identity, and they must protect that anima from the dark portions of themselves. Threats arise especially from figures that typify the chaotic unconscious (and the sexual nature) or else the hyperconscious, liberated reason—ratiocination, as Bulwer conceives it, divorced from the moral sense. These evil figures belong more to the material than to the immortal aspect of the identity and would destroy the soul before it can return to its true home.

Bulwer may nevertheless tend increasingly to portray the need for an accommodation with those material aspects and to emphasize the career of the soul here even beyond the promise of an immortality hereafter. As the "vague something" seems to inhere more and more fully within the physical world, the novels also associate immortality less with the individual soul than with the universal human identity. The cause of the lonely ego is consequently subordinated ever more definitely to "the deep cause of the great family of Man." Where the historical novels, for example, recognize the sacrifice of the individual as tragically necessary, the Caxton novels go further and affirm the sacrifice as comically desirable.

Yet Bulwer has remained stubbornly committed withal to the images and the "fairy gold" that do not have their counterparts in this world. As the last four novels especially testify, he has wished his works, unlike Schiller's poem, to maintain the split between the Ideal and the materials of Life that can never adequately clothe it. The immortality for which he longs must exist literally beyond the material world as well as in the consciousness of beings tied to this realm.

So unique as to be incommunicable to another, the soul is the very identifying idea of a man. That idea remains constant through all the physical changes and experiences that constitute earthly life, and it is indeed quite distinct and separable from its material manifestations. The noblest and purest of ideas, the idea of individual identity also seems to Bulwer to lie behind and to sustain all the values of art and civilization. Insofar as individuals have possessed an "intense conviction" of the ideal significance of identity, they have been inspired to preserve and enrich what they perceive as the larger extensions of that identity. Still the larger identities of family, nation, and race must ultimately refer back to "the consciousness of individual being ... one and indivisible." Issuing from God himself, the idea of "an integral, earnest, original unity" is the first cause of all creation.

Bulwer's fiction may suggest the diffusion of his being: "Scarcely any one of the romances I have woven together," he once observed, "resembles its neighbour,"[36] and sometimes his works—most notably *What Will He Do with It?*—even dispute the value of the pure identity. But the diffusion and the contradictions are nevertheless calculated to point to a unifying, ideal wholeness behind themselves. Thereby working out so many of the ramifications of the idea of identity, the novels and romances keep protesting against what Bulwer sees as the growing materialism of his age. And fortunately, as the ensuing chapters seek to show, something of the earnest intensity that went into the works may yet remain active. In the mortal and Victorian elements, one may still discern the outlines of the immortal, mythic abstractions which this most idealist of Victorians has so passionately loved.

CHAPTER II

The Dangerous World Within

Alas, how seldom are these worlds akin,
The world without us and the world within.
"The Tale of a Dreamer," 1824

From the outset of his quest for the "new regions," Bulwer rejects the claim of "conventional morality" that "there is much in the human heart which ought not to be described." All psychological knowledge, according to his defenses of both *Falkland* and *Pelham*, is "moral," and he compares fictional research into "the constitution of the mind" with the researches of philosophy and medicine. The novelist who has properly dedicated himself to the acquisition and dissemination of accurate knowledge debases his art if he uses it for "the trite illustration of any moral maxim however excellent."[1]

But while they both derive from the same devotion to knowledge, Bulwer's first two fictions seem to propose opposite answers to an epistemological problem and to come up with opposite conceptions of man. The epistemological opposition resembles the traditional one between idealism and empiricism, and it reflects too, of course, an initial version of Bulwer's sense of his own duality. Before discussing the structure of each novel, it may thus be useful to observe very briefly some of the biographical factors that help to illuminate the duality of *Falkland* and *Pelham*. Bulwer often employs in this context the terms Cave and Agora to refer to the two spheres in which the philosopher-artist must live and seek his knowledge.

To the idealistic Bulwer all knowledge was a form of self-knowledge, and the cave lay within his own mind: "I begin to believe, with Bishop Berkeley," he told Mrs. Cunningham in a letter of 1828, "that the world itself is a lie, and that there is nothing true in the universe but one's own mind."[2] The belief has so overwhelmed the narrative technique of *Falkland* that the reader often finds himself uncertain about what is actually and literally happening. Confessing that he has not shared "the ordinary ambition of tale-writers" to deal with "the external event," the narrator has determined to show only "the interior struggle" and "to chronicle a history rather by thoughts and feelings than by incidents and events; and to lay open those minuter and more subtle mazes and secrets of the human heart, which in modern writings have been so sparingly exposed" (F 2).

In looking for knowledge within the cave, Bulwer discovered a more Byronic than serenely platonic kind of truth. The devastating effects of Byron's death, the loss of his first love, and the affair with Lady Caroline continued to unnerve and enrage him. Alternating moods of reckless ferocity and extreme depression caused him to move restlessly back and forth in 1825 and 1826 between the dissipations (especially gambling) of Paris and the misanthropic solitude of his lodgings at Versailles. Mrs. Cunningham, certainly his best friend in Paris, would address him as "My dear Childe Harold" and try gently but unsuccessfully to tease him out of his "Diogenes mood." As the principal literary product of the residence in France, *Falkland* therefore reveals what Park Honan terms a "Bulwer Byronized." The work not only indulges the "touching egotism" that Bulwer had so fervently admired in Byron but also celebrates the terrifying, anarchic implications of the recognition that the ego alone is real.[3]

Pelham on the other hand resulted from a concern for the life of the agora. As a newly married man busily planning a career in both literature and politics, Bulwer had the impression in 1827 that he was rejoining the human community. And in fact he wrote *Pelham* quite literally for the marketplace: since his mother had cut off his allowance, he found he "must write for the many or not at all. I cannot afford to write for the few."[4] The novel happily did more than repay his labors, for it created a sensation—even to changing the fashion in men's evening dress—and firmly established his reputation as one of the most important novelists of the age. With its story also set in the bustling realm of society, *Pelham* illustrates Bulwer's notion of the empirical avenue to truth. The dandy protagonist sets forth to seek "knowledge of the world" and of his "species" rather than of the "subtle mazes" within himself. Concentrating frankly upon external "trifles," he nevertheless gains important insights: "Nothing is superficial to a deep observer!" runs one of the maxims added to the second (1828) edition. His careful observation of the "facts" on the surface enables him to recognize certain deeper "principles" too—a process that his supposedly intense study of Bentham, Mill, and Ricardo definitely helps. Basic to the whole structure of wisdom he goes on to erect is what he terms "the first piece of *real* knowledge I ever gained": "my interest was incorporated with that of the beings with whom I had the chance of being cast: if I injure them, I injure myself: if I can do them any good, I receive the benefit in common with the rest" (Pe 2:16). Since Pelham's experiences continually reinforce that truth, Bulwer believed that the story as a whole successfully realized his intention to demonstrate "that the lessons of society do not necessarily corrupt."

In effect, the lessons of society lead Pelham to challenge the egoistic, gloomily Byronic knowledge gained in the cave: "In all sentiments that are impregnated with melancholy and instill sadness as the moral," he remarks to a misanthropic friend, "I question the wisdom and dispute the truth" (Pe 2:17). And with some evident reason Bulwer would claim later on that *Pelham* had helped to discredit Byronism in the eyes of his whole generation: "I think, above most works," the preface to the edition of 1840 modestly states, "it contributed to put an end to the Satanic mania,—to turn the thoughts and ambition of young gentlemen without neckcloths, and young clerks who were sallow, from playing the Corsair, and boasting that they were villains."

Yet *Pelham* did not put an end to every aspect of the Satanic mania in Bulwer's own life and art. Although he would term *Falk-*

land his *Werther*—maintaining that the expression of the "perilous stuff" had exorcised it—much of the stuff has actually remained in *Pelham* and the subsequent works. The benevolent lessons of society were no more finally persuasive than the perilous recognitions of the cave. While "every good novel has one great end—the same in all—*viz.* the increasing our knowledge of the heart" (Pe 2:15), novels may still apply opposing epistemological methods and reach contradictory truths about man.

The uneasy conviction of the duality of truth provides the structural basis for each novel in itself too. For while they view the duality from opposite sides, each novel does define the same two terms—"the world without us and the world within"—and does dramatize the same irreconcilable discrepancy. An analysis of the two works may suggest not only their hostility but the subtle sense in which each from its own perspective may reinforce the message of the other.

"Thus is it with human virtue," the narrator of *Falkland* observes when a jealous woman betrays her best friend for her supposed good: "the fair show and the good deed without—the one eternal motive of selfishness within" (3).[5] That division, so basic to human nature, also suggests the main structural principle of the story. While the two terms usually refer to the external and internal aspects of the same personality, Bulwer has separated them in the allegory and assigned them respectively to heroine and hero. The insipid Lady Emily represents the fair and virtuous appearance deriving from no motive at all while Falkland is the eternal "selfishness within" unable to relate itself to any apparent virtue. Their hopeless, destructive love affair indicates that the hidden energy of the ego can never manifest itself creatively through the fair shows demanded by society. In struggling to make those appearances serve its purposes, the ego continually undermines them, and the war between the inner and outer worlds is ultimately to the death.

[29]

Bulwer's control of imagery in particular keeps the allegorical conflict clear. Although he composed *Falkland* as a largely epistolary romance in order to emphasize the characters' mental responses, the colorful prose does not convey psychological complexities so much as it serves the interests of the allegory. Falkland's highly metaphorical, if often bombastic descriptions of his career prior to the opening of the story are especially helpful in this regard. While confusingly unchronological, scattered, and unspecific in reference, these descriptions nevertheless do coalesce to create a symbolic context for his present love affair. It will thus be useful to observe first the imagery that defines the individual backgrounds of Lady Emily and Falkland and then the mingling of images in their love story.

Most coherent and pervasive is the imagery of surfaces and depths, which becomes associated as well with certain kinds of landscapes. Lady Emily, to begin with the simpler figure, thereby seems representative of a bland smoothness that implies the triumph of civilization over all the interesting unevenness and passion of nature. She exhibits "that polished surface of manner common to those with whom she mixed" (1). Staying at her country home with some lady friends—mainly "persons of *ton* who, though everything collectively, are nothing individually"—she also devotes her days to playing with her infant son on the smooth lawns. The grounds themselves—"laid out in a classical and costly manner" —constitute a civilized rejection of "the wild and simple nature of the surrounding scenery" (2). But perhaps the description of her husband Mr. Mandeville, a commonplace Tory politician, best epitomizes the tame superficiality of her environment: "Neither in person nor in character was he much beneath or above the ordinary standard of men. He was one of Nature's Macadamized achievements. His great fault was his equality; and you longed for a hill though it were to climb, or a stone though it were in your way. Love attaches itself to something prominent, even if that something be what others would hate. One can scarcely feel extremes for mediocrity" (1).

Depths exist only in potentiality beneath the macadamized surfaces of her world. Although "the deeper recesses of her nature . . . hid the treasures of a mine which no human eye had beheld" (1), she seems never to become conscious of the treasures. Her illicit love does grant her a new level of awareness, but "to separate herself from the herd, was to discover, to feel, to murmur at the vacuum of her being" (2). In the unavoidably sexual imagery of the story, "the bitter knowledge of *herself*" continually refers to the feeling of emptiness—the "abyss," the "void," the "blank"—that she both longs and fears to have filled. She remains in herself little more than a polished surface.

Falkland, on the contrary, is in no sense equable or macadamized. An unstable combination of heights, depths, and all manner of contradictory passions, he typifies pure energy, and the lands surrounding his hereditary home differ accordingly from those of the Mandevilles: "Even the short distance between Mr. Mandeville's house and L—— wrought as distinct a change in the character of the country as any length of space could have effected": "Dark woods, large tracts of unenclosed heath, abrupt variations of hill and vale, and a dim and broken outline beyond of uninterrupted mountains, formed the great features of that romantic country" (2, 3). The setting provides, in fact, more than a suggestive image for Falkland's character because he has grown up as a Wordsworthian child, and such scenes have actually "educated" him. He has, moreover, never quite transcended the undisciplined, passionate quality of the earliest stage of his relationship with nature: "the wild delight which he took then in the convulsions and varieties of nature" have marked him with "that fitfulness of temper, that affection for extremes [which have] accompanied [him] through life" (3, 1).

As an aspect of his "affection for extremes" perhaps, he has oscillated during much of his mature life between the worlds of men and of nature—"mingling today in the tumults of the city, and tomorrow alone with [his] own heart in the solitude of un-peopled nature" (1). Although the urban and solitary settings naturally recall the macadamized surfaces and empty depths of Lady Emily's environment, the values of the two levels are now reversed. Falkland finds emptiness in the realm of collective humanity and plenitude in the depths of his individual being.

In the human world, to treat its emptiness first, he has supposedly wasted himself and others in a vain quest for meaning. He had loved a woman to madness, for example, until he had lost her and realized that he had simply "shaped out in his heart an imaginary idol . . . and breathed into the image the pure but burning spirit of that innate love from which it sprung!" (1). And a subsequent philanthropic passion has further revealed the vacancy of the external world. Love of nature having progressed in vaguely Words-worthian fashion to love of man (though "at a distance"), he has sought universal "knowledge" for man's sake. But his studies, while originally empirical and utilitarian in their bias, have only carried him to the position of "Faustus," who had found "nothing in knowledge but its inutility" (1). To love or to know a thing has been to observe its disintegration: every "phantom I had wor-shipped melted into snow. Whatever I pursued partook of the energy, yet fitfulness of my nature" (1). The urge to know—whether carnally or intellectually—may even have concealed a perverse wish to impose himself on those external forms and so to prove their nullity. "All who had loved him, he had repaid with ruin" (4), and his intellectual researches have similarly amounted to an aggression against nature. He refers to having "penetrated the womb of nature" and having "erect[ed] a tower, which shall reach the heavens," and concludes that these aspirations have only isolated him more fully from mankind and from external truth (2).

Regardless of the question of blame, his failure to make contact with some palpable truth has reduced him to a sense of cosmic desolation. He has existed at times in "a waste, a stillness, an infinity, without a wanderer or a voice"; he has "made the universe one wide mausoleum of the lost" (3, 4). The effort, in the phrases of Coleridge's ode, "from outward forms to win/ The passions and the life whose fountains are within" has drained the vitality of both regions. In his first letter Falkland thus indicates that one may even wish to close off those dangerous avenues to empirical knowledge, the five senses: "We are the dupes and the victims of our senses: while we use them to gather from external things the hoards we store within, we cannot foresee the punishments we prepare for ourselves."

When he returns at the other extreme, then, to "the solitude of unpeopled nature," Falkland goes back in imagination to the ideal sources that antedate the ill-fated establishment of human society. Precisely because of the "stillness" and "loneliness" of "the solitudes unbroken by human footstep," they also suggest a greater plenitude than do "the tumults of the city." They possess all the richness of potentiality and thereby recall the energies that had existed as potentialities in Falkland too before he had squandered them among human beings. In the secure fastness of his "own empire of thought *and self*," these energies begin to stir once more. He compares himself to Prospero and glories in his ability to "feel all the powers, and gather together all the resources of [his] mind" as he reclines, apparently unoccupied, in his favorite retreat—"surrounded by the trees, the waters, the wild birds, and the hum, the glow, the exultation which teems visibly and audibly through creation in the noon of a summer's day!" (1). The mere consciousness of teeming fertility, powers, and resources now suffices him, and he dare not again employ these energies on behalf of civilization. As Chateaubriand had also understood in *Atala* (although his "execution" had fallen far short of his "design"), nothing can be more "sublime, than the vast solitude of an unpeopled wilderness, the woods, the mountains, the face of nature cast in the fresh, yet giant mould of a new and unpolluted world; and, amidst those most silent and mighty temples of THE GREAT GOD, the lone spirit of Love reigning and brightening over all" (1).

At its source the energy that identifies Falkland therefore remains divine, and the affair with Lady Emily should be the supreme attempt to use it creatively. Like the breath of life, his passionate spirit should awaken her to an awareness of unique individuality; their union should symbolize the formation of a vital new identity. As I have intimated, however, the creative attempt fails, for man evidently cannot repeat in this manner the work of "THE GREAT GOD." While Bulwer's alleged horror of adultery may also provide a mundanely ethical explanation for the failure, the more important factor is that baffling "metaphysical" hostility between different levels of being. The imagery of the love story emphasizes two aspects of that hostility in particular: Falkland's visionary idealism seeks to dissolve Emily's empirical understanding of reality, while his anarchic, uncontainable energy destroys her actual material body.

With respect to the antagonism between conceptions of reality, Falkland seems frequently to be luring Emily into areas of vision inimical to her mental health. She first sees him lying asleep; a search for her child's lost ball has carried her from the safety of the lawns into the grove where he likes to doze and to play Prospero. For the rest of the day, "the face haunt[s] her like a dream," and she will find herself drawn ever further into a mysteriously unreal existence. "Like the music of an indistinct and half-remembered dream," his voice rings in her ear at night while the reflections in the lake where they meet suggest "the dream-like remembrance of a former existence" (1, 4). As the narrator explains in attempting to describe the phenomenon, their love has disinterred the enchanted setting of some distant past: *"We remove the lava, and the world of a gone day is before us!"* (3).

Like Bulwer's own recollected paradise with its hidden Venus, the ideal landscape is an image of identity, and Falkland seems practically to wish he could assume Emily bodily into that setting. She must cease to take pleasure in her husband's house and garden and must learn to see all the precise contours of Falkland's imagined world around herself. Indeed if she would only realize it, his letters keep assuring her, she already exists within that realm of his ego. She reflects his "earliest visions of beauty and love" and from time immemorial has been dwelling as the "divinity" within his "temple" or the "idol" above the "altar of [his] soul." In urging elopement to Italy, he even seems to invite her on an all but literal journey to "the world of a gone day"—back to one more version of his own mythic, unpeopled solitude: "We will go, my Emily, to those golden lands . . . where the breezes are languid beneath the passion of the voluptuous skies; and where the purple light . . . invests all things with its glory. . . . Amidst the myrtle and the vine, and the valleys where the summer sleeps, and the rivers that murmur the memories and the legends of old; amidst the hills and the glossy glades, and the silver fountains, still as beautiful as if the Nymph and Spirit yet held and decorated an earthly home; amidst these we will make the couch of our bridals, and the moon of Italian skies shall keep watch on our repose" (3).

However alluring, such invitations give Lady Emily a sensation like vertigo. Because she is so essentially the representative of empiricism and civilization, she cannot grasp the reality of imagined, pre-civilized settings that have no basis in her actual experience. "Their love," says the narrator, "was their creation; beyond all was night, chaos,—nothing!" and the void seems to terrify her more than the dream-like creation reassures her. "I shudder at the abyss," she confides to her journal after their first admission of love, and when she finally agrees to leap, "[she] felt as if the very earth had passed from [her] feet" (2, 4). Indeed she does fall into nothingness because his recollections of the rich, primeval settings melt "like the baseless fabric of [Prospero's] vision." After the consummation of their love, "Emily's bosom . . . was a dreary void —a vast blank": "Like the period before creation, her mind was a chaos of jarring elements, and knew neither the method of reflection, nor the division of time" (4). Without restoring them to a setting of infinite potentiality and fertility, their regressive love has simply undermined the achievement and eroded the rational order that civilization has slowly established through the millenia.

While threatening to dissolve everything into an impalpable vacancy, the passion is also portrayed—in its other destructive aspect—as a fund of energy that resists material containment. Particularly significant in this context is the imagery of rising waters. A stream runs through the grove in which Emily first sees Falkland asleep, and her eye falls on an appropriate line in the book lying open beside him: " 'The course of true love never did run smooth!' " From this point, the narrator observes some pages later, one may "trace through all its windings the formation of [their] affection," and Emily's problem especially will be an inability to control those windings. When a woman has experienced "the deeper sources of affection," she may find that they resist "flow[ing] into one only and legitimate channel" (2). An excursion to the seashore makes the process appropriately dramatic: the tide sweeps in to separate the lovers from their party, and in facing death, they rapturously avow their love and embrace. Although an undesired rescue intervenes at the last moment, the ocean has clearly revealed the weakness of the ethical laws and civilized customs that would contain and channel the forces of the deep. Soon, regardless of Emily's most virtuous resolutions, "the various streams with which the country abounded were swelled by late rains into an unwonted rapidity and breadth; and their voices blended with the rushing sound of the winds, and the distant roll of the thunder" (3). That night Falkland recklessly submits to a sense of destiny and "track[s] the stream; it wound its way through Mandeville's grounds, and broadened at last into the lake"—on the banks of which the love will finally be consummated.

Still more pervasive than the external imagery of the ocean and swelling streams may be the references to equally palpable and un-controllable forces within the circulatory systems of the lovers. These forces, whose full pressure will destroy Emily, naturally seem to originate in Falkland. He mentions *"the tumultuous ocean of my heart,"* and there would appear to be a literal disorder in the actual biological organ. "The love which had so penetrated and pervaded his whole system" refers similarly to his very real blood: "a fever had entered his veins" (3, 2). "The blood rushed into my cheek," he observes on a typical occasion: "I felt choked with con-tending emotion. . . . I heard my very heart beat," and he goes on to echo *Childe Harold* perhaps as well as Bacon: "Oh God! if there be a curse, it is to burn, swell, madden with feelings which you are doomed to conceal! This is, indeed, to be 'a cannibal of one's own heart' " (2). In fact, he does not contain those pressures within his heart, for the internal love becomes progressively more physical in its outward manifestation. It is "revealed by the eye," next "re-corded by the lip" in words, and then recorded by the lip in still more palpable fashion—"that long, deep, burning pressure!—youth, love, life, soul, all concentrated in that one kiss!"(2). Fi-nally, of course, there is the sexual intercourse which suggests an eruption of the irresistible liquid energy: "His kisses were like lava; the turbulent and stormy elements of sin and desire were aroused even to madness within him. He clasped her still nearer to his bosom: her lips answered to his own: they caught perhaps something of his spirit which they received: . . . the bosom heaved wildly, that was pressed to his beating and burning heart" (4).

Although Falkland has supposedly suffered from a literal heart problem, the medical history of Lady Emily indicates still more graphically how destructive that amorous energy must be to physi-cal health. Her very life depends on her ability to control her blood pressure, and more frequently and heroically than Falkland she must resist the "fever" and endure those "choking" spells. Ulti-mately his passion infuses more energy into her than her physical organization can possibly bear. A weak blood vessel that has burst at a crisis earlier in the story breaks again when her infuriated husband confronts her, and she expires from massive hemorrhaging: "the blood gushed in torrents from her lips."

The love has therefore been destructive in both its spiritual-platonic and its physical-sexual manifestations. It has constituted the supreme instance in Falkland's career of the inability of the egoistic energy within to combine creatively with the materials of the world without. Insofar as Falkland has typified the eternal principle of selfishness in all men, the romance has clearly established its allegorical or metaphysical point too. The individual tends ultimately to identify himself through his mysterious recollections of a pre-existence in which he has ruled in unchallenged and divine supremacy. Hence derives his inevitable aggression against whatever would socialize and subdue the wildness of his individuality—especially if the enemy should "embody," as Emily has done, an aspect of himself. According to the grim logic, which Edgar Allan Poe seems incidentally to have relished in another early Bulwer story too, the discovery of an alter-ego or double may even drive certain egoists to murderous desperation.[6]

The only false aspect of the allegorical love story has resulted from Bulwer's occasional payment of lip service to "conventional morality." His narrator has felt obliged to assure the reader that his pages constitute not "an apology for sin" but "the burning records of its sufferings, its repentance, and its doom" (3). The final visions and actions of the hero may therefore be interesting because they carry the quest for metaphysical truth so unequivocally beyond the limits of ethical categories. Suggesting an epilogue, these last events endow the myth of the individual identity with all the resonance of a cosmic struggle between the forces of anarchic freedom and of physical containment. In this struggle it also becomes clear that far from typifying sin, the egoistic energy and demonism of Falkland have remained allied to a divine principle of freedom. The destructivenes of his career is even transformed into a manifestation of the process that will ultimately liberate the universe.

In a delirium for weeks after Emily's death, Falkland first has visions that represent the awesome, punishing powers that seek to contain and suffocate his energy. He finds himself in a "vast and blazing prison" and wanders amidst the flowers, trees, hills, and streams that appear to be precise infernal counterparts of the "golden lands" of his pre-existence. All consists of lurid, scorching fire, and his paradise lies ruined, as he understands, "For Ever." Then in another vision reminiscent of those of De Quincey, he seems to experience an even more hideous form of the everlasting bondage to mortality. It begins with the full horror of death, as if in that "tumultuous ocean" of his passion: ". . . the lengthened and suffocating torture of that drowning death—the impotent and convulsive contest with the closing waters—the gurgle, the choking, the bursting of the pent breath, the flutter of the heart, its agony, and *its stillness*." He evidently falls to the abysmal deeps to which he had consigned Emily, and there, "chained to a rock round which the heavy waters rose as a wall," he feels his body rot piece by piece through endless ages. Revolting sea-serpents and monsters, apparently suggestive of the ugliness of sexuality, swim about him glaring "with a livid and death-like eye."

Falkland refuses, however, to submit to the enemy that punishes him for his anarchic energy. Recovering from his delirium, he devotes himself to a cause that results in a vision of the apotheosis of freedom. With his uncle, who has been urging such a step throughout the story, he returns to his sources in Spain, the land of his birth, and joins the forces of the Constitutionalists in the Pyrenees. (One thinks here, of course, not only of Byron's trip to Greece but also of the subsequent visit of Tennyson and Hallam to the camp of Ojeda in the Pyrenees.) Although the immediate prospects for the band embodying "the last hope and energy of freedom" are bleak, their leader Riego has "lived solely for Freedom" and he confidently prophesies victory over all the material powers of tyranny:

It is in vain that they oppose OPINION; anything else they may subdue. They may conquer wind, water, nature itself; but to the progress of that secret, subtle, pervading spirit, their imagination can devise, their strength can accomplish, no bar: its *votaries* they may seize, they may destroy; *itself* they cannot touch. If they check it in one place, it invades them in another. They cannot build a wall across the whole earth; and, if they could, it would pass over its summit! Chains cannot bind it, for it is immaterial—dungeons enclose it, for it is universal. Over the faggot and the scaffold—over the bleeding bodies of its defenders which they pile against its path, it sweeps on with a noiseless but unceasing march. Do they levy armies against it, it presents to them no palpable object to oppose. *Its camp is the universe; its asylum is the bosoms of their own soldiers.* Let them depopulate, destroy as they please, to each extremity of the earth; but as long as they have a single supporter themselves—as long as they leave a single individual into whom that spirit can enter—so long they will have the same labours to encounter, and the same enemy to subdue.

The apocalyptic fantasy indicates the lofty extremism of Bulwer's idealism. The struggle between material tyranny and ideal freedom will proceed until one has annihilated the other. So long as there exists "a single individual into whom that spirit can enter," tyranny must feel itself threatened and so must continue to depopulate and destroy the earth. Eventually the single, individual self-consciousness will remain—the only reality amidst the collapse of the entire material creation.

Far from being able to manifest or express the energy of the ideal, matter is the doomed adversary of the eternal idea behind itself. The final event of the story—Falkland's suicidal death in the cause of freedom—thus seems designed to imply the victory of the essential ideal ego over the imprisoning physical form: "He stood in this world a being who mixed in all its changes, performed all its offices, took, as if by the force of superior mechanical power, a leading share in its events; but whose thoughts and soul were as offsprings of another planet, imprisoned in a human form, and *longing for their home!*" The ending raises again, to be sure, the possibility (more disturbing to the religious scruples of Bulwer's mother than the story's treatment of adultery) that the sense of an immortal soul may have been a ghastly illusion. Beneath the polished surfaces may lie only vacancy and night. Yet as death claims Falkland at the same hour in which Lady Emily had died, he appears to have some vision that leaves him in serenity. He has presumably returned to the divine wilderness and solitude from which all the energy of life has flowed.

With its emphasis upon civilized environments rather than the "unpeopled wilderness," *Pelham* appears to present an extraordinary contrast to *Falkland*. Henry Pelham dreads the darkness and solitude of the idealist's cave, and his utilitarianism leads him to evaluate life in terms very different from those of Erasmus Falkland. He criticizes his scholarly friend Clutterbuck, for example, because the life of the latter has been "cautiously excluded from a single sunbeam" and has thus remained "elaborately useless, ingeniously unprofitable; and leaving at the moment it melts away, not a single trace of the space it occupied, or the labour it cost" (2:26).[7] Pelham himself has been turning a steady profit from all his labors ever since his school days, when his mother had first taught him the importance of seeking in all things for his own "advantage": "Remember, my dear," she had written him at Eton, "that in all the friends you make at present, you look to the advantage you can derive from them hereafter; that is what we call knowledge of the world, and it is to get the knowledge of the world that you are sent to a public school" (1, 2).

Despite the outrageousness of the advice, the profitable "knowledge of the world" need not entirely contradict all ideal values and truths, and Pelham will eventually gain some awareness of the soul. His experience continually enforces the lesson, however, that any high truth depends for its value or utility upon its being viewed obliquely. He approaches self-knowledge, then, not through introspection but through his knowledge of mankind—and so escapes the isolating ramifications of the "perilous stuff." For the advantage and profit of the reader, moreover, he has tried to maintain the veil over the deeper meanings implicit in his retailed life story. Not until the end of "the motley course of my confessions" does he admit "that I have sometimes hinted at thy instruction when only appearing to strive for thy amusement. But on this I will not dwell; for the moral *insisted upon* often loses its effect, and all that I will venture to hope is, that I have opened to thee one true, and not utterly hacknied, page in the various and mighty volume of mankind" (3:22).

The "laughter" that Lord Vincent, a character in the story, terms "a distinct indication of the human race" is thus designed to insinuate a humanizing awareness (2:15). Or as the preface of 1828 emphasizes, "the appearance of frivolities [is] not indulged for the sake of frivolity" but in order "to inculcate the substance of truth." Although Diogenes Teufelsdröckh failed to perceive it, that obliquely and comically inculcated truth may even constitute Bulwer's version of a clothes philosophy. The story dramatizes the enjoyment of semblances and clothes for their own sake precisely to hint at the inadequacy of a life in which all value exists on the surface.

Yet while the story successfully implies the deeper levels, it does not go on to define a useful interaction between the superficial vestments and the profounder truths. The clothes continue to function as disguises rather than as expressive symbols for the truth that one dare not view directly. Pelham is indubitably, as the 1840 preface states, "something wiser—nobler—better" than the "men of the world" about him, but his better nature remains hidden and somewhat irrelevant to the world in which he must live. Since the hostility between the ideal and the material thus endures, his career may even seem as uncreative and as unprofitable in its way as Falkland's.

The external world, to begin with the comically superficial aspect of Pelham's knowledge, does not initially appear to contain the mysterious and ungovernable natural forces that had figuratively overwhelmed all social restraints in *Falkland*. Although a violent storm once overtakes Pelham as he rides through dangerous country at night, he waits calmly for its abatement and observes at last without a trace of awe: "the beautiful moon broke out, the cloud rolled heavily away, and the sky shone forth, as fair and smiling as Lady —— at a ball, after she has been beating her husband at home" (2:27). So determined is Pelham to condescend to natural settings that he even finds the magnificent old groves of his ancestral estates less impressive in themselves than as "the witness of [the antiquity] of the family which had given them existence." And as the sun sets gloriously over the lake, it "ting[es] the dark firs that overspread the margin, with a rich and golden light, that put me excessively in mind of the Duke of ——'s livery." For nature as for man the clothed appearances alone matter; whatever lies hidden from view, Pelham suggests in the next paragraph, has ceased for all practical purposes to exist: "As Providence made the stars for the benefit of earth, so it made servants for the use of gentlemen; and, as neither stars nor servants appear except when we want them, so I suppose they are in a sort of suspense from *being*, except at those important and happy moments" (1:34).

Human society assigns the value—and thus gives meaningful existence—to all individuals and things. Pelham's flippant suspicion that the trees and stars have no being apart from his consciousness of them betrays not genuine solipsism but a conviction that man is the proper study of mankind: "I study nature rather in men than fields, and find no landscape afford [*sic*] such variety to the eye, and such subject to the contemplation, as the inequalities of the human heart" (2:25).

In the human landscape too, though, the varieties and inequalities appear entirely superficial at first. Wherever Pelham goes, he finds people whom he can readily classify according to their obvious functions in society. He travels among "species of bipeds" and is always collecting typical "specimens"—from "the baronetage," for example, or from the class of "*le chevalier amoureux.*" Since underlying differences among individuals do not count for very much, everyone apparently tries to wear as well as he can and without question the outfit prescribed for his social identity. Men of fashion, especially, resemble the servants of "the man in one of Le Sage's novels, who was constantly changing his servants, and yet had but one suit of livery, which every new comer, whether he was tall or short, fat or thin, was obliged to wear" (1:8). In assuming the color of a certain duke's livery, the sun itself provides an appropriately artificial lighting for the theatrical settings and the sometimes ill-fitting costumes.

Pelham's absurdly passionate liaison with the "Byronic" duchesse de Perpignan helps to indicate the peril of seeking for some truth beneath the surface of an individual's personality. Hiding in a closet from the duc one evening, Pelham comes upon a wig and a set of false teeth, and "from that moment the duchesse honoured me with her most deadly abhorrence" (1:23). She attempts to poison his coffee, to stab him with a paper cutter, and to embroil him fatally in a duel. But however ludicrous her efforts to model her behavior upon episodes in the *Turkish Tales*, she does depend on the attractive appearances and romantic poses for her very existence. When an eruption threatens her complexion, she must therefore cure it at any cost. Dangerous drugs permit her to appear at an important social event as radiant as ever but in the course of the evening a stroke paralyzes her. Learning that her face will remain drawn on one side, she kills herself. Once the mask is gone, such a figure must collapse altogether. Or like the stars and servants who are in a "suspense from *being*" when not wanted, characters who cease to play their roles and who retire from the social scene thereby cease to exist. It is impossible to go on living backstage.

As if to indicate Pelham's own derivation from the theatrical milieu—rather than from a realm of platonic pre-existence—his parents also live with the majority of characters on the figurative stage. The Hon. Mr. Pelham hides his henpecked insignificance with a better than average histrionic skill, and his moment of greatness arrives when he learns of his wife's elopement with a wealthy man. Concealing the delight occasioned by the prospect of the damages he will win, "he called for his dressing-gown—searched the garret and the kitchen—looked in the maids' drawers and the cellaret—and finally declared he was distracted. I have heard that the servants were quite melted by his grief, and I do not doubt it in the least, for he was always celebrated for his skill in private theatricals" (1:1).

Lady Frances Pelham, the most egregious and amusing worldling in the novel, similarly lives in terms of her costumes and theatrical propensities. When she unexpectedly inherits twenty thousand pounds, for example, she dresses as a sultana, receives nine hundred people in a tent, and becomes the sensation of the season. This enables her pretentiously to enjoy the attentions of the most sought-after man in town, with whom she virtuously refuses to elope until the season ends. But her complacent artificiality becomes especially marvelous whenever she enacts the role of "affectionate mother." Expressing maternal solicitude in her rather famous letters, she worries about Pelham's complexion, his clothes, the people of fashion he visits, and his religion—insofar as church-going is equated with good taste in Cachemires. (In the same vein, a vulgar countess Pelham meets at Cheltenham confounds "morality" with the observance of fashionable hours.)

Typified by such characters, society therefore manages to do without authentic emotions or values. The affectation of strong passions—love, hatred, jealousy, grief—substitutes for the real thing, and by tacit consent everyone has agreed to take the counterfeit at its face value. Lady Frances, who had thought she could not appear at important events without her diamonds, thus finds she can do as well with paste. Indeed no one desires a true currency, for true standards would threaten the comfortable artificiality to which man has reduced his environment and his life. The majority of society, Pelham observes, "would conceive it an insult to be thought of sufficient rank to be respectable for what they are" (1:3).

As he collects knowledge of this world, Pelham seems initially to resemble its fashionable inhabitants, for he too fails to exemplify a profound awareness of what he is individually. Bulwer intended, according to his son, that Pelham be "a person who took to himself the form and colour of the society in which he moved,"[8] and like a good chameleon Pelham does reflect the colors of his environments. Strolling into the Faubourg St. Germain, he finds his "feelings, thoughts—nature itself— . . . [are] tinged, refined, ennobled by a certain inexpressible awe." He imagines himself a survivor of the ancien régime and "tread[s] the gloomy streets with the dignity of a man, who is recalling the splendours of an ancient court where he once did homage" (1:23). More spectacularly and amusingly, he absorbs the tinges of each elector's house when he canvasses a Parliamentary borough in his uncle's possession. The capacity to be all things to all men allows him not only to alter his personality to fit each household but also to hint at his adherence to quite contradictory political philosophies. And the same negative capability may contribute to his linguistic facility; he readily picks up new tongues, including "Flash," to suit the countries and strata of society he visits.

The indeterminacy of his underlying identity becomes of most obvious thematic significance as the novel develops the motif of mirrors. A thorough dandy, Pelham naturally spends many hours before his mirror considering the propriety of new colors and styles of dress, and wherever he goes, he looks instinctively for mirrors. "I was ushered into a beautiful apartment," he observes typically, "hung with rich damask, and interspersed with a profusion of mirrors, which enchanted me to the heart" (2:9). He conceives of the reflected image almost as if it were his entire and literal being and so seems to depend on mirrors to reassure himself of his existence. Yet since the mirrors do not always reveal the same image, he also tends to approach them with a certain anxiety. He dreads visits to country homes, for example, where he may be lodged in a room "with a looking-glass, that . . . distort[s] one's features like a paralytic stroke" (1:8). An unexpected reflection in the mirror of a hotel room similarly causes him to shrink back "aghast": "I . . . had the pleasure of seeing my complexion catch the colour of the curtain that overhung the glass on each side, and exhibit the pleasing *rurality* of a pale green" (2:2). Instead of reflecting his own true colors, mirrors may thus impart their shade to his chameleon-like nature, and insofar as possible he looks for glasses of an attractive color. For his own apartment, he tells Lady Rose-ville, he has purchased "Bohemian glasses": "I have one which I only look at when I am out of humour; it throws such a lovely flush upon the complexion, that it revives my spirits for the rest of the day" (2:8).

Despite the comic exaggeration and insolence of such statements, Pelham does gradually realize that a kind of guilt attaches to the creature who possesses no inner authenticity of being. He thus comes to criticize his mother because in having "lived, moved, breathed, only for the world," she has wanted "self-dignity" (3:7). But the potential guilt of worldly superficiality emerges still more clearly in the career of the confidence man Job Jonson. "My morals," Job tells the protagonist, "are all that I can call my own, and those I will sell you at your own price." His morals, that is, resemble those of the fashionable people who unquestionably adopt the conventions of their set, and Job even claims his own right to the status of gentlemen: "I belong to no trade—I follow no calling: I rove where I list, and rest where I please: in short, I know no occupation but my indolence, and no law but my will. Now, Sir, may I not call myself a gentleman?" (3:5).

Indeed Job functions as one of the alter-egoes of Pelham, the "Gentleman" of the novel's subtitle. More adept and plausible as an actor than Pelham, he is able to victimize the latter a couple of times in quick succession and so to earn his honest admiration. In one disguise he even appears as a dandy more resplendently gorgeous and more outrageously pretentious than Pelham himself, and Pelham enlists him as a companion for some of his adventures. When the plot requires Pelham to descend to the criminal underworld, he gets the incredible Job to teach him "Flash," to create a costume for him, and to coach him for his most fantastic role. Job transforms him, in fact, beyond recognition. Shorn of his precious locks, covered with makeup, and disguised in rusty clerical attire, Pelham experiences what may be his moment of greatest panic before a mirror: "Had I gazed at the reflection for ever, I should not have recognized either my form or visage. I thought my soul had undergone a real transmigration, and not carried to its new body a particle of the original one" (3:17).

The tremendous recognition that he can exist in any form, shape, or color that Job may choose to give him does not, however, overwhelm him with a horror of his own essential nullity. For by this time Pelham has learned that the soul does exist as an individualizing principle apart from all the superficial costumes and colors of man's external, collective being. Although the novel does not, like *Falkland*, use frequent imagery of landscapes to define it, certain hints do suggest the vitality of the whole world within. Lady Roseville seems to allude, for example, to its often intense anguish when she and Pelham meet at a ball: " 'How little,' said Lady Roseville, 'can the crowd know of the individuals who compose it. As the most opposite colours may be blended into one, and so lose their individual hues, and be classed under a single name, so every one here will go home, and speak of the *"gay scene*," without thinking for a moment, how many breaking hearts may have composed it' " (3:7).

While pursuing knowledge in such scenes, Pelham becomes aware that four members of the crowd in particular possess "individual hues" and lead valuable lives backstage. Through them he gains his indirect self-knowledge too. Where Job and other figures had reflected something of his artificial aspects, these four conceal profounder secrets and suggest the more "metaphysical" dimensions of his hidden self. They are the pedantic young Lord Vincent, the widowed Countess of Roseville, the genuinely Byronic Sir Reginald Glanville, and Glanville's sister Ellen, who becomes Pelham's wife.

Although it baffles most people, the secret "buried deep beneath the surface of [Lord Vincent's] character" is perhaps the least difficult for Pelham to penetrate: "I recognized in the man, who as yet was only playing a part, a resemblance to myself, while he, perhaps, saw at times that I was somewhat better than the voluptuary, and somewhat wiser than the coxcomb, which were all that at present it suited me to appear" (1:14). Behind their playacting, in other words, lies an unusually sophisticated level of intellectual awareness, and their friendship deepens as they discuss literary and political topics and perceive the similarity of their critical insights. Committed and ambitious students both, they arrive finally at the moment of confession so rare for individuals in their society; "in a sort of nervous excitement," Vincent removes his figurative mask: " 'Pelham,' said he, at last, 'it is for the sake of moments like these, when your better nature flashes out, that I have sought your society and your friendship. *I*, too, am not wholly what I appear' " (2:6).

Yet Vincent threatens Pelham's ethical well-being, for it becomes apparent that he serves on the allegorical plane as the representative of man's potentially immoral intellectual capacity. While profoundly versed like Pelham in the writings of the utilitarians, he has not really admitted the degree to which his self-interest must merge with the general interest. His intellect thus degenerates into the somewhat ruthless instrument of his own political advancement, and he tends, like most of Bulwer's intellectuals, to adopt an end-justifies-means ethical theory. In a critical episode he tempts Pelham to give up some of the purity of their political principles and to join in his intrigues with the most undemocratic of the Tories. A sort of compromise with principles would enable Pelham to take a seemingly justifiable revenge on his own wily party chief and would get him into Parliament, where he could thereafter be his own man. But Pelham resists the temptation, and his cooling friendship with Vincent demonstrates that man must not give free reign to the intellectual aspect of his personality.

Lady Roseville, with whom Pelham also establishes "a sort of freemasonry," begins the series of beautiful, faintly tragic, and aristocratic women that feel a half-romantic, half-maternal tenderness for Bulwer's young protagonists. Pelham meets her early in his quest, and while her air of subtle mystery fascinates him, he assumes at first that her only secret is that ineffable one of perfect breeding: "Her manners constituted her chief attraction: while they were utterly different from those of every one else, you could not, in the least minutiae, discover in what the difference consisted: this is, in my opinion, the real test of perfect breeding. While you are enchanted with the effect, it should possess so little prominency and peculiarity, that you should never be able to guess the cause" (1:3).

As Pelham soon realizes, though, her "difference" consists in more than her breeding: under "a veil which no superficial observer could penetrate," "she possessed great sensibility, and even romance of temper, strong passions, and still stronger imagination" (1:5). These passionate and imaginative qualities evidently correspond to the "higher and deeper feelings" which she claims, during their moment of most profound communication, to have discerned in Pelham (3:7). Unfortunately, these qualities also prove as perilous in their way as the intellectual prowess of Lord Vincent, for they have involved Lady Roseville in an unrequited and increasingly uncontrollable passion for Sir Reginald. The division between her social and passionate natures becomes ever more tragically acute. She ceases to function as arbitress in the great social sphere and takes to wandering at night, literally veiled now, outside the house of the ailing Glanville: then, "the last news we received of her, informed us, that she was living in Sienna, in utter seclusion, and very infirm health" (3:22). In solving the entire mystery about her,

Pelham has therefore recognized not only his own potentially very passionate sensibility but also the necessity for keeping it too under strict control.

For like Lady Roseville, Pelham has been particularly susceptible to the spell of Glanville, whom he has known ever since he had first been sent to gain knowledge of the world at Eton. There, he recalls, Glanville had been "the one, who of all my early companions differed the most from myself; yet the one whom I loved the most, and the one whose future destiny was the most intertwined with my own" (1:2). As the seeming opposite of the highly civilized Pelham, Glanville has assumed the function of his demon shadow and has returned periodically to haunt him. Pelham often comes upon his wild friend suddenly and unexpectedly—in a cemetery at night, for example, or in gambling hells—and at such moments Glanville's penetrating gaze expresses a "ferocity and defiance, . . . which made me start back and feel my heart stand still" or "a joy so malignant and fiendish, that no look of mere anger or hatred could have so chilled my heart" (1:6, 19). There is, of course, a deep mystery here, which slowly but inevitably engulfs Pelham and threatens with its lurid sensationalism, as Bulwer later admitted, to burst the seams of the predominantly comic novel.[9]

Pelham nevertheless manages at last to control the demonic energy that emanates, as it were, from his own unconscious being. To clear the "metaphysically" but not legally guilty Glanville of a murder charge, he makes the journey that has, in Jerome J. McGann's observation, "all the trappings of a descent into [the] underworld."[10] His safe passage through the ordeal, which incidentally entails his killing of a criminal, proves his mettle once more.[11] He has confronted at least metaphorically all the energies hidden in the depths of the human personality and has either exorcised them or reasserted civilized and ethical control over them. While giving him self-knowledge, his discovery of the secrets of Vincent, Lady Roseville, and Glanville have thus alerted him as well to the dangers of the world within. A surrender to the inner man may involve a guilt as great as that of the worldling who surrenders all "self-dignity" to live entirely on the surface.

The marriage to Ellen may have been intended to suggest the proper sort of reconciliation with the energies of the world within. Typifying the anima, Ellen seems to exist as a milder and more innocent version of each of Pelham's other allegorical counterparts—Glanville, Vincent, and Lady Roseville. Her brother has loved her above everyone save his own lost mistress, and when he expires from fever and consumption on her wedding day, he leaves her, as the best part of himself, to Pelham. Her connection with Vincent may be less obvious. Yet Pelham had first seen her in Vincent's company, and although he had feared to "have her presence profaned" by the latter's pedantry, she actually resembles Vincent in her unexpectedly intellectual and ambitious aspect: "her knowledge was even masculine for its variety and extent, [though] she was averse to displaying it," and "she was, at heart, perhaps, as ambitious as myself; but . . . [her] aspirations . . . were softened by her timidity, and purified by her religion" (2:4; 3:4; 2:20). And like Lady Roseville, whose protégée she becomes, she possesses a deeply ardent nature that moves Pelham to exclaim at one point, "Thank Heaven, *she was alive*" (2:16).

The marriage may fail, however, to unite completely the various aspects of Pelham. As he had emphasized in proposing for Ellen's hand, their love can have nothing to do with his dandiacal nature: "*that* love was not to be mingled with the ordinary objects of life—it was too pure to be profaned by the levities and follies which are all of my nature that I have permitted myself to develop to the world" (3:12). Her "pure and holy love" finally withdraws him altogether from the levities and follies; after their wedding they retire to the country where he plans to devote two calm years to reflection and study.

Although he wants to return one day to the world and devote his energies and ambitions to the service of mankind, it remains uncertain that he will find the way. To judge from his experience hitherto, the world simply does not offer any very adequate or productive channels for the hidden energies and ambitions of individuals. Those who have possessed deep passions have ended up broken and destroyed like Glanville and Lady Roseville, corrupted like Lord Vincent, or rather touchingly pathetic like a gourmet called Lord Guloseton. The strength of Pelham himself has resulted not from his ability to convert the hidden energy into useful actions but from his ability to live with the tension. He has merely accepted the absolute necessity for a fragmented existence and enjoyed the irrelevant costumes while somehow maintaining an impalpable integrity.

To the extent that *Pelham* has owed its thematic and structural coherence to its acknowledgement of the discrepancy between the external and internal realms it has also repeated the lesson of *Falkland*. Although "knowledge of the world" need not corrupt and although it may lead indirectly to a profounder self-knowledge, the two sorts of truth remain separate. To know the member of the species is not to know the individual soul, for there can still be no symbolic correspondence between the two.

As if dissatisfied with each truth in itself, Bulwer did not wish readers to identify him too exclusively with either Erasmus Falkland or Henry Pelham. He assured his fiancée that Falkland was "quite a different character [from himself] and meant as such," and "the silly error" that kept him associated with Pelham would exasperate him for many years.[12] He had modelled Pelham on a friend,[13] and precisely to suggest their essential disparity, he prefixed a long, amusing, and rather convincing dialogue between the "Author" and "Mr. Pelham" to early editions of *The Disowned*. Still, if neither of the first two protagonists was Bulwer himself, they did embody the two major tendencies in him and represent the duality of the truth about man. In the succeeding novels he would continue to state that duality, but as he slowly altered its terms, he would also begin to resolve some of its destructive antagonisms.

CHAPTER III

Communications from beyond the Tomb

This commune between the living and the dead—this intercourse between that which breathes and moves and *is*—and that which life animates not, nor mortality knows—annihilates falsehood, and chills even self-delusion into awe. Come, then, . . . and as the shadows and lights of a checkered and wild existence flit before you, watch if in your own hearts there be aught which mirrors the reflection.

Autobiographer's Introduction to *Devereux*

Bulwer did not follow up the success of *Pelham* with further satires of fashionable life. Not only did his publisher advise him that the public was tiring of such light-hearted works but also he began to associate the attitudes he had celebrated in *Pelham* with his own immaturity. What he would call the period of "my first *beaux jours*, the early tickets for Almacks and my first fine lady love," had definitely passed. And as Clare Greville, a dandy of far more bitterly sarcastic flippancy than Pelham, remarks in an unfinished novel of 1828, "Nothing can again restore the hour of glory in one's *glass* and splendour in one's flower!"[1] So *Pelham* and its "follies" belonged with *Falkland* and its "perilous stuff" to a phase that must not be prolonged.

In the new phase, as I have suggested, Bulwer seems to have looked for more mature ways to relate the energies of the world within to the appearances of the world without. Or in the terms that *Wilhelm Meister*, Bulwer's "metaphysical" novel par excellence, develops, he may have envisaged life as a "fortuitous mass" upon which he needed to impose "some form, the pattern of which originated in his spirit."[2] The pattern gained a firmer outline during the twenty months that he and his wife remained in Oxfordshire after the publication of *Pelham*. He studied and worked conscientiously—thereby following the scheme that Pelham had devised for his own proposed two years in retreat—and accumulated additional capital from the successes of *The Disowned* and *Devereux*. Then in January 1830 occurred the long anticipated move into Hertford Street and the commencement of the more public efforts to shape that "fortuitous mass" of modern life.

"Edward and Rosina came gleefully," in the description of Michael Sadleir, "to the assault on London," and an assault it certainly appeared to be. The purpose was not simply to collect Pelham's harmless "knowledge of the world" but to obtain, as Bulwer would tell Lady Blessington in 1834, "what, when I was a boy, I made the object of my life—a career of some honour and a name that shall not die."[3] For nearly four years he slaved with almost superhuman energy and devotion on behalf of that object—as novelist, essayist, editor of the *New Monthly Magazine*, reforming Member of Parliament, and, not least arduously, as man of fashion.

Predictably enough, however, the various "career[s] of some honour" soon overwhelmed him with the crushing immediacy of their pressures. As the larger sense of the purpose behind them even threatened to vanish, he had to force himself to maintain his commitment. Disraeli has reported, for example, a conversation of January 1833 in which Bulwer confessed that only a certain pride kept him from succumbing to the temptation to retire once more from the "stage": "[Bulwer] turned round and pressed my arm and said in a tone the sincerity of which could not be doubted: 'It is true, my dear fellow, it is true. We are sacrificing our youth, the time of pleasure, the bright season of enjoyment—but we are bound to go on, we are *bound*. How our enemies would triumph were we to retire from the stage! And yet,' he continued in a solemn voice, 'I have more than once been tempted to throw it all up, and quit even my country, for ever.' "[4]

Within about nine months Bulwer would in fact throw up many

of his responsibilities and go abroad. In the meanwhile, though, he had to continue in his political, literary, and social careers and persuade himself that he was fulfilling the high destinies and the vows of his boyish self. For as he became older, that impression of the promise of his boyhood seems to have entranced him more deeply. He frequently sought "consolation," as Sadleir suggests with respect to the unfinished "Lionel Hastings," "in the memory of his unshadowed youth."[5] Or going even further into the past, he tried to persuade himself of the lasting vitality and validity of his glorious ancestry. A determination to be the worthy ambassador of his ancestors to the public of his own age even became a sort of governing factor in his commitment to his career.

In leaving the stage of *Falkland* and *Pelham* behind, then, Bulwer has not so much escaped that hostility between the dangerous Cave and the artificial Agora as he has redefined it. He has translated the opposition between the worlds within and without into the relationship between the past and the present, and his novels now seem to locate their "metaphysical" dimension in the past. The Cave is even associated quite literally at times, in the novels I wish to consider in this chapter, with a tomb containing the bones of the past. By dealing so persistently as they do with the theme of inheritance, these works also imply that the dead have communicated their values and destinies to the living. While by no means an unmitigated blessing, the heritage of the past contains the key that will help men first to discover and then responsibly to affirm the principle of order in their present, daily lives.

The relationship of past and present within the novels also tends to be reduplicated in the relationship Bulwer implies between the eighteenth-century setting of each work and his own nineteenth century. In *The Disowned* and *Eugene Aram*, for example, the nineteenth-century narrator occasionally suggests that the events of the story somehow lie in his own past, and *The Disowned* concludes with his musings at the tomb of one of his protagonists. *Paul Clifford* depends for some of its effect on the parallels between eighteenth-century highwaymen and nineteenth-century politicians. As one of the first *Tendenzromane* in Britain, its treatment of crime in the previous century also has a direct relevance to the penal philosophy which Bulwer's own day has inherited—and which imprisons the whole society of his present.[6] But *Devereux*, which is incidentally relevant to current debates on Catholic Emancipation,[7] provides in the coherence of its whole temporal and narrative structure the best treatment of the large themes of time and inheritance. (Bulwer was himself understandably fond of this work because its "execution more exactly [than in any of his previous novels] corresponded with the design.")[8] Supposedly the autobiography of an early eighteenth-century soldier of fortune, it has been designed expressly for a later age, which the autobiographer trusts will appreciate him better than his own. His fascinated awareness of the separation in time between his readers and himself most conveniently helps—as the following passage may illustrate—to articulate the double perspective that informs all four novels: "I am writing for the children of an after age, to whom the very names of those who made the blood of their ancestors leap within their veins will be unknown. . . . This history is a union of strange contrasts! like the tree of the Sun, described by Marco Polo, which was green when approached on one side, but white when perceived on the other—to me it is clothed in the verdure and spring of the existing time; to the reader it comes covered with the hoariness and wanness of the Past!" (De 2:6).

Despite the hoariness and wanness, however, events seem to become fully meaningful in these novels only in retrospect. A man lives through the green present, in a sense, chiefly in order to gain a past, which then becomes—as Wordsworth had thought too—his most precious possession. Indeed he must fashion his very soul from his store of memories. Only insofar as he has gained his revelatory communication from the tomb of his past, can his living career escape the appearance of fortuitousness and exemplify "some form, the pattern of which originated in . . . spirit."

With their generally double plots, these novels tend to define two compartments of life, and it will be useful to consider each in turn. The first compartment suggests the poverty of the present when it is cut off from its roots in the past. Each of the four works treats the career of a youth who is in some sense disowned and who must try to carve out his own way in the world. Leading inevitably to pain and despair, the career finally culminates at the Cave or tomb that contains the essential communication from the regions of the dead. Then the protagonist may gradually discern as if in retrospect the pattern that has been unfolding all along, though unbeknownst to him, in the more "metaphysical" compartment of the plot.

The first stage involves a sort of expulsion from Eden, and it receives its most complete treatment in *Devereux*. The orphaned son of an English adventurer ennobled by Louis XIV, the young Count Devereux lives at first in a troubled Eden at Devereux Court, the home of his uncle on the English coast. Jacobite intrigues continually shroud the atmosphere with mystery, and Devereux appears to encounter a major temptation when the Abbé Montreuil, the family's dashing, animally magnetic, Jesuit confessor, waits on him in his special tower. In a scene charged with overtones of *Faust*, the Abbé offers an ambiguous pact of friendship and then, to obtain a proof of his power, disappears for two years. He returns from France (despite the wars hindering most such travel) with a sword that King Louis has sent to the son of his servant, the late Count. The sword may typify knowledge of evil in its association with the virility derived from the father and in its function as a badge of the "enemy." Still Devereux seems to hold his innocence so long as he maintains a pure love for his seraphic, younger brother Aubrey. In its reciprocity, their idyllic but curiously passionate relationship shows "that the love of brotherhood can pass the love of woman."

Then Devereux may betray Aubrey. Falling in love with the ideal Isora, he kisses Aubrey (who will spend his life praying for him) farewell and leaves for London, where he secretly marries Isora. As an apparent result, a series of dramatic events seems to bar the gates of Eden to him forever. The mysterious enemy fatally stabs Isora, and Devereux becomes a sort of disillusioned cynic overnight. Next, his uncle's fear of the Jacobites prompts the literal closing and barring of the pleasantly furnished cave on the coast, which had functioned as a center of family life and from which a passage leads to the hero's own tower. When his uncle dies and astoundingly disinherits Devereux in his last will, the sentence of exile from Devereux Court becomes irrevocable. Yet the news that Aubrey—who has recently felt "predestined to the power of the Evil One"—has taken to strenuous religious devotions and died may constitute the worst blow of all. Not only closed, the innocent past has wholly disintegrated.

With somewhat less detail the other novels similarly imply that unknown gods have decreed the hero's exile from his early home. Disappointed in love, Walter Lester thus sets forth in *Eugene Aram* from the explicitly Edenic village of Grassdale to start the quest for his missing father. The initially unnamed protagonist of *The Disowned* has suffered a still more literal banishment, which the ending of his first happy adventure in the camp of the gypsy "kings of Fairyland" may seem to reinforce. But since he has never known a genuine Eden, the orphaned Paul Clifford may be the most unfortunate of all the protagonists. He grows up in a parodic paradise amidst the squalor of Thames Court—from which he is nevertheless expelled when the gates of Bridewell close behind him. More specifically than the others, he is henceforth condemned to follow the paths of sin.

Cut off from his heredity, each hero takes his sword or pistol and tries in the second stage of his career to win honor and riches on his own. The protagonist of *The Disowned*, for example, begins to make his fortune when he bravely saves the rich Talbot from housebreakers and accordingly becomes his protégé and heir. (Later he must also fight a duel with Lord Borodaile, his rival for the hand of Lady Flora.) The adventures of Walter Lester follow a chivalric pattern too, for he constantly plays Quixote to the earthy, selfish Sancho of his companion, Corporal Bunting. And again providing one of the fullest instances, Devereux travels throughout the continent for a decade as a soldier of fortune in the service of the French Regent and later of the Czar, Peter the Great.

Paul Clifford uses the sword and pistol not only in his exciting adventures as swashbuckling highwayman but also in an interestingly figurative sense as man of letters. His career properly speaking begins when MacGrawler, the great Scottish literary critic and editor of the *Asinaeum*, teaches him about the three branches of criticism—"namely, 'to tickle, to slash, and to plaster.' " With the help of the inimitable Augustus Tomlinson too, he begins to see how the forceful, cavalier use of words can enable one to emerge victorious over the most intransigeant of moral realities. Since all "depends upon the language applied to the action," says Tomlinson, "we are never rogues so long as we call ourselves honest fellows; and we never commit a crime so long as we can term it a virtue" (PC 10). Highway robbery becomes an especially exquisite form of chivalry, and the novel propounds, as one of its major themes, the notion that criminals are really no worse than lawyers and politicians. Far from possessing a mature knowledge of good and evil, the post-Edenic world exhibits an ethical relativism and lawlessness that have made everyone an unprincipled adventurer and desperado in the realms of language: "Half of us [admits Brandon, the lawyer who prosecutes the outlaws] are employed in saying white is black, and the other half in swearing that black is white. There is only one difference . . . between the clever man and the fool; the fool says what is false while the colours stare in his face and give him the lie; but the clever man takes, as it were, a brush, and literally turns the black into white, and the white into black, before he makes the assertion, which is then true. The fool changes, and is a liar; the clever man makes the colours change, and is a genius" (PC 13).

Only material appearances seem to count in the public worlds of all four novels, and amidst the falseness the heroes naturally have the strength and cleverness to succeed more brilliantly than anyone else. Each of them except Lester becomes in some sense a marvelously skillful impostor—rather in the tradition of Pelham.

Their tragedy, however, is that they have remained idealists. With their memories of Eden they have been looking for something that neither the tremendous wealth nor the social position they have achieved can purchase. Above all, perhaps, their quests have been for the ideal authenticity, which the heroines who cannot be changed from white to black must typify. The so-called Clarence Linden of *The Disowned* thus discovers to his grief that the mystery surrounding his origins—and the suspicion of "puddle blood" —must forever disqualify his pretensions to the hand of Lady Flora. And no matter how much he impresses the world of mutable colors in his guise as Captain Lovett, Paul Clifford can never hope to marry the pure Lucy Brandon. The sad recognition may even carry the hero, as it does in the case of Devereux, to a religious crisis of truly Victorian proportions. Confronting ever more fully the philosophical materialism of his own age (he has also had a valet who reads and spouts Leibnitz), Devereux admits that the dead Isora must probably remain inaccessible to him throughout all eternity. Only this ever-changing, ever-decaying world of present appearances exists according to "the dark doctrine which teaches that man is dust, and that all things are forgotten in the grave" (De 5:6).

The third stage therefore leads the heroes to the hopelessness of their respective caves or graves, where they also receive after all the blessed communication from the dead. In *Devereux*, again to take the neatest example first, the soldier of fortune becomes a pilgrim and journeys in his despair to Italy. Divesting himself of the signs of his wealth, he lives as a religious penitent in a grotto in the Appenines. His faith begins to return, and at the moment of crisis he discovers a mad and desperately ill monk in a nearby cave—who turns out to be his supposedly dead brother Aubrey! In dying, Aubrey bequeaths him a very long manuscript—"THE HERMIT'S MANUSCRIPT"—which finally explains all the mysteries of the past and enables Devereux to discern the significant pattern of his entire life.

Although it does not actually contain his manuscript, the quest of Walter Lester similarly culminates at a deathly cave. He unearths the bones of his father, murdered some fifteen years previously, at St. Robert's Cave, and his universe seems to collapse when he further understands the worthlessness of the father he had idealized. Yet he regains a reason for living in his anxiety to bring the murderer to justice and so to disinter the full truth of the past. After the trial of Eugene Aram has accomplished some of the process, Walter successfully persuades the condemned man, in a battle of wills, to relinquish the proud determination to carry his secret to the grave. Aram leaves behind the long written confession that constitutes the penultimate chapter of the novel, and Walter too can discover the principle of meaning in life.

The other two novels do not develop the motifs of the cave and the manuscript so fully, and yet I believe the same patterns operate implicitly in both of them. In *Paul Clifford* it is interesting that the treacherous MacGrawler, who was associated with Paul's original setting forth, should turn up at the end as the cook in the cave of the robbers. (Bulwer squanders a page of spaced exclamation points, comprising all of chapter xxvii, upon the coincidence.) As in Devereux's discovery of the mad Aubrey, Paul has found in the cave a perverse remnant of his youth, and although MacGrawler betrays him to authorities, that betrayal confers an indirect blessing upon him. Through his trial and its aftermath Paul will come, like Lester at the trial of Aram, to know the truth.

Lacking a cave, *The Disowned* has an equivalent symbol in the tomb of Mordaunt, which figures so prominently at the end. Linden had first known Mordaunt at the outset of his quest, and the final return to Mordaunt's tomb thus implies Linden's return to his origins too. He has gained the equivalent of his manuscript as well in the form of Mordaunt's long autobiography, the "History of One Human Mind." Although Mordaunt had delivered the history as a speech some months before his death, it had conveyed rather funereal overtones even at the time: "Something there was in Mordaunt's voice and air, and the impassioned glow of the countenance, that, long after he had ceased, thrilled in Clarence's heart, 'like the remembered tone of a mute lyre' " (Di 62). And still more suggestive of a voice from beyond the tomb, the final discourse of Mordaunt has lingered in the memory; an assassin's bullet had struck him just as he finished that discourse. Briefly despairing at that juncture, Linden has nevertheless found a sublime reassurance in the very last words of the friend who has expired in his arms.

All four heroes have received the figurative *Mémoires d'outre-tombe* that contain the meaning of life. While the various communications and manuscripts do not all deal in specific terms with the literal events of each protagonist's past, they do all typify the deeper truth about his career. They enable him, as Devereux reflects on his voyage back to England, to discern and so to complete a pattern: "Thus, as I leant over the deck and the waves bore me homeward, after so many years and vicissitudes, did the shadows of thought and memory flit across me. How seemingly apart, yet how closely linked, had been the great events in my wandering and wild life! . . . By the finest, but the strongest, meshes, had the thread of my political honours been woven with that of my private afflictions. And thus, even at the licentious festivals of the Regent of France, or the lifeless parade of the Court of————, the dark stream of events had flowed onward beneath my feet, bearing me insensibly to that very spot of time, from which I now surveyed the past and looked upon the mist and shadows of the future" (De 6:5).

The "spot of time"—as Wordsworth had also termed it—may

permit the hero to intuit the meanings which the reader has already seen unfolding in the more "metaphysical" compartment of the plot.

Representing what *Eugene Aram* calls "that deep cave—the human heart—" this other compartment deals with the interactions of archetypal figures whom it will be convenient to refer to the categories of demon, anima, and mediator. As this last seeks to protect—or fails to protect—the anima from the power of the demon, the significant, underlying drama of man's life proceeds. And as the protagonist eventually discerns the degree to which the process has corrupted that mediating figure, he may recognize the quality of his own guilt or innocence. So he will come to authentic knowledge of himself at last.

Bulwer found "a gloomy and profound sublimity" in the notion that each man possessed his evil demon: "What a world of dark and troubled secrets in the breast of every one who hurries by you! Goethe has said somewhere that each of us, the best as the worst, hides within him something ... that, if known, would make you hate him" (EA 4:5). So hateful are the demons in these novels that one tends to think of their malignance as utterly unmotivated despite Bulwer's lame efforts to account for it. Houseman, for example, reveals an excessive delight in his ability not only to blackmail but to torture Eugene Aram psychologically: "I enjoy, I hug myself in your torments. I exult in the terror with which you will hear of each new enterprise" (EA 3:2). Even more unholy in his joy, the principal demon of *The Disowned* resembles the Satan who had sought to make Job curse God. Although based on an actual forger named Fauntleroy,[9] the pious-seeming Crauford appears less interested in profit (his supposed motive) than in getting Mordaunt to foreswear his noble idealism. He secretly reduces his once-wealthy victim to the most abject poverty. Then denying him every chance to earn a livelihood, he gloats while Mordaunt helplessly watches his wife die of starvation.

In its connection with original sin, evil may become somewhat less mysterious, and Bulwer often associates the demon with the father who transmits a heritage of guilt to the son. The fascinating, inscrutably powerful Montreuil has thus given Devereux the sword of his father, while Brandon, the best example of all, is literally the father of Paul Clifford. The most vigorous character in the novel and the seeming first cause behind all the events of the plot, Brandon also typifies in his character as lawyer and judge the corrupting power of the entire social system.[10] He believes firmly—as does the vengeful old law of the traditional penal philosophy, which the novel is out to attack—in man's innate depravity. Accordingly meting out the punishments that will deprave men in fact, he makes the new generation bear the weight of hereditary crime and injustice. When Paul, whose mother he has also deeply wronged, comes before his court, he therefore commits the hitherto innocent youth to Bridewell—and to certain corruption. And at the final trial he ignores Paul's most impassioned appeals to the new law and condemns him to the death that remains the inevitable penalty for original sin.

At the other extreme the figure of the anima typifies a radical innocence and a loving mercy that are as imponderable and unmotivated in their way as the malevolence of the demon. When he had first seen Madeline Lester, says Aram, "a sudden and heavenly light seemed to dawn upon me. Her face—its still, its serene, its touching beauty—shone down on my desolation like a dream of mercy—like a hope of pardon" (EA 5:7). Indeed Madeline extends pardon automatically, for nothing can induce her to believe in Aram's guilt. While resembling many saintly heroines of nineteenth-century literature, she seems a stronger version of Psyche too when she obeys without question her mysterious lover's injunction not to seek to learn more about him.[11] She possesses, as Bulwer observes of Lucy Brandon, "so pure a credulity in the existence of unmixed good, so firm a reluctance to think that where we love there can be that which we would not esteem" that even the

[65]

testimony of the beloved against himself fails to shake her faith in his innocence (PC 29).

Whereas the demons embody a depravity that may issue as much from heredity and environment as from the soul itself, the anima may suggest a quality that is indisputably and purely innate. Bulwer associates Lucy with "the germ of perfectibility" in all men, while Isabella typifies the "Virtue" that Mordaunt has worshipped "in the depths of [his] soul." "All-sufficient to itself," that Virtue refers not only to an ethical value but to the irreducible *virtù* that constitutes the very identifying essence of the individual personality. It can, as Mordaunt's long, autobiographical discourse affirms, survive any ordeal (Di 62).

With the exception of Lucy, these females do nevertheless die, for that *virtù* or germ is ultimately so pure that it can scarcely exist —even symbolically—as a visible, tangible presence. Somewhere, the woman seems to say, the eternally incorruptible idea will always endure, and having implied this truth, she returns to the ideal regions herself. By proving the ideality and immortality of her all-pardoning love, her death has become her most expressive action: "The love I bear to you," muses Isora as she attempts to indicate the meaning of her death shortly before the event, "I can but feebly express now.... It seems to me that I was made only for one purpose—to love you; and I would fain hope that my death may be some sort of sacrifice to you—some token of ... the whole object of my life" (De 3:5). She dies a few pages later, having sacrificed herself to save Devereux and murmuring, "it *is* dearer to die for you than to live!" (De 3:7).

The demons, on the other hand, usually dread death as the greatest of calamities. During a last night alive that resembles Fagin's, the condemned Crauford faces the implications of annihilation and goes mad; his materialism has prevented him from conceiving even the possibility for an afterlife. Besides the forces of good and evil, the anima and demon therefore represent that part of man which can hardly exist on earth and that part which can exist nowhere else.

Between the two irreconcilable extremes, the mediator must attempt to strike some sort of balance. He seems invariably to fail, and yet his efforts do help to bring the typical problem of man's life into an interesting ethical focus. The discrepancy between the worlds within and without is here perceived especially as a contradiction between the ideally Good and that which is practically good for the flesh.

Reminding one of Mill's interest in Bentham and Coleridge, Algernon Mordaunt has tried to achieve the compromise by reconciling the ethics of utilitarianism and idealism. He defines the utilitarian "sense of the common interest" as a lofty moral imperative: "Yes! it is the most beautiful truth in morals that we have no such thing as a distinct or divided interest from our race. In their welfare is ours; and by choosing the broadest paths to effect their happiness, we choose the surest and the shortest to our own" (Di 62). That is "one stage of virtue" and the next stage would appear simply to restate in idealistic terms his conception of the "virtue" for which the entire race must share a common longing: " 'our souls are *indeed* of the same essence as the stars,' and . . . the mysterious yearning, . . . to mingle with their glory, is but the instinctive and natural longing to re-unite the divided *portion* of an immortal spirit . . . with the original lustre of the heavenly and burning *whole!*" (Di 86).

Despite the ingenuity of his lengthy, rhetorical efforts to reconcile the two conceptions of virtue, however, his life places all the emphasis upon idealism and fails to admit the claims of the flesh. On behalf of "Virtue," he would sooner starve—and have Isabella and their child starve—than make even minor concessions to Crauford for their practical common interest. While enduring the testing I have compared to that of Job, he also likens the service of "Virtue" to the torments of the bound Prometheus. In the ordeal of life everything is to be endured, nothing to be done, and, appropriately enough, his assassination occurs at the outset of a Parliamentary career—just as he might need to begin doing something as a practical legislator. Prophesying not the redemption but the destruction of the material universe, his last speech joyfully transforms his death, precisely in the manner of *Falkland*, into a victory for the glorious idea.

Surprisingly similar to Mordaunt, the scholarly Eugene Aram has also sat for long hours in his observatory and aspired toward the stars. His indulgence of a rather solipsistic idealism (he "regard[ed] the pomps of the world as shadows and the life of his own spirit the only substance") has even made him the "forerunner" of Goethe and Byron. Like the "sublime discontent" of Faust in particular has allegedly been his "yearning for the intellectual Paradise beyond, which 'the sworded angel' forbids us to approach" (EA 2:4).

Yet however extravagant, his longing for the ideal does not in itself undo him. As in the case of Mordaunt, the difficulty arises rather from his attempt to reconcile idealism with a philanthropic utilitarianism. He considers using practical means toward his ideal end and decides that for the greatest good of the greatest number he may justifiably commit a crime against one single and utterly worthless individual (a vicious rapist): "Is it not for the service of man," he asks himself in devising a teleological suspension of an ethical absolute, "that thou shouldst for once break the law on behalf of that knowledge from which all laws take their source? If thou wrongest the one, thou shalt repay it in boons to the million" (EA 5:7). Succumbing to Houseman's blandishments, he then finds himself involved in a murder and forever enmeshed in a web of multiplying guilt. He continues to love the Good, but the "spectre" of the blackmailing Houseman, whom he can never "exorcise" now, obscures his vision of it. Whereas Mordaunt had known that "guilt and sorrow, and this world's evil mysteries, [would] roll away like vapours before the blaze" (Di 56), Aram thus sees only the deathly shadows: "what is this world . . . but a stupendous charnel-house? . . . When we rifle nature, and collect wisdom, are we not like the hags of old, culling simples from the rank grave, and extracting sorceries from the rotting bones of the dead? Everything around us is fathered by corruption, battened by corruption, and into corruption returns at last. . . . All are one vast panorama of death! But it did not always seem to me thus" (EA 3:6).[12]

The corruption of the grave comes to taint the other two mediating figures as well. They fall, though, not only because their reason fails to subordinate utilitarianism to idealism but also because their fleshly natures simply overpower them. The religious Aubrey Devereux wishes to renounce his devotion to God's creatures in order to maintain the purity of his ideal devotion to the Creator. Yet his supposedly holy love for his brother obsesses him to the point that it becomes an all-consuming jealousy. Foreseeing that his brother and Isora will fall in love, he tries desperately to make Isora love himself instead and to this end haunts and threatens her. Then as he falls ever more helplessly into the power of the craftily goading Montreuil, he becomes Isora's murderer and the forger of the will by which his brother is disinherited. (In the perverted mind of his Jesuit tempter, these crimes are again justified because they will tend in practical if not ideal ways *ad majorem Dei gloriam*. Any means that will secure the Devereux properties to the Catholic and Jacobite cause are permissible.)

In *Paul Clifford* the practical, fleshly considerations that overthrow ideal loyalties become still more mundanely physical. The noble bandit is betrayed by his cook, MacGrawler, and in the more metaphysical compartment the gourmet Lord Mauleverer occupies the position of mediator between the demonic Brandon (his crony) and the pure Lucy (for whose hand he is Paul's rival). Although capable of gallant speeches and theoretically devoted to high, aristocratic principles, the aging Mauleverer really care only for the pleasures of the table. His "digestive organs . . . stood proxy for a heart," and all conceivable evils are as nothing to the horrors of dyspepsia. He represents, moreover, an entire society that has effectively confused the soul—whose longings for "the heavenly and burning *whole*" Mordaunt had described so platonically—with the stomach: "the yearnings of an indigestion," says Tomlinson, the philosopher of this society, "we denominate yearnings after immortality—nay, sometimes 'a proof of the nature of the soul!'" (PC 18).

On the yearnings of the digestive system, then, the world has established its ethics: "With Stupidity and sound Digestion man may front much," Mauleverer might have said, if he had wished to anticipate Diogenes Teufelsdröckh: "But what . . . are the terrors of Conscience to the diseases of the Liver! Not on Morality, but on Cookery, let us build our stronghold."[13] During Paul's last trial Mauleverer accordingly urges Judge Brandon to despatch the criminal hastily to the gallows so that all the guests can assemble as soon as possible at the great banquet his cook is preparing. And that banquet becomes still more disturbingly emblematic of the world in which men live to eat or to be eaten when the defeated Brandon arrives as a corpse. To such repugnant levels of corruption does the universe fall once man permits his concern for the good of the flesh to outweigh his loyalty to the ideal Good.

In showing life as a process whereby the flesh corrupts the yearning soul, the message from the charnel cave conveys primarily a knowledge of guilt to the protagonist. He recognizes not only the original sin for which he has been expelled from Eden—whose gate "the sworded angel" now guards—but also the subsequent guilt of his career. Walter Lester finds himself implicated, for example, in the guilt of the murderer whom he ought mercifully to have forgiven instead of hounding vengefully to justice. He has become responsible for the death of Madeline too, and henceforth a "dread and gloomy remembrance never forsook his mind." Devereux similarly sees in Aubrey the guilt of his own self-infatuation and in Montreuil the more seriously evil temporality of his wandering quest for fame and fortune. By creating his new identity in terms of *fortuna*, he has lost sight of the *virtù* within.

While fearful, however, the communication from the dead bestows a certain comfort as well. It suggests the pattern of destiny amidst the fortuitousness of life and enables the protagonist finally to impose *virtù* upon *fortuna*. Devereux thus recognizes his evil demon in Montreuil and after a long pursuit kills him with his sword in the very cave that provides the entrance to his old tower at Devereux Court. So ends his estrangement from himself and his long career as soldier of fortune. Since his other brother (the owner of the Court during his exile) conveniently dies in the sword fight too, he takes possession of the now ruined estate and uses his fortune to rebuild it. His quest has taken him through good fortune and desolation precisely to lead him back with greater wisdom and humility to his past. Although he cannot regain that past in its vitality, he perceives in his memories the true image of himself. It is enough to know that he has experienced and learned so fully the "lessons" his life has been designed to teach him: "If love exists for me no longer, I know well that the memory of that which has been is to me far more than a living love is to others. . . . If I have borne much, and my spirit has worked out its earthly end in travail and in tears, yet I would not forego the lessons which my life has bequeathed me, even though they be deeply blended with sadness and regret. No! were I asked what best dignifies the present and consecrates the past; what enables us alone to draw a just moral from the tale of life; . . . I would answer, with Lassus, it is 'Experience!'" (De 6: Conclusion).

In helping to create memories, experience has even preserved his soul. For he has learned in particular that he possesses the ideal Isora far more fully in memory than he ever could have maintained her as "a living love." While all that lives grows corrupt, memories alone remain pure, and so he understands at last why she had found it "dearer to die for [him] than to live": "That love *of ours* was never made for after years! It could never have flowed into the common and cold channel of ordinary affairs! It could never have been mingled with the petty cares and the low objects with which the loves of all who live long together in this sordid and most earthly earth are sooner or later blended!" (De 3:2).

The desire for a purity that will not blend with "this sordid and most earthly earth" has similarly moved Walter Lester. In his own way too, he has found that desire fulfilled in his recovery of the truth of the past: "even the criminal is not all evil," Aram's written confession assures him: "the angel within us is not easily expelled; it survives sin, ay, and many sins." By teaching him that truth about human nature, his manuscript has offered him—in more helpful fashion, perhaps, than the "moral" of Devereux's "tale of life"—ethical rules to guide his subsequent existence: "the darker secrets . . . in which the true science of morals is chiefly found, taught him the twofold lesson,—caution for himself and charity for others." As with the other protagonists, then, the "gloomy remembrance" becomes a blessed principle that exercises thereafter "the most powerful influence over the actions and motives of his life" (EA 5:8).

The memories and the knowledge of the past can evidently provide the basis not only for a "science of morals" to regulate private life but also for a public science of laws. Clarence Linden, whose recovery of his true identity has been accomplished by the inheritance of an earldom,[14] will thus attempt to apply in the Lords the ethics he has inherited from Mordaunt. The difficulty of establishing a practical body of laws upon the ideal recognition of the good "angel within us" still obtains, but with time and caution Bulwer evidently believes it may prove possible. Owing much of its inspiration to William Godwin,[15] *Paul Clifford* even hints that if the legal system founded itself upon man's perfectibility rather than his innate depravity, a utopia might result. Lucy, the representative of that "germ of perfectibility," thereby sees only the innocence in Paul and redeems him from the oppressive old law when she helps him to escape the penal colony. Rising from strength to strength, she takes him to post-Revolutionary America, where he preaches to the happy society of the future: "Circumstances make guilt, . . . let us endeavour to *correct the circumstances*, before we rail against the guilt!" (PC 36). As legislators correct the circumstances, "this world's evil mysteries [will] roll away," to recall the prophecy of Mordaunt, "like vapours before the blaze!" Eden may at last be restored in fact.

In the meanwhile, however, Bulwer emphasizes that the memory of Eden must substitute for the possession of it, and the dénouement of *Paul Clifford* is somewhat exceptional and unconvincing in its optimism. The more typical conclusion to *Eugene Aram* shows Walter Lester adjusting himself to the diminished conditions of life in the present. After seeking to expiate his sin during some years in the service of Frederick the Great, he returns to Grassdale and marries the far less sublime, though good-hearted sister of the dead Madeline. The noble values always lie buried in a man's past, no matter what the age in which he actually lives.

To appear complete and meaningful, any present life must probably define itself as the relic or monument of the past. The youthful narrator of *The Disowned* thus regrets on the last page that so much vitality and ambition continues to move him restlessly forward in life. He still has so many years to live before he can look back serenely on his completed pilgrimage: "I have stood there," he says of Mordaunt's grave, "in those ardent years when our wishes know no boundary, and our ambition no curb; . . . I would have changed my wildest vision of romance for that quiet grave, and the dreams of the distant spirit whose relics reposed beneath it." By the same token Devereux takes a calm satisfaction in observing that he has become the spent hulk or relic of his former self: "I have exhausted the sources of those feelings which flow, whether through the channels of anxiety or of hope, towards the future; and the restlessness of my manhood, having attained its last object, has done the labour of time, and bequeathed to me the indifference of age" (De 6: Conclusion). As the survivor or heir of his youth, he no longer needs to live as a mature being in his own right. Indeed he is all but a corpse now, and the composition of his autobiography often enables him to refer to himself in the third person as the decomposed corpse he has literally become to his reader: "the very worms are starving upon his dust."

Only his memories have value, and when the body that serves simply as the sepulchral storehouse of those memories has fully decayed, his mémoires will preserve their immortality.[16] Like Aubrey already, he will then belong wholly to the regions of memory; he will have become in his turn an impalpable voice from beyond the tomb. And so Bulwer, the supposed heir of his manuscript, hopes to follow in his own turn to some realm of ideal, unchanging authenticity. Although his career as radical politician and man of letters was the practical manifestation of the ideal destiny buried in his past, "yet," he would tell Disraeli, "I have more than once been tempted to throw it all up, and quit even my country, for ever." In this life, as Falkland too had known, there can be no stable reconciliation between the utilitarianism of the material regions and the heritage of idealism.

CHAPTER IV

Leaving the Haunts of the Nymph

The occasional song of the birds . . . floated with a peculiar clearness . . . along the deserted haunts of the Nymph. . . .

"And here," thought he, ". . . every one who has tasted the loves of earth, and sickened for the love that is ideal, finds a spell more attractive to his steps—more fraught with contemplation to his spirit than aught raised by the palace of the Caesars or the tomb of the Scipios."

Godolphin

By sending forth communications, as if from beyond the tomb, Bulwer had represented his hope that the sympathy of kindred souls could transcend temporal barriers: "watch if in your own hearts," Devereux had urged his readers of the next century, "there be aught which mirrors the reflection." The appeal for sympathy had become even more curiously direct in *Eugene Aram*, for to the confession of the criminal and the concluding chapter, Bulwer had added a plea in his own voice: "when thou hearest the malice that wrongs affect the candour which should judge, shall [the author] not find in thy sympathies the defence or in thy charity the indulgence,—of a friend?"

After *Eugene Aram*, however, the insinuated appeals on behalf of the misunderstood inner man become less urgent and evident. Bulwer continues to transmit supposed messages from the dead, but a new motive apparently underlies the device. Far from wishing to communicate the special quality of his own identity, the "compiler" of the anonymous *Godolphin* thus hopes to elude detection by triumphantly carrying his secret to the grave. His fast-approaching death will enable him to outwit "the idlers who have leisure to waste on trifles," and his story—"woven from real events" in the lives of others—will be judged simply on its own merits.[1] The

[75]

elaborate explanations of the alleged editor-translator of *Zanoni*, too, surround the identity of the author of the inherited, eighteenth-century manuscript with the atmosphere of an impenetrable mystery. With its formal complexities and ambiguities *Zanoni* in particular avoids the semblance of the confessional plea.

For Bulwer did want to bury some of the traces of the dangerous world within himself. Suffering chronic bouts of depression throughout the decade of his thirties, he desired not to immortalize but to escape his painful self-consciousness: "I feel how necessary it is," he told his mother in 1834, "for me to divert my thoughts, anyhow and anywhither, from myself and my own situation, which, from whatever point of view I look at it, is dark without one ray of comfort." He was intermittently "overpowered," according to another letter of the same day, "not by any ordinary melancholy, but by a profound dejection which leaves me literally crushed and helpless." On the conscious level the anxiety derived from his shattering marital problems and their reverberations, which continued endlessly even after the separation from Rosina in 1836: "those dead passions," he wrote in a letter thanking Lady Blessington for her praise of *Maltravers*, "have ghosts no exorcism can lay. . . . I cannot long be alone with the Past. I must ever be busied with little anxieties created for myself, in order to escape from the terrible stillness within. . . . I hate my *métier*, but I go on with it, and still fancy, like the tradesman behind the counter, that the day will come when I may be happy and retire. Vain hope!"[2]

In giving up many of his public roles and responsibilities in 1833, he had not, then, escaped to the dolce far niente (in his frequent phrase) of private life. While he effectively retired from politics, disappointed by the failure of the Radicals to form a viable coalition under his friend Lord Durham, he redoubled his efforts in literature—launching, for example, his successful career as dramatist. He had at all events to keep working: "I had no resource but to fly from myself," he recalled as he analyzed the reasons for his nervous collapse of 1844, "—to fly into the other world of books, or thought, or reverie—to live in some state of being less painful than my own. As long as I was always at work it seemed that I had no leisure to be ill. Quiet was my hell."[3]

The flight from himself did not, however, lead him merely into blind busy work. While avoiding what Tennyson's "Soul" would term "the abysmal deeps of personality," he was evidently looking for his own Palace of Art, and so his career entered its most aesthetic phase. He pondered the history of art, and the need to escape all the sordid mire and blood of everyday reality caused him especially at this point to formulate his theories about the "Ideal" schools. Of particular note may be his contributions to what would become, as Mario Praz has shown, a very general Victorian debate about the relative merits of Italian and Dutch painting. Unlike Trollope and so many of their contemporaries who preferred "the real matrons of Rembrandt" to "the idealized Madonnas of Raphael,"[4] Bulwer of course defended the stylized impersonality of the latter. The "Familiar" or "Dutch" school's "imitation of actual life" degraded the viewer, he feared, by arousing an unfortunate "sympathy for something low," while the "Intellectual" or "Italian" style elicited an ennobling "admiration for something high"—and this, it is interesting to observe, as a function more of the artist's idealizing manner than of the initial moral worth of his matter: "There is nothing high," to repeat Bulwer's favorite example, "in a boor's head by Teniers—there is nothing low in a boor's head by Guido."[5] (Ruskin would develop an extremely similar distinction between Teniers and Titian but would place far more emphasis upon the moral value of the subject chosen in the first place.)[6]

His admiration for the Italian school led Bulwer to wonder how a literary artist could "sit down to compose a fiction as a painter prepares to compose a picture." It should be possible, he decided, for the author "who resigns the Dutch art for the Italian" to learn not to imitate surfaces but to set himself an abstract or intellectual problem in design. And here the great German writers of the last generation offered some help, for in their work the idealism of

Italian painting appeared already to exist as a literary phenomenon too. Bulwer thus studied the ideal or aesthetic aspect of the Germans more assiduously than ever—as he prepared, for example, his translation of Schiller's poetry for Blackwood's and won recognition as one of the chief spokesmen for German letters in England. The works of Goethe, in particular, continued to enthrall him because instead of "the broad splosh, the thick brush, lots of outline, and a burly chap in the foreground," Goethe offered "perfectly pure *art*": "Such effects with such ease," Bulwer exclaimed to Forster of the *Wahlverwandtschaften* in 1838: "The interior meaning (without which no romance, no novel is worth much) so delicate, so noble; and yet the crowd of readers would call it the most ridiculous nonsense!"[7]

As the reference to an "interior meaning" suggests, Bulwer did not, even in his most aesthetic phase, think a novel should be utterly without a moral or philosophical message. By the all-important element of "*composition*" (his italics), he meant a pattern of ideas or intellectual concepts—or a subtly advanced argument. The characters and incidents of the story should embody the agreeably balanced terms and logical divisions of this argument. Insofar as the story dealt with "*typical* meanings" rather than the "distinct and definite things" characteristic of "allegory," the argument would also exist on enough different planes to give the novel an interestingly complex texture. In this intellectual way, then, the subject matter of a fiction might become less significant for itself than for the manner of its arrangement, and the verbal composition would possess analogies with more plastic compositions. And in fact the intellectual abstractions of the argument might take on such multiple meanings—as the clever pattern of cross references acquired increasing complexity—that the argument could result after all in an utterly aesthetic ambiguity. The "pure *art*" of a fiction like the *Wahlverwandtschaften* would finally use its very intellectuality for the purpose of teasing the reader out of thought: "It takes the thought," as the 1853 note to *Zanoni* describes such a parabolic narrative, "below the surface of the understanding to the deeper intelligence which the world rarely tasks. It is not sunlight on the water, it is a hymn chanted to the Nymph who hearkens and awakes below."

Owing loyalty only to that invisible muse, the fiction would seem to be a self-contained artifact with a strange life of its own. At least Bulwer contemplated such a possibility, and the mysteries of the writer's craft sometimes came to fill him, despite the complaints about his difficult *métier*, with an immense awe. It was quite wrong, he now suspected, to treat literature merely as a communicative or confessional vehicle through which a writer offered or solicited sympathy. Perhaps the literary man must sacrifice both the concern for an audience and any lingering self-preoccupation on the altar of a higher art. Like the "Italian" artist who "must continue through the dark to explore the principles upon which he found[ed] his design," the dedicated author should at last care only to tap those occult energies that enabled a creation to grow into harmony with itself. The "pure delight" of such an act of creation would then confirm the author in his splendid isolation and sublime indifference to both the Many and the Few: "My affection for my work is rooted," the dedication of *Zanoni* assures the serenely detached sculptor Gibson in Rome, "in the solemn and pure delight which it gave me to conceive and to perform. If I had graven it on the rocks of a desert, this apparition of my own innermost mind, in its least-clouded moments, would have been to me as dear; and this ought, I believe, to be the sentiment with which he whose Art is born of faith in the truth and beauty of the principles he seeks to illustrate, should regard his work."

The reader about whom Bulwer professes not to care may, in fact, share the author's satisfaction with the results of his aesthetic labors. The works of this period do constitute interesting illustrations of the principles that have inspired them, as they combine— to take an obvious example first—the atmosphere of the land of Raphael with "the truth and beauty" of German idealism. On the one hand, a large portion of each novel is set in Italy and recreates the mood of dreamy exaltation that had intoxicated Bulwer near Como and in "my beloved Naples"—and which he seems to have associated with the canvases of Guido Reni. Especially through-out *Zanoni*, the masterpiece of Bulwer's aestheticism, does there breathe, according to an Italian reader, the purity of a noble "italia-nità." Yet Goethe, on the other hand, has provided the sources for many characters and situations in all three novels, and *Ernest Maltravers* is actually dedicated "to the Great German People, a Nation of Thinkers and of Critics." *Zanoni*, as R. L. Wolff has furthermore shown, draws very heavily not only on Goethe (and a very occult neo-platonic tradition) but also on Schiller, Novalis, and E. T. A. Hoffmann. Some of Bulwer's contemporaries even recognized the Germanic influence as the prevailing one. Harriet Martineau thus praised the originality of the work in the British context by noticing that this "sort of poem" must appear "new . . . to English readers who are not conversant with the German, and to whom the language of the Ideal region may be more unfamiliar than its thoughts." And the same Germanic qualities evidently im-pressed Carlyle—who had presumably repented his denigration in *Sartor Resartus* of Bulwer's *Pelham* and had come by now to recog-nize something of an ally in Bulwer. After glancing through the copy of *Zanoni* Bulwer had sent him, he could therefore predict that it would—like his own works, one supposes—help to arouse its readers to an awareness of the ideal element in life: "it will be a liberating voice," he assured Bulwer in his favorite style, "for much that lay dumb imprisoned in many human souls; . . . it will shake old deep-set errors looser in their rootings, and thro' such chinks as are possible let in light on dark places very greatly in need of light! I honour much the unwearied, steadfast perseverance with which you prosecute this painfullest but also noblest of human callings, almost the summary of all that is left of nobleness in hu-man callings in these poor days."[8]

In a somewhat unintended sense, the reference to Bulwer's calling may also emphasize what must remain even more significant about these aesthetic works than their relationship to specifically Italian or German (or Greek) sources of inspiration. Of more significance to this study, at least, is the fact that these novels and romances constitute the most successfully original products of Bulwer's absolutely committed devotion to his own muse. The most important fact about *Godolphin*, as Michael Sadleir has stated, is "that it *is* a unity, and that in this novel and its spiritual successors, Bulwer achieved for good or ill his individuality." Although Sadleir mentions only *Maltravers* and *Alice*, which compose the two halves of the same story, among those "successors," one must, as I have intimated, also include *Zanoni*—"this well-loved work," in Bulwer's phrase, "of my matured manhood." In these novels Bulwer was "admirably" the "one kind of novelist which he really longed to be," and they must "represent the maturity of the author of *Pelham*." By most freely indulging his wish to deal learnedly with intellectual traditions and abstract ideas, Bulwer has somehow managed to create, as Wolff may imply too, some of his most passionately vigorous, appealing, and vital fictions.[9]

Besides its manifestation in these aesthetic qualities, Bulwer's fascination with the theory of his art has determined the explicit themes of the three works of fiction. For the intellectual argument, which provides the important principle of organization in each work, has taken the form of a debate about the sources and goals of art. The epistemological and ethical oppositions between the worlds without and within have thus been translated into an aesthetic opposition: histrionic public art is seen in contrast to the hymns addressed to the "Nymph who hearkens and awakes below." As if in a Palace of Art, removed from both the turmoil of the Agora and the perilous stuff of the Cave, Bulwer also seems now to discover the possibility for a reconciliation. A career devoted to the service of mankind need not, when properly conceived, represent a denial of "pure *art*"! This highly theoretical resolution to Bulwer's characteristic dilemma also differs in its emphasis from the reconciliation that his recent fictional communications from the dead had proposed. Whereas those novels had subordinated the life without to the values buried within the tomb, the more aesthetic novels—perhaps paradoxically—urge the sacrifice of the unseen ideal to the visible realities of life. The "apparition of my own innermost mind" and the "hymn chanted to the Nymph" thus seem curiously, but with a useful ambiguity, to impart a message that challenges the validity of their own hermetic aestheticism.[10]

Roughly suggestive of the dialectical pattern of thesis, antithesis, and synthesis, the debate involves first the recognition and rejection of both the external and internal worlds and then the discovery of a realm that fuses aspects of the two. The world without is the rational, civilized realm that demands a certain amount of play-acting and gives rise to artifice rather than true art. It brings "to the training and formation of the poet," in the phrases of Bulwer's essay of 1837 on Thomas Gray, "[the] rules and arcana registered and classified by the clearest lecturer, or the most disciplined academician."[11] Opposed to this realm are the internal haunts of the nymph wherein the artist seeks the ideal muse. There, to appropriate the phrases of Pater's essay on Leonardo, the artist is "smitten with a love of the impossible" and seems "to those about him as one listening to a voice silent for other men." Unfortunately for him, his nymph is actually a Belle Dame sans merci who will reveal herself to her adorer only to enchant him. ("To see a nymph," as Bulwer also explained in a footnote to *The Last Days of Pompeii*, "was to become mad, according to classic and popular superstition.") In his nympholepsy the artist would find himself haunted by the spectres of a strange guilt and increasingly unable to create.

Finally there is the third realm that Bulwer calls "Nature" but which suggests his version of Carlyle's natural supernaturalism. Beneath the apparently arid surfaces of the external and artificial world lies a beneficent, powerfully dynamic, and fertile principle, which seems to reveal—to the inhabitants of Pompeii, for example—"the hand of God" (Po 5:5). When the artist renounces his pursuit of the ideal nymph, he may thus find his deity here amidst the palpable immediacy of natural life. The true fountains of the muse turn out to be not the sources that inspire the "pure delight" of a private creation but the rivers and waters that sustain the joyful harmony of the universal creative system. Nature, it may furthermore appear, has been subtly guiding the artist back to herself even during the years of his seeming estrangement from her. For the development of the great artist, as the essay on Gray maintains, has proceeded in mysterious accord all along with the influences emanating from natural sources:

Had Shakespeare been asked through what paths Nature had conducted him to the inner temple of her mysteries, he could have given us no chart of his progress. As springs, that supply the fountain, work under ground, so latent and concealed are the deep and unfailing streams that gather into those reservoirs, which give delight and freshness to the world: yet, not the less for our want of a clue, has the long journey been undertaken—not the less for their silence and darkness, have the streams flowed through countless veins and strata of earth, in order that the waters of the fountain might sparkle in the face of day. From the hour of birth to the hour when genius breaks suddenly into fame, the education of the unconscious artist must noiselessly progress.[12]

Respectively subtitled "The Eleusinia" and "The Mysteries," *Ernest Maltravers* and *Alice* most obviously deal with the "paths" through which "Nature" conducts the artist toward his initiation within "the inner temple of her mysteries." But *Godolphin* and *Zanoni* are *Künstlerromane* too and attempt to chart at least the main stages in the education of the artist. It will thus be useful to consider the various artists and artists-*manqués* in all these works as the aspects of Bulwer's archetypal aesthetic hero who journeys through three stages to an eventual creative synthesis. His progress shows, according to the preface of 1840 to *Maltravers*, how art may come to treat "life in its spiritual and mystic as well as its more visible and fleshly characteristics."

[83]

Various barriers, as *Zanoni* in particular describes them, divide the universe into zones, and from the human perspective these barriers may serve a protective function: "There may be things around us that would be dangerous and hostile to man, if Providence had not placed a wall between them and us, merely by different modifications of matter." When he comes upon the walls that surround the "regions of Custom and Prescription," the reasonable man therefore tends to respect them: "who, in an age in which reason has chosen its proper bounds, would be mad enough to break the partition?" (Z 2:1; 7:9).

Yet within these regions of rational, civilized life, the true artist will lack for inspiration, and each of the novels seeks to imply the inadequacy of the art of this sphere. It becomes steadily more apparent, in fact, that reason may have chosen bounds that are too narrow, for both art and the society it reflects show signs of a self-defeating sterility. At last a sort of moribundity prevents the denizens of these regions from holding back the more irrational forces that begin once more to sweep, as it were, through the barriers.

Devoting the most attention to this realm within the barriers, *Godolphin* emphasizes its artificiality in terms of Bulwer's characteristic imagery of the stage. The barriers may seem similar to a proscenium arch, for the very prominent voice of the narrator does not let the reader forget that the characters are moving about on "our stage." Composing what he likes to call "a spectacle" or "scenes" or an "allegory of real life," he may even believe that his tableaux are more interesting for their theatricality than for their supposedly genuine vitality: "Here let us drop the curtain upon Lucilla," he remarks typically, satisfied with the effect of his stage picture: "Often, O reader, shalt thou see her before thee—alone and broken-hearted—weeping in the twilight streets of Rome!" (G 43).

Within the story the aesthete and mentor of the protagonist, Augustus Saville, demonstrates how the theatrical values of the narrator may inform a man's entire existence. Essentially a spectator and manipulator whose chief pursuit, aside from gambling, is going to the theatre, Saville all but literally stages the central event of the plot—the reunion of hero and heroine halfway through the novel. It would be amusing, he thinks, to bring the former lovers together again after so many years now that both his erstwhile protégé and the widowed countess happen to be in Rome. So he arranges a surprise meeting at the Colosseum and steps back "with a sardonic yet indifferent smile"—as if to watch the circus. Although the intensely genuine emotions of his actors are at first disquieting, he is soon relieved when "the habitual hypocrisy" of the countess restores a certain comfortable artificiality to the spectacle. As he has foreseen too, the ensuing marriage is as hollow an event as all the other spectacles he has arranged for his delectation. Husband and wife sleep separately while keeping up the pretences appropriate to their highly civilized ménage.

In a final display of the style for which he has lived, Saville stages his own deathbed without any of the troubling realism that had perhaps marred the performance at the Colosseum. Then as the scene ends, he complacently pronounces the epilogue: "I have played my part decently—eh? . . . I am very glad I die before the d——d Revolution that must come; I don't want to take wine with the Member for Holborn Bars. I am a type of a system; I expire before the system; my death is the herald of its fall." His allegorical—or artificial—value, which he has created himself, exceeds the value of his literal humanity. His favorite actress, Fanny, who has arrived in her costume from the theatre, and Godolphin stand around the corpse and observe that "the world is indeed a stage": "It has lost a consummate actor, though in a small part" (G 65).[13]

Playing a far larger part, the heroine, Constance, Countess of Erpingham, provides the ultimate instance of consummate style attempting to redeem the futility of life within the regions of Custom and Prescription. In fact, she has aspired to do far more than exemplify style for its own sake. Her embittered and dying father had sworn her to the holy cause of reforming the fundamental values of the cynical, hypocritical society that had brought about his own downfall. For this high purpose, then, she had rejected Godolphin, married the Earl, and painstakingly created her coterie —casting too "the spell" that had captivated even Lord Byron and Mme. de Staël. As a founder and Lady Patroness of Almack's, she has established the very stage and prescribed the very roles wherein fashionable society has discerned the meaning of life.[14]

Emblematic of her commitment to noble principles have been a stern portrait of her father and the mirror that reminds her at every critical juncture of a beauty to be used on behalf of her goal. These emblems also come to manifest, however, the emptiness of the values on which her career is founded. One fatal day the mirror shows her the signs of age, and she confronts the growing realization that despite the showiness of her apparent victories her life has accomplished very little: "Was she, after all—was she right to adhere so rigidly to her father's dying words, and to that vow afterwards confirmed by her own pride and bitterness of soul? She looked to her father's portrait for an answer [the portrait hangs opposite the mirror]; and that daring and eloquent face seemed, for the first time, cold and unanswering to her appeal" (G 59).

The nullity of her career onstage has already begun to obsess her: "the Something of life was wanting"; "political intrigue could not fill up the vacuum of which Constance daily complained"; her object "does not fill up all the spaces of time. The intervals between the acts are longer than the acts themselves." As the time of the Reform Bill approaches—"the d——d Revolution that must come" —the events begin to threaten her stage; those unpredictable forces are breaking down the barriers that her Exclusivism has established for its protection. She has lost control and can only wait helplessly in a strange state of fascination: "The bright countess listened to [the Radicals'] harangues, pondered over their demonstrations, and mused over their hopes. But she had lived too much on the surface of the actual world, her habits of thought were too essentially worldly, to be converted, while she was attracted, by doctrines so startling in their ultimate conclusions. She turned once more to herself, and waited, in a sad and thoughtful stillness, the progress of things—convinced only of the vanity of them all" (G 55).

When the progress of things overtakes them, the figures corresponding to Saville and Constance in the other novels will similarly find that their careers have been in vain. Meanwhile they tend like Lumley Ferrers in *Maltravers* and *Alice* to manifest the more sinister implications of the vision that recognizes no significance beyond the bounded, civilized regions. Whereas the histrionic successes of Saville and Constance have proved relatively harmless to others, Ferrers becomes in his ruthless pursuit of materialistic self-interest one of Bulwer's most vicious confidence artists. As one of the evil demons, in fact, of the story, he plots his rise to power at the particular expense of pure females—especially those with whom the hero has fallen in love. (In his habit of turning up to spoil each affair, he reminds one of the demon of E. T. A. Hoffmann's amorous adventures.) Most absorbing perhaps is the complex episode in which his efforts to keep Evelyn Cameron separated from Maltravers serve indirectly to destroy the soul of Caroline Merton. To enlist her help in his schemes, he persuades Caroline (who genuinely loves him) that they are "too wise" for conventional marriage and must enter into a more modern sort of pact. While they remain lovers in secret, he provides her with an advantageous husband in the form of Lord Doltimore, and she works to get Evelyn for him.

Since Ferrers' behavior represents what Bulwer takes to be the logical consequence of materialist rationalism, the analogous personalities in the eighteenth-century world of *Zanoni* are those who associate themselves with the "Age of Reason." These include, besides Condorcet, Malesherbes, and other philosophes, the prominent painter Jean Nicot who consistently deplores the evidence of priestcraft in the soulful art of past centuries: "the soul—bah!— we are but modifications of matter, and painting is modification of matter also" (Z 3:4). On this material basis, then, a whole vast civilization is relentlessly destroying the soul and creating the new forms whose emptiness and artificiality it fails to recognize. Cut off from the genuine sources of vital inspiration, it is also weakening itself on behalf of its Nemesis. When the "d——d Revolution" does come, the forces of the irrational will break through the modern "modifications of matter." For these new modifications have ignored, where Providence had originally designed them to counteract, the "things around us . . . dangerous and hostile to man."

In his second or antithetical phase, the artist will discover the full meaning of that avenging spirit. His search for a higher inspiration beyond the barriers of the rational leads him to the recognition not only of beauty but also of guilt and horror; the "hymn chanted to the Nymph who hearkens and awakes below" seems inevitably to arouse a devil along with the nymph. Or the nymph and the devil may signify the two aspects of the same mysterious, irrational energy. When the idealist cannot control that energy, then, he understands that his high art bears the seeds of its own defeat just as surely as the artificial histrionics of the world's stage.

Godolphin identifies the entrance into the "immeasurable regions" beyond "Custom and Prescription" most explicitly with the haunts of the beautiful Nymph. Having been rejected by Constance and disgusted by "the paint and canvass" he sees wherever he looks in the "actual world," Percy Godolphin journeys to Italy and walks one day outside Rome: "Scarcely conscious whither he was wandering, he did not pause till he found himself in that green still valley in which the pilgrim beholds the grotto of Egeria." There he comes upon Lucilla, "who seemed almost to restore to the deserted cave and the mourning stream their living Egeria," and his romantic liaison with the strange, fey creature begins (G 31).[15] Possessed of clairvoyant abilities, she can also "awaken" in others, as the important speech delivered during her madness much later in the story indicates, "that great power thou callest the IMAGINATION":

... that power which presides over dreams and visions, which kindles song, and lives in the Heart of Melodies; which inspired the Magian of the East and the Pythian voices—and, in the storms and thunder of savage lands originated the notion of a God and the seeds of human worship; that vast presiding Power which, to the things of mind, is what the deity is to the universe itself—the creator of all. I would awaken, I say, that Power from its customary sleep, where, buried in the heart, it folds its wings, and lives but by fits and starts, unquiet, but unaroused; and by that Power thou wouldst see and feel and know, and through it only thou wouldst exist. So that it would be with thee as if the body were not: as if thou wert already all-spiritual, all-living. (G 61)

This is not, however, the creative secondary imagination, and Egeria cannot actually turn her lover into a poet. Although Godolphin "has the soul of the poet" and wanders in those "all-spiritual" ideal regions, he does not "discover the magic wand that . . . would have reduced the visions into shape and substance" (G 65). He falls an impotent victim to that "most common disease to genius . . . nympholepsy," and as "the Ideal having no vent in [him], preys within," his mind supposedly undergoes a steady "deterioration" (G 20, 15, 6). The awareness of the ideal beauties that remain so disembodied and so irrelevant to man's actual life evidently constitutes a curse—and a curse, moreover, which the idealist can never escape. For when he leaves Lucilla and returns to Constance, Godolphin finds that his guilty disease has only intensified. Now crazed, Lucilla has pursued him back to England and haunts him like his very devil.

As the same pattern seems to repeat itself with each new love affair, the career of Ernest Maltravers may associate guilt and madness even more inexorably with the adoration of the ideal muse. He begins as a student fresh from Germany, where he had "filled a dozen common-place books with criticisms on Kant" and had lived "up to his ears in the moonlit abyss of Plato" (EM 5). Since he is "half unconsciously a poet, . . . and woman [is] his muse," he readily falls in love with the extraordinarily innocent Alice and attempts to live creatively with her. In fact she becomes pregnant (Lucilla had also borne Godolphin a child that had not survived), but events separate them before Maltravers discovers the fact. Feeling that he has betrayed his muse and increasingly obsessed by a sense of sterility, he also starts to gain a persuasion of the power of the devil—who would seem incarnated at this stage in Alice's monstrous father Darvil.[16]

His pursuit of the *Ewig-Weibliche* leads him into four important affairs, which may associate the operations of the devil quite simply with an inability to harmonize his own cross-purposes. Requiring on the one hand an ideal muse, he forgets that he and his particular beloved "are made of clay." The oversight tends, as in the liaison with Mme. de Ventadour, to enable the clay to assert itself suddenly and powerfully; the guilt of adultery thus threatens to attaint the ideal woman. On the other hand he does also need a woman of clay who can tame him and "restore him," in Evelyn's words, "to his race." But if he then neglects the ideal muse, she will take her revenge, and the awful punishment for his courtship of Evelyn is to learn that she may be his own daughter by Alice. Failing to find the ideal and real in the same female, he violates both types and loads each aspect of himself with remorse. The "ghosts," in the frequent term of the novel, of his past loves reduce him over and over again to "a crushing sense of impotence."

In one phase he does appear to discover "the magic wand" that had eluded Godolphin and to become genuinely creative: on the shores of Como, where Godolphin and Lucilla had lived, he one day takes "the wand of the simple pen" and gives "a palpable form to the long-intangible visions . . . the beautiful ghost of the Ideal" (EM 3:2). Yet the books he thereby publishes lead him into the affair with Lady Florence Lascelles (who has been sending him thrilling, anonymous missives), and this hectic affair serves most completely to emphasize the violence of his cross-purposes. His two rivals for the hand of Lady Florence are his two most important alter-egos—the undisciplined, irrationally idealistic poet Castruccio Cesarini and that coolly disciplined, hyper-rational materialist Lumley Ferrers. Goaded into frantic jealousy by the crafty Ferrers, the unstable Cesarini eventually becomes a raving maniac. Lady Florence succumbs in the meanwhile to the bitterness that the rivalries, misunderstandings, and conflicting demands upon her physical and spiritual energies have entailed. She dies of consumption, leaving Maltravers more hopelessly ghost-ridden than ever. The last sight of her haggard face in the lamplight would never "cease to haunt the heart of Maltravers": "When shall that altered aspect not pass as a ghost before his eyes?" (EM 9:4).

His lifelong quest for inspiration in the haunts of the nymph has led him to discover only "the impotence of human agencies" and the omnipotence of the devil. At the end he flees with the ghosts of his guilty and sterile past to the only landscape that now suits his vision of the universe: ". . . those swamps and morasses that formerly surrounded the castle of Gil de Retz, the ambitious Lord, the dreaded Necromancer" (A 10:2).

In giving the typical story its most fully mythic overtones, *Zanoni* may help most satisfactorily to indicate the connection between the aspiration for the ideal and the discovery of the devil. For however seemingly noble, the aspiration may involve a Hubris that relates the idealist to Lucifer. The painter Clarence Glyndon thus indulges the "godlike dream" of freeing himself of the trammels of mortality when he journeys up to the castle of the immortal sage Mejnour in the Appenines. He does not even pretend to seek the nymph who will inspire him to artistic creativity but longs instead for the condition of ethereality that Lucilla had described: ". . . as if the body were not: as if thou wert already all-spiritual, all-living."

The path to his version of the grotto of Egeria takes him deep into his own psyche. Far from existing as an external source of inspiration, his Egeria must be discerned as the most nearly "all-spiritual, all-living" principle inside himself: "The music of the fountain," Mejnour assures him, "is heard in the soul *within*": "Not in the knowledge of things without, but in the perfection of the soul within, lies the empire of man aspiring to be more than man" (Z 3:18). The attainment of the ideal state therefore involves an absolute denial of the external and physical empire, and Glyndon engages in a strenuous regimen of mortification of the flesh. Instead of redeeming or fulfilling his humanity, his asceticism would destroy all signs of it. By the end of the process of dehumanization, only the pure, utterly passionless "all-spiritual" part of him will remain. He will also discover at last the identity of his own psychic empire with "the farthest and obscurest regions in the universe of ideas" (Z 4:5).

When he destroys the barriers surrounding the ordinary human consciousness, he too discovers, of course, his devil rather than his Egeria. He discovers, more precisely, that the ethereal Mejnour had possessed a hitherto invisible demonic counterpart, and that the development of man's superhuman capacities must first entail a full recognition of this demonic element. In the dread shape of the "Dweller of the Threshold," Glyndon indeed encounters Bulwer's most fearful representation of the terrifyingly chaotic and ugly forces lurking within the unconscious. The spectre addresses him as "my mortal lover" and taunts him for the scorn he has shown toward the condition of ordinary mortality. Appalled, Glyndon wanders abroad and like the Ancient Mariner periodically confesses —in one such episode making his young virgin sister fatally conscious of the Dweller too. In the general desolation of his life, his capacity for artistic creativity has naturally withered as well, and when he attempts to draw, he can depict only his own criminality.

In all three novels, therefore, the artist sins when he seeks to transcend the barriers and to live amidst "those visions of the lovely and perfect which never can," in the phrases of *Godolphin*, "descend to the gloomy regions wherein mortality is cast" (G 20). Yet those gloomy regions of mortality have been similarly unable to offer authentic inspiration, and it is fully apparent by now that a guilty sterility may overtake the artist whether he courts a material or an ideal muse. The very same guilt, indeed, attaches to those

[92]

who have denied the soul as to those who have sought to deny their physical being.

The culminating events of the novels accordingly suggest that the same Nemesis may bring down both sorts of Hubris. Those perverse, demonic energies—which the idealists have unleashed, as it were, in the regions beyond the barriers—now burst into the civilized sphere to overwhelm the rational materialists too. As *Alice*, for example, economically represents the cataclysm, the raving Cesarini grows strong as a wild beast, breaks out of his asylum, and tracks down and murders his coolly self-possessed enemy Ferrers.[17] (The symbiotic relationship between these two antagonists who typify opposing drives within the hero himself is, of course, similar to the relationship between the Dweller of the Threshold and Mejnour.)

In the other novels the avenging force of the irrational swells into an even more spectacular threat to the rational facade of a whole fruitless civilization. The mad Lucilla, at one time as innocent as Egeria, thus becomes not only the private demon of Godolphin but a portent of the "d——d Revolution." Lord Saltream sees in her arrival in London an especially ominous sign of the times, and he becomes in his own person too an emblem of the irrationality that is bringing down society. A public madman and a rather poignant figure, whom like Cassandra no one takes seriously, he gloomily apprehends his own death and the apocalypse to come—while on the eve of Reform there are indeed "fires and insurrections in the provinces; convulsions abroad and turbulence at home" (G 55).[18]

Zanoni manages to expand the individual Nemesis into the apocalyptic horror of the French Revolution. Glyndon arrives in Paris during the Reign of Terror, where "seeing crime and vice in all their hideousness, and in so vast a theatre, he . . . found that in vice and crime there are deadlier horrors than in the eyes of a phantom-fear" (Z 7:6). Like an outbreak of the collective human unconscious, the enlarged Dweller of the Threshold will destroy the moribund Age of Reason.[19] Condorcet, Malesherbes, Nicot, Robespierre must all die. Individual after individual who has denied the significance of the regions beyond the barriers must enter those regions via the guillotine of the Barrière du Trône.

The cataclysms have revealed the danger of polarizing the universe between those two regions and of affirming the absolute value of one at the expense of the other. Life and art must evidently draw their sustenance from both regions at once, and fortunately the cataclysmic events do seem to open the way for a synthesis. Or they enable the civilization and, more particularly, its sick and haunted artists to discern as if with fresh eyes the synthesis that has obtained all along in the fruitful life of Nature.

The synthesis, as I have suggested, may resemble the mysteries of natural supernaturalism: "Look round all being," Zanoni urges Glyndon in a typical passage, "is there not mystery everywhere? Can thine eye trace the ripening of the grain beneath the earth?" (Z 7:9). Those mysterious, dynamic processes imply the very "soul" of nature, for the true soul exists not as an utterly pure, ideal entity but as the immanent life-force. It reveals itself especially in those aspects of nature that seem to be in perpetual, purposeful, life-giving movement: "Like the soul of the landscape is the gush of a fresh stream; it knows no sleep, no pause; it works forever—the life, the cause of life to all around. The great frame of nature may repose, but the spirit of the waters rests not for a moment" (G 68).

This restless, immanent spirit not only sustains life but, as Bulwer implies in other passages, constitutes a destiny that would make every aspect of nature develop in proper accord with its potentiality. Human nature too must submit to its powerful guidance because "as the soul of the landscape is the soul of man, in our deepest slumbers its course glides on, and works unsilent, unslumbering, through its destined channel" (G 68). While recalling Lucilla's references to "a creative spirit within," that rushing soul evidently resembles as well what *Wilhelm Meister*, in a passage to which I have already alluded, calls "the creative force, which out of these [things without us] can produce what they were meant to be."[20] Nature seems, that is, to wish to lead each individual toward his own appropriate fate, and the secret of the creative life is to co-operate in the working out of that destiny: "Depend upon this, Ernest Maltravers [writes his guardian], that if you do not fulfil what nature intended for your fate, you will be a morbid misan-thrope, or an indolent voluptuary—wretched and listless in man-hood, repining and joyless in old age. But if you do fulfil your fate, you must enter soon into your apprenticeship. Let me see you labour and aspire—no matter what in—what to. Work, work—that is all I ask of you!" (EM 2:4).

Since Nature exhibits a vast panorama in which every element is continually performing its appropriate function, work rather than contemplation relates a man to the general scheme of "what Nature intended." The work that has constituted the human apprentice-ship may provide too an especially good instance of natural super-naturalism. For while the apprentice has been working—"no matter what in"—some quasi-supernatural principle or "creative spirit within" has been presiding over the process. "Unsilent, unslum-bering," it has been helping him to create from the elements of his life "what they were meant to be." It may finally require, as in Goethe and Carlyle, some kind of sacrifice or resignation (*Ent-sagen*)—as if to enable the guilty nympholept to escape destruc-tion in the cataclysm—but then the apprenticeship will end in "the inner temple of [Nature's] mysteries." Now an initiate, the hero will discern his unity with his true soul and creative spirit.

In addition to their treatment of the creative principle in Na-ture and in the *Bildung* of human nature, the novels also grope to-ward definition of the analogous principle in artistic creativity. Bulwer apparently wished to typify the process whereby the work of art might come into being—not through the inspiration of the dangerous, private Egeria, but through the agency of Nature and the artist's love for humanity. With such considerations in mind too, then, it may be interesting to assess the increasingly successful presentation of apprenticeships and other patterns of "natural" development in the three novels.

Godolphin represents the rushing course of the soul "through its destined channel" most consistently in the imagery of water. A river flows from the glassy lake of Godolphin Priory, where hero and heroine first meet, and at every moment of crisis thereafter, the hero will encounter an irresistible river, lake, fountain, or storm. These include the spring of Egeria and the Lago di Como, for example, as well as the fountains of the Villa d'Este, amidst whose booming Godolphin proposes for the second time to Constance. Since he has come to deal "*con amore* with fatalities and influences," he apparently finds that it is his destiny to return by the roundabout course to Constance. Their marriage may thus imply the fortunate and fated merging of what one passage terms the "two streams of existence—the one belonging to the actual, the other to the imaginary" (G 20). His tendency to live in the imagination must now interact with her career of calculated action upon the public stage— the career that had made her long, of course, for the "Something" profounder in life. The synthesis of his noble sense of ideal beauty and her extreme resolution and discipline should prove fruitful, and in their mutual creativity each should find he has fulfilled "what Nature intended for [his] fate."

As I have mentioned, however, the aesthete Saville has staged their marriage, and it proves at first a futile affair. Nature evidently demands a sacrifice, which Bulwer seems to arrange in the form of the self-effacing action of Stainforth Radclyffe. The spokesman for "Benevolence" and the other chief representative in the story (besides Saville) for the narrator, Radclyffe is able to establish the marriage on a new creative basis. He has fallen deeply in love with Constance himself, but when she one day sadly confesses to him the emptiness of her marriage to Godolphin, he resists the temptation to urge his own love. Instead he advises her toward greater humility; then assuring Godolphin in many conferences that "Benevolence is the sole cure to idealism," he becomes the successful intermediary between husband and wife. Each resigns his private schemes or ideals, and "this reconciliation," the often cynical narrator observes, "was not so short-lived as matters of the kind frequently are" (G 60). They return to their sources at the Priory: "they stood by the very rivulet" where they had first met. Restored thus to harmony with the soul, and having lost their pride and regained their naturalness, they may go on to create children: "Again and again, in the slumbers of the night, she stretched forth her arms to feel that he was near; all her pride, her coldness seemed gone as by a spell; she loved as the softest, the fondest love" (G 67).

Unfortunately, for the sake of the creative or apprenticeship pattern, the process does not end here, and the concluding events emphasize that Godolphin never was a very successful husband or apprentice.[21] As if to show the inescapability of his nympholepsy, he leaves the arms of Constance one stormy night to obey the summons of Lucilla to attend her deathbed. Afterwards he drowns in the swollen torrent of the river near the spot at which he had experienced in one of the early chapters an inexplicably "shadowy and chilling" sensation. Bulwer has wished perhaps to imply that any artist must, at the critical moment, ignore the sensible advice of Radclyffe, leave the civilized Constance, and heed the call of the irrational, demonic muse. Yet despite the degree to which references to rising waters prepare for it, the catastrophe does seem false —as Bulwer himself came to believe. He had intended to write what one of his characters in the story calls a "natural romance" but his catastrophe emphasized the romantic and supernatural out of all proportion to the natural: there was, the preface of 1840 admits, "exaggerated romance" in the avenging reappearance of Lucilla and "the admission of *accident* . . . out of keeping with the natural events" in the flood.

The other two stories do not err in the same way. Instead of treating the nymph of the fountain as the only muse, they find elements of the inspiring female in even the most worldly of women.

And instead of identifying the guiding soul of Nature with waters that sweep the protagonist away into the darkness, they allow him to recover his vision of Nature within the regions of civilization. The series of incarnations of the *Ewig-Weibliche*—which constitutes the guiding element in Ernest Maltravers' career—has thus been luring him not into the region of ghosts but beyond and out of it. Far from desiring an ideal nymph, he even perceives in retrospect that the source of his inspiration and the goal of his quest have always been a fully human and civilized female—who has, as it incidentally turns out, also become a baroness. Maltravers comes to rest, then, at the opposite pole from Godolphin.

The circumstances leading Maltravers into his last stage, in particular, are supposed to demonstrate that the supernatural element, which had wrecked the conclusion to Godolphin's story, has wholly fused itself into a naturalistic process. For even though Maltravers may appear to see a *genuine* ghost at this point—in the only event of the story "to savour of the Supernatural"—yet, maintains the author, "it is easily accounted for by ordinary agencies, and it is strictly to the letter of the truth" (A 10:2). He has a dream involving his mother's portrait (which had previously been associated in a complex manner with Evelyn and her singing of an air out of his past). The voice of his dead mother, like the true call of the eternally feminine, then summons him home to England, and his obedience leads directly to his ecstatic reunion with his original muse Alice. In her "Nature . . . claim[s] her fairest child": "Here," he exclaims, "have I found that which shames and bankrupts the ideal!" And at the end of his speech "there went a melodious voice that seemed as if Nature echoed to his words, and blest the reunion of her children" (A 10:5; 11:The Last).[22]

There is, however, a possible theoretical weakness in Bulwer's handling of that reunion. The process of "The Mysteries" seems in principle to require an individual to renounce his idealism before permitting him to recover something far better than his ideal in Nature. Mme. de Ventadour, for example, who "had preceded her younger admirer through the 'MYSTERIES OF LIFE,'" had needed to resign herself humbly to very bleak realities before achieving her final serenity (A 6:1). Maltravers, on the other hand, has not clearly reached the point of renunciation; despite the tremendous batterings of fortune, he retains the taint of pride and of nympholepsy. As in the rather similar conclusion to Ibsen's *Peer Gynt*, he has had to do nothing himself but to return to the heroine. She has waited for him chastely through the years, and although he has sinned mightily against her, his true self has somehow preserved its spotlessness in her heart. (Alice assures him that she is "unpolluted" in one of her very first excited utterances after their reunion and typifies like Lucy Brandon the radical innocence at the core of Nature.)

Yet if Maltravers has failed to renounce idealism before recovering Alice, he does certainly do so afterwards, and the termination of his apprenticeship leaves him cured of nympholepsy. "The haughtiness of his temper [is] subdued" too, and he accepts, as it were, the lesson of Radclyffe, upon which Godolphin had only been meditating at the time of his death: "Benevolence is the sole cure to idealism." That truth is, moreover, far from an abstract principle in Maltravers' thinking because Alice has fully embodied the "mysterious beauty and immortal holiness . . . [of] our human nature" and so elicited his love for all men: "Your fidelity to my erring self," he tells her, "has taught me ever to love, to serve, to compassionate, to respect, the community of God's creatures" (A 11:The Last). She will, as the 1840 preface emphasizes, inspire him especially to practical action on behalf of the community: while "in 'Wilhelm Meister' the apprenticeship is . . . that of theoretical art," Maltravers' "apprenticeship is rather that of practical life." Although the novel remains somewhat vague about the career he will pursue, one assumes it will be political. He will take his place, in any event, within the larger, living wholeness of the natural scheme of things and thus become appropriately creative: "No longer despising Man as he is, and no longer exacting from all things the ideal of a visionary standard, he was more fitted to mix in the living World, and to minister usefully to the great objects that refine and elevate our race" (A 11:The Last).

The apprenticeship thus ends in a far more appropriate manner than Godolphin's. And yet one other aspect of the conclusions to both *Alice* and *Godolphin* may still trouble the reader: both novels have dealt with essentially artistic temperaments, but Bulwer has not indicated what the role of art may be in the beneficent natural order of the "living world." In fact, "theoretical art" may have no place in "practical life." Radclyffe, the benevolist and arranger of the reconciliation of Constance and Godolphin, had specifically confessed to "know[ing] nothing of the Fine Arts" while Maltravers' attainment of practical benevolence has probably entailed his complete renunciation of art. The artists have therefore remained sterile, and insofar as the physical unions of the two couples have tended to symbolize the hope of artistic creativity, they too have failed to bear fruit. (Now that he has given up art, Maltravers' marriage to Alice may produce children to replace the daughter of their illegitimate union, who had died in infancy.)

It may therefore be especially interesting that in *Zanoni* Bulwer does at last dramatize the possibility for successful aesthetic creativity. As before, the artist must first be roused from his entranced and sterile worship of the ideal Egeria and awaken, like Adam from his Keatsian dream, to the real Eve beside him. But now the actions inspired by the real Eve (again, in part, typifying Nature) possess not only a practical but also an aesthetic value. The practical commitment to Nature—to be expressed in Maltravers' mode of life— no longer has to cancel out the commitment to an ideal art, which Godolphin had expressed in the mode of his death. Instead of a choice of one side over the other, a synthesis can at last resolve the problem of the divided loyalties.

The resolution is possible on the individual level because Nature herself has come in *Zanoni* to resemble a work of art, and all actions performed in harmony with her—no matter how practical—become artistic. The artist will thus be able to manifest his devotion to ideal beauty even in the conduct of his trivial daily affairs: "in conduct, as in art," we read in the important chapter on aesthetic principles, "there is an idea of the great and beautiful by which men should exalt the hackneyed and the trite of life" (Z 2:9). The "Benevolence" that motivates all worthy human actions may come in this way to operate less as Radclyffe's cure to idealism than as the appropriate expression of a lofty idealism. The artist has finally discovered in this life a medium that is adequate to his vision.

Two aspects of Nature—the medium of the divine Creator—receive special emphasis in *Zanoni* and help to suggest how initiation into the natural "Mysteries" now enables the individual artist to become creative. First there is the hierarchical (or spire-like) organization that forever maintains the distinction between creation and Creator: "Throughout all creation, from the archangel to the worm, from Olympus to the pebble, from the radiant and completed planet to the nebula that hardens through ages of mist and slime into the habitable world, the first law of nature is inequality." "And *this*," Zanoni further assures the apprentice Glyndon, "is not a harsh, but a loving law—the *real* law of Improvement"—because it assures perpetual aspiration upward (Z 2:7). The reach of every individual is constantly impelled, as it were, to exceed its grasp.

The "loving" quality of the law may become even more apparent, however, in connection with what would seem to be the second and complementary aspect of Nature. While in one sense distinct from his creation, the Creator is also immanent in this second aspect of it: in the principle, namely, of self-sacrificing love that constitutes, as it turns out, the very sustaining essence of created life. When he gave up his own self-sufficient purity and loved the materials he brought into being, God identified the self-sacrificing impulse as his chief attribute. And his creation—while deriving thus from the idea of self-sacrifice—perpetually reaffirms the idea and perpetually sustains its identity through constant actions of self-sacrifice performed by its individual members. Each individual fulfills, in effect, his own reason for being when he intuits the self-sacrificing essence of the creation and acts on the basis of that intuition. In this way those who exist on the upper levels of the hierarchy are forever moved to sacrifice themselves for those on lower levels; the ideal that provides the basis for all created life is exemplified and communicated from Olympian heights to the lowest pebble.

This self-sacrificing movement downward rather paradoxically sustains, moreover, the upward tendency of the creation. For each individual act of self-sacrifice tends to raise those for whom it was performed to a perception of a higher level of love and so to make them more nobly self-sacrificing in their turn. The more and more complete communication of divine love, even to the lowest levels of creation, is thereby assured and the entire universe is progressively recreated at ever higher stages of ideality. The material creation gradually becomes in this manner a medium that is adequate to the idea it manifests.

Such a perception of the universe, as I have suggested, once more makes individual artistic creativity possible. Inspired by his "faith in whatever is self-sacrificing and divine," the artist can participate—even more fully than other men perhaps—in the natural-supernatural processes of life. That participation also involves him now in an apprenticeship that of course transcends the traditional pattern of *Bildung*. Going beyond the "Mysteries" that had taught Godolphin and Maltravers the virtues of Resignation and Benevolence, the artist can now enact a divine self-sacrifice and his work can provide a vehicle for the cosmic energy that the Platonist of the introduction terms "the enthusiasm of Love." His career will not simply "minister usefully [like Maltravers'] to the great objects that refine and elevate our race," but will guide the race toward its quite mythic apotheosis. For the artist above other benefactors seems to promise victory in "the perpetual struggle of Humanity to approach the Gods" (Z 2:9).

Right from its first episodes, *Zanoni* illustrates the creative interdependence of Art and Nature—and of the Gods and Humanity—in the cosmic struggle. Instead, that is, of revealing only in retrospect the meaning of the rushing waters (for Godolphin) and the various incarnations of the *Ewig-Weibliche* (for Maltravers), the romance tends to suggest immediately a universe in which the self-sacrificing "creative spirit" is operating. That spiritual energy seems, moreover, not simply to be operating as a guiding, motivating force now, but actually to be penetrating and transfiguring materials. Nature, for example, does even more than inspire the artist: it depends now on art for its own fulfillment, and indeed for much of the allegory, Art and Nature work through the medium of each other. At certain points too, as a summary of three especially symbolic actions may indicate, the process brings into sudden focus an image for the identity towards which both elements in Bulwer's eternal antitheses are forever struggling. The symbolic child, which could not quite be born in the earlier novels, is now effectively brought to birth.

The first symbolic action brings an artist's natural child and his aesthetic offspring ("his other child") into a fleeting identity and so shows Nature and Art serving as vehicles for each other. The process begins, though, with the artist's neglecting Nature and living in the haunts of the nymph. The Neapolitan composer Gaetano Pisani listens, that is, to the voice of a siren who remains inaudible to everyone else. Absolutely possessed, indeed, by a nympholepsy that may suggest the beginnings of the *Sturm und Drang*, he can compose only a wild opera called "The Siren," which is considered far too anarchic to be produced. Nor can he pursue his artistic destiny as a performer himself since his inner demon prevents him from obediently submitting, as a member of the San Carlo orchestra, to the maestro. (Bulwer may, as Wolff incidentally speculates, have modelled his enchanted violinist on Paganini, who had died in 1840.) [23]

In contrast to the siren, Pisani's neglected daughter Viola typifies both Nature and, as Harriet Martineau stated, with Bulwer's approval, "Human Instinct."[24] The work of art can thus come into being when love for her poor mad father moves the self-abnegating Viola to scheme to have his wild opera produced. Herself an aspiring opera singer, she dares to make the role of the siren the vehicle for her stage debut, and her success emphasizes an important aesthetic truth. She is herself, the amazed Pisani observes, "fairer than the very Siren he had called from the deeps of melody." And other enraptured witnesses of the performance would seem to agree that in Viola, the offspring of his love for a humble Englishwoman, Pisani has produced, after all, his masterpiece. "It was the daughter that interested me," says Zanoni of that evening, for the natural mystery of a daughter's love may be far more thrilling than the supernatural voice of a siren. Yet for those moments onstage the daughter has remained nearly inseparable from the siren, and the image does not suggest (like the conclusion to *Alice*) that Art must always seem sterile beside the plenitude of Nature. Art can, on the contrary, approach sublimity because it can provide the necessary medium for the expression of natural instincts and reveal the divine beauty that is in Nature.

In uniting Art to Nature, the image seems to reveal in particular the single identity of the two muses that had opposed each other in *Godolphin*. Whereas the demonic Lucilla had once called Godolphin from the safe love of the civilized Constance and had lured him to a watery death, the two women now sing with one voice. The siren still sings, that is, in the voice of the soprano on the world's stage (to recall the theatrical metaphor pervading Constance's career too), and is present in the daughter's love for a father (which had similarly provided Constance's chief motive). Perhaps, in fact, the siren lure of death always informs and intensifies "whatever is self-sacrificing and divine" in life; whenever love for humanity moves the artist toward self-sacrifice, he is somehow remaining loyal to the darker muse as well.

So occult, however, remains the suspected relationship between what one might consider the creative and destructive instincts that the operatic medium can bring their energies only momentarily together in a single image. Quickly enough, too, the other elements in the synthesis fall apart. Viola herself becomes aware of the artificiality of the operatic milieu, and as time passes she seems more and more to lose the ardent awareness of the supernatural within Nature—an awareness that had often made the expression on her face resemble that of a pre-Raphaelite or in this context, perhaps, Raphaelite model.[25] Exemplifying a universe in constant need of redemption, the novel must depict a new struggle on the part of art to conceive the image in which nature may again become divine.

The second and far grander aesthetic struggle grows out of the first, in that Viola's initial enactment of the siren continues to serve as the image of the muse. In particular, Viola's action offers the immortal Zanoni—who claims verily to typify "ART"—a sudden vision of divine love in its purest form, and he longs to give complete and absolute expression to that vision. To do so, he must become even more godlike himself and must discover a far more sublime stage than that of the San Carlo on which to manifest the holiest of passions. Naturally enough, though, the quest for a divine medium leads him to the vast arena of human life, and the "aspiration to be more than man" expresses itself as a decision "to be man at last" (Z 4:9). Since the very essence of divine love is always "utter abnegation of self," the god shows the degree of his divinity precisely in the degree of his willingness to exchange it for humanity. Only on the human stage, then, can all the implications of an Annihilation of Self (as Carlyle's worthy Editor translates *Selbsttödtung*) be responsibly, progressively, and fully worked out. And so while he still heeds the siren, Zanoni obeys within the human medium her divine call toward annihilation. The love for the dark muse is fruitfully concealed within the love that prompts his self-sacrificing devotion to living humanity.

Whenever Art identifies itself in love with the cause of humanity, works that again show the godlike dimension in human affairs must result. (As in the performance of Pisani's opera, Art has redeemed Nature even while Nature was saving Art from the sterility of an ideal purity.) In the broadest possible terms, then, the human career of Zanoni reveals that, far from being a degraded state, mortal life still constitutes the most appropriate material for the ideal work of art. Two particular events may help to bring this allegory into focus.

Zanoni's decision to father a human child provides the first notable instance of the use of mortal means for the expression of a divine love. (God, as Browning's Pompilia was also given to understand, "grew likest God in being born.") For Bulwer the action manifests its exquisitely self-sacrificing—and therefore divine—character in the fact that the father irrevocably commits something of his own precious identity into the keeping of a child over whom he must lose control. Through what he terms the "medium" of the child, Zanoni thus resigns his ideal purity and dares even to deliver himself a hostage to the cycles of mortal life. He feels henceforth that "fetters" are binding him ever more firmly, but since these fetters have now become instrumental to the revelation of a divine love, they have themselves become blessed.

The other event that brings the divine degree of Zanoni's self-abnegation into focus is his actual death. When Viola and, metaphorically, all mankind find themselves prisoners of the Terror, Zanoni renounces the last vestiges of his own ideal freedom and divinity and accepts the ultimate implication of his choice of mortality. He substitutes himself for Viola in the tumbrels carrying the condemned to the Barrière du Trône (thus incidentally helping to inspire Dickens' treatment of the Terror some seventeen years later).[26] "I go," he says, "with my free will into the land of darkness" (Z 7:14). After his death on the guillotine, a visionary sequence transforms him at once into an "IMAGE"—"radiant amidst the radiant"—and into "an IDEA of joy and light!" The culmination of his self-immolation has therefore provided the image that can fully express the very idea of his identity, and in that image all the various antitheses of the story once more fuse.

In particular, life has again been reaffirmed, redeemed, and re-created through the medium of death. For while culminating his secret devotion to the siren, his death has also served as a culminating and fruitful act of devotion to the benevolent muse of humanity. His last deeds have supposedly provided just the impulse needed to bring down Robespierre and to save mankind from the Terror. In conveying his redeeming love into the cell of Viola, he has also reawakened her to a faith in the natural-supernatural universe—"the faith which, seeing the immortal everywhere, purifies and exalts the mortal that beholds." ("*The laws of our being*," he then assures her, "[*have*] *become the same*.") And finally he has left in their child, the offspring of a once more briefly identical Art and Nature, an actual emblem for that recreated universe. To the eye of faith (or of the imagination), the mortal and material nature which the child has inherited from the mother itself testifies to what must have been the courageous and ideal degree of the aesthetic father's self-sacrificing love. "Smil[ing] fearlessly" on the last page, the child is the creation that always remains to show the spot whenever a Creator has dared to refine himself out of existence.

And the destructive-creative process will continue through endless cycles, as what I have termed the third significantly symbolic action of the romance seems to show. This action naturally takes its rise from the inspiration of Zanoni's career (as that career had originally been inspired by Pisani's creation), and it shows the divine impulse not only allegorically but again literally creating a work of art. Zanoni, the type of "ART," has ministered near the end of his life to Glyndon, the actual artist, and has set him on the path toward creation, as one guesses from several clues, of the actual novel we read![27] As in the case of the symbolic opera and the symbolic child, moreover, the novel is to be appreciated not just as a finished product but also for the process by which it came into being and to which it still testifies.

At each stage that process has again involved sacrifice. First Glyndon has had to give up his dream of attaining a vision of the absolute. His ideal, if it is to be found anywhere, must be sought within the human and natural "regions of Custom and Prescription," and the subject of his art too naturally becomes the return of the artist to these regions. Such a subject remains, of course, a very lofty one, and so the sacrificial process has also continued as an Editor has translated the tale Glyndon has written in a mystic cypher into the vulgate. That translation has indeed entailed two sorts of sacrifice. More obviously, the editor has found he must sacrifice some of the sublimity of the original: "it was not possible to do justice" to the "poetical conception and design." But almost more significantly, the editor has had to sacrifice his own work and to devote many painful years of his own life to the labor of translation. Such a sacrifice has fortunately engaged him in his turn in the cosmic process that translates God's love into ever new media and thereby redeems those media. Insofar as the novel still bespeaks the process that has produced it, then, it may exemplify after all the most divine aspect of its original conception and design.

Like *Sartor Resartus*—with its Editor, its metaphor of translation, and its self-reflexive interest in its own composition—*Zanoni* thus provides in its very form one of its own most active symbols for the natural-supernatural creation. (*Zanoni* in fact constitutes an especially notable example of the Carlylean influence that Kathleen Tillotson has discerned everywhere in the novels of the 1840's.) [28] Of course Bulwer's symbol also differs in some fundamental respects from Carlyle's because for Bulwer this actual creation can seem to *be* precisely the ideal one at only the most fleeting instants of focus. While the materiality and imperfection of the creation does speak eloquently to Bulwer of the Creator's hidden perfection, the distinction between the two remains at least as extreme as that between the "archangel" and the "worm." Still, Bulwer would seem to have agreed with Carlyle in the most significant area of their faith: these regions of Custom and Prescription, which the reason of man has created for himself, can by an act of the imagination be seen as a medium adequate to the working out of man's divine mission. Although no single creation may finally and fully reward a single individual's efforts, his loving commitment to his materials and the process of his constant struggles may themselves, in the last analysis, be the adequate translation into the human medium of the serene and radiant ideal.

To some readers the images for the process that translates the ideal may seem so essentially tragic in *Zanoni* as to render the work a less than triumphant assertion of the possibility now for art. While an anti-novel like *Sartor Resartus*, this tale of an artist's failure to do what he had originally wished may also remind one of a poet's dejection ode. Bulwer has shown why lofty "ART" must face its doom and may even have implied, from this perspective, that the chief subject for art must now be the decline of art. Finding it more and more difficult to discover and celebrate the ideal quality in life—like the principle of "Joy" that had redeemed Nature for the Romantics—the isolated artist must come to dramatize his own sterility. Or he must try through acts of self-destructive devotion to the siren (and similar Belles Dames) to uncover simply the embers of the divine vitality that had once permitted creation. The image of Zanoni at the Barrière du Trône may seem as desperate in this context as the attempt of Empedocles on Etna to transform a supreme act of self-annihilation into a creative assertion of freedom. At the expense of extinction, as Frank Kermode has pointed out, such victories become pyrrhic.[29]

Yet Zanoni's deed is not necessarily one of desperation. Nor does it represent, like the magnificently futile death of Falkland, an ideal rejection of the entire medium of mortality. Symbolizing, on the contrary, precisely the immersion of the isolated individual in the concerns and cycles of ordinary mortality, it may tend to dispute the value of any grandiose individual gesture. Although an ambiguity definitely remains, the emphasis may fall less on the actual individual's extinction than on the allegorical individual's rejoining the "community of God's creatures" and there recovering the nobility of his life. "THE UNIVERSAL HUMAN LOT," in Miss Martineau's summation of the positive moral of the romance, "IS, AFTER ALL, THAT OF THE HIGHEST PRIVILEGE."

As it conveys its vision of that human lot (often through images of parenthood and of human compassion in the face of death), *Zanoni* also seems to offer Bulwer's most satisfactory symbolic portrayal of the Mysteries of Nature. More specifically than in *Godolphin, Maltravers*, and *Alice*, Nature now enables human society to submit along with the other elements of the cosmos, to the "loving law" and so to perform its destined function in the grand scheme. And as the artist is led to a position of quite crucial and profound participation in Nature's operations (taken through those "paths ... to the inner temple of her mysteries"), he especially becomes creative. In this sense far from a dejection ode, *Zanoni* indicates the road through to aesthetic action in particular.

An ultimate ambiguity still resides, of course, in the fact that the actual author of *Zanoni* has not yet followed that road back toward rediscovery—with fresh eyes—of the regions of Custom and Prescription. In this romance practically above all his others, Bulwer may even have lingered in those dangerous haunts—chanting, as his note of 1853 has it, "a hymn ... to the Nymph who hearkens and awakes below." While the story so forcefully enunciates self-sacrificing, altruistic theories, Bulwer claims in his dedication to have given shape to "this apparition of my own innermost mind" simply to indulge himself. With its constant typology of conflicting abstractions and its sustained apostrophes to the imagination, *Zanoni* may indeed stand as the most hermetic and fascinating product of Bulwer's egoistic loyalty to a private muse.

Yet the divine principle so mysteriously implicit in Nature has led Bulwer at least to the recognition that he could remain creative only if he too left the haunts of the fatal nymph. He too must cease

to contemplate the static shapes of his own innermost mind and begin again to participate in the dynamic struggles of mankind in the
marketplace. For a time he hesitated—and the fact may help to explain why he would indeed go through something like a "dejection"
crisis in 1844 and would write that dedication of *Zanoni* to Gibson
in 1845. But the same recondite influences that had guided his
"long journey" into its most aesthetic phase would eventually seem
to lead him through the crisis and enable him to find a new vein of
aesthetic inspiration. Resisting the temptation, expressed in the
introduction to *The Last of the Barons,* to give up fiction, he would
instead enter into the most popular stage of his fictional career. As
the divine principle would then be celebrated in still another medium and inspire one more cycle of self-sacrificing action, the theories
of *Zanoni* would at last bear their "practical" fruit. Bulwer would
be reenacting the sacrifice himself this time, for by resigning his
beloved "Italian" art for a lower "Dutch" mode, he would actually
be demonstrating his altruistic solidarity with ordinary humanity.
The lofty and tragic idea behind Zanoni's career would receive,
especially in the last of the Caxton novels, a fully complete and
adequate translation into the comic medium of everyday life.

CHAPTER V

The Cornfields of History

The opinions I have here put forth are not in fashion at this day. But I have never consulted the popular, any more than the sectarian, Prejudice. Alone and unaided I have hewn out my way, from first to last, by the force of my own convictions. The corn springs up in the field centuries after the first sower is forgotten. Works may perish with the workman; but, if truthful, their results are in the works of others, imitating, borrowing, enlarging, and improving, in the everlasting Cycle of Industry and Thought.

Preface of 1845 to *Night and Morning*

Until the end of the 1840's, Bulwer continued to treasure his aloofness and to conceive of his art as designed rather for the ages than for his own troubled times. He had retreated again from the public stage—perhaps literally as well as figuratively in that he had ceased after the success of *Money* in 1840 to supply his friend Macready with plays. Playwriting had become, he told the actor, increasingly uncongenial to him, and it would be especially difficult now to write the comedies that the public apparently desired. He was willing to keep trying, but he confessed to Forster in a typical remark of 1847: "though I have tried hard to write the comedy, I have not been able. It baffles me. The hearty laugh of comedy is not natural to my Muse. Had Macready called for tragedy he should have had one long since."[1] He had, in fact, proposed a tragedy based on Warwick, the Kingmaker, or on King Harold, and his romances on these subjects thus seem in their tragic aspect to reveal the type of art most congenial to his muse. Like himself, his historical heroes found themselves living in unsympathetic ages; in the battles in which they fell, they had been able only to sow the corn for future ages to harvest.

[112]

Yet the historical novels do not treat the hostility between the idealist and his times simply as an allegory of the individual quest for identity. By considering the individual chiefly as a representative of a social group or nation, Bulwer extends the principles of *Bildung* to the process whereby a whole people develops its highest potential capacities. The relationship between the actual and ideal aspects of the individual personality is thus translated into the relationship between a society at a particular stage in history and the "eternal People"—the mystical, enduring national or racial identity.

Bulwer does not, moreover, envisage the struggle between the representatives of the ideal and the society of the present as a straightforward conflict between good and evil. Although unwilling to immerse himself, as it were, in his own age, he nevertheless tries in these novels to show the positive value of each particular age, no matter how inimical to ideals. The principle of *Alice* and *Zanoni*—that the individual should sacrifice his ideal freedom and merge himself with the public causes of his day—thus continues to operate powerfully, if abstractly. The timeless ideal must fulfill itself in temporal and material forms, and Bulwer seems to consider each age as an essential step in that progressive fulfillment of the idea of human freedom.

Still, the division between the immediacy of mortality and the intuitions of the immortal idea—and the separation of the period of sowing from the period of fruition—remains tragic. No single individual or generation can expect to fulfill its longings; the ultimate fulfillment will emerge only as the sweep of history reveals the vast wholeness of all finite human experiences. Despite intimations of the divine tendency, furthermore, any given moment in time appears as a grim ordeal to test the endurance of the idea. Acceptance of the teleological view therefore includes a recognition of the horrifying extent and reality of evil in the world. While technically optimistic, Bulwer's philosophy of history involves a mood of pessimism that is not so pronounced in the Germans—mainly Kant,

Herder, Hegel, and Goethe—from whom he has surely derived his theories.

Night and Morning and *Lucretia* express Bulwer's determination to confront in modern times the historical problem of evil, and a brief discussion of them may help introduce the concerns of the actual historical novels. Like *Zanoni* these two novels associate evil especially with the French Revolution. In this "type of all upheaval,"[2] at once the most horrifying and the defining event of the present age, the forces of temporality and materialism have revealed the full measure of their hostility to the pure idea. But whereas *Zanoni* culminates in the Revolution, these works issue from it and deal with the world that has resulted from the apparent elimination of the divine Zanoni. As novels of crime, they show the post-revolutionary world suffering from the criminal burden of the more original revolutionary sin of aggression against the ideal. Bulwer thus demonstrates in action the menacing principle that applies, according to his essay of 1842 on the Reign of Terror, even more "to nations than to individuals": "The sins of the fathers are visited on the sons."[3]

To refer the principle first, though, to individuals, "The Children of Night "(the subtitle of *Lucretia*) are often quite explicitly the offspring of the Revolution. *Lucretia* opens in Paris during the Terror, and in the first chapter the cruel father of the unfortunate young Gabriel Varney takes him to witness the execution of his mother. The appalling experience destroys Gabriel's moral sensibility and haunts him for the rest of his life—which Bulwer has modelled on the life of the murderer and forger Thomas Wainewright.[4] Portrayed as a crony of Robespierre and later as a Napoleonic double-agent, the father Olivier Dalibard also becomes the tutor, corruptor, and husband of the heroine Lucretia. He involves her too in a career of endlessly proliferating crimes against the representatives of innocence and legitimacy. In *Night and Morning* the confidence man William Gawtrey similarly carries on the work

of the Revolution when he corrupts the bold and wrongfully disinherited protagonist Philip Morton. (Philip and his brother Sidney distinctly recall Balzac's Napoleonic desperado Philippe Bridau
and his gentler brother Joseph.) [5] As a coiner during the Restoration, Gawtrey seems especially to be continuing the retributive
aspect of the Revolution:

He was, in fact, the incarnation of that great spirit which the laws of
the world raise up against the world, and by which the world's injustice
on a large scale is awfully chastised; on a small scale, merely nibbled
at and harassed, as the rat that gnaws the hoof of the elephant: —the
spirit which, on a vast theatre, rises up, gigantic and sublime, in the
heroes of war and revolution—in Mirabeaus, Marats, Napoleons: on a
minor stage, it shows itself in demagogues, fanatical philosophers, and
mob-writers; and on the forbidden boards, before whose reeking lamps
outcasts sit, at once audience and actors, it never produced a knave
more consummate in his part, or carrying it off with more buskined
dignity, than William Gawtrey. (NM 3:4)

The English and French nations suffer because of the enduring,
irreconcilable division, which had become so terrifyingly visible
during the Revolution: on the one hand, the respectable establishment, and on the other, the everlastingly disaffected and criminal elements. Although Bulwer tries to criticize both sides even-
handedly, he seems to direct his most virulent attacks against the
hypocrisy of the respectable establishment of "our sickly civilisation." *Night and Morning* attempts to expose those grasping individuals in high places who believe they have a corner on virtue
while they actually create the atmosphere that nourishes crime. In
the eminently respectable churchman Robert Beaufort, for example, the novel unmasks a prototype, as Bulwer believed with possible justice, for Dickens' Pecksniff.[6] And the most depraved villain
in the novel, Lord Lilburne, similarly functions as a member of the
ruling class.

In *Lucretia* the social division corresponds even more nearly to
Disraeli's "Two Nations"; Bulwer incidentally coins the terms

"*have-nots*" and "*haves*," which have since proved so useful, to indicate the split (L 2:9). More powerfully perhaps than any of his other novels, *Lucretia* delves into the conditions of life among the have-nots of London, who so dangerously expect every impossible blessing from the impending Reform Bill. The plight of the crossing sweeper Beck is particularly memorable—"this joyless temperament," as Bulwer once apostrophizes him, "this age in youth, this living reproach, rising up from the stones of London against our social indifference to the souls which wither and rot under the hard eyes of science and the deaf ears of wealth" (L 2:6). The story of Beck also seems to anticipate, as has been shown, the story of Jo in *Bleak House*.[7] Through such details of plotting and characterization and through motifs such as that of the spider and flies, *Lucretia* seems constantly to emphasize that aggression has become the law of life in modern society. Whether naked or disguised, the aggression continues not only between the two hostile nations, but also, and more anarchically, within each camp.

All the specific acts of violence, fraud, and injustice are the effects of a more underlying cause, and as usual Bulwer associates the cause, at least in part, with the eighteenth-century emphasis upon the materiality of the universe. The more important criminals have experiences that one might even term materialist epiphanies. When the moral and other values in which they have tended to believe collapse, they confront the horror of a universe empty of ideals. They see, in the pervasive imagery of the novels, the awful "blackness," "night," "vault," or "abyss" within others as well as themselves. In desperation they cling then to the palpable sense of the ego as to the only possible absolute; they make "*self* the centre of being" to the point where it becomes a "monomania" (L 2:9). Lucretia and her husband Dalibard provide some of the best examples, for life seems purposeful to them chiefly insofar as their schemes to amass material property enable them to feel their egos encountering and subduing other egos. Eventually psychological and financial considerations make each recognize the desirability of the other's death, and they engage in a long, silent duel wherein each plots murder while craftily protecting himself. Lucretia emerges the victor in the contest that epitomizes the life of the civilization founded upon the principles of materialism. And although she does, to be sure, finally go mad, Bulwer has specifically tried in both these novels to avoid dealing out "the soft roses of poetical justice" (NM 5:The Last). Poetic justice would soften and falsify his stark vision of potent, material evil.

In addition to the horrified recognition of the darkness, the novels imply that evil serves some positive and teleological function, and so they attempt to define a response that goes beyond terror. It is first of all good for a man to make himself look calmly at the evil that lurks just under the surfaces of life: "It is well to be awakened at times from the easy commonplace that surrounds our habitual life—to cast broad and steady and patient light on the darker secrets of the heart—on the vaults and caverns of the social state over which we build the marketplace and the palace" (L 2:Epilogue). Secondly, the awareness of the depths may enable one to feel a certain awe before the mystery of the universe, and so the materialist view is curiously challenged: "Below the glass of that river," we read at the end of *Lucretia*, "the pike darts on his prey; the circle in the wave, the soft plash amongst the reeds, are but signs of destroyer and of victim. . . . Not with fear, not with doubt, recognise, O Mortal, the presence of Evil in the world. Hush thy heart in the humbleness of awe" (L 2:Epilogue). Thirdly, the sensation of the awe-inspiring mystery may even lead a man on to God. Like the night of *Night and Morning*, evil is woven into the divine order, and Philip Morton can affirm that "in spite of evil God is good" (NM 3:8). Since, indeed, "from the depth of a sea comes its music" (L 2:Prologue), Bulwer recognizes God's goodness precisely in the phenomenon of evil: "the mystery of evil," he observes in a footnote to the Epilogue of *Lucretia*, "whatever its degree, only increases the necessity of faith in the vindication of the contrivance which requires infinity for its range, and eternity for its consummation. It is in the existence of evil that man finds his duties, and his soul its progress."

The logical next step might be to cultivate, like many artists of the ensuing decades, the flowers of evil. And *Lucretia* created, in fact, a scandal of rather phenomenal proportions because its first critics and readers believed that Bulwer had actually taken this step.[8] Without choosing a side in that old controversy, it is at least interesting to notice that *Lucretia* comes closer than any of Bulwer's other novels to expressing an aesthetic appreciation for evil. In the chapter titles and elsewhere the remarkably beautiful Lucretia is consistently likened to a serpent, while the novel indicates as well that serpents fascinate the artist with their graceful charm. A scene that recalls both "Lamia" and a similar event in Bulwer's *Pompeii*,[9] for example, involves Gabriel, the future painter, in a struggle with the serpent guarding the hollow tree that contains Lucretia's love letter: "He gazed spelled and admiringly with the eye of an artist. Had he had pencil and tablet at that moment, he would have dropped his weapon for the sketch, though the snake had been as deadly as the viper of Sumatra. The sight sank into his memory, to be reproduced often by the wild, morbid fancies of his hand. Scarce a moment, however, had he for the gaze; the reptile sprang, and fell, baffled and bruised by the involuntary blow of its enemy. As it writhed on the grass, how its colours came out —how graceful were the movements of its pain!" (L 1:4).

With their fearful symmetry the beautiful serpent and the beautiful criminal have a necessary place in the divine scheme, and the artist must dare to discern sublimity and grandeur even amidst depravity. Bulwer appeals in his many defensive comments on *Lucretia* to the Greek tragedians, to Shakespeare, and to Goethe in order to prove that "great crime is the highest province of fiction": "it is moral, and of the most impressive and epic order of morals, to arouse and sustain interest for a criminal."[10] While often excruciating, the aesthetic vision of injustice and cruelty evidently operates in some purifying manner upon the beholder. Bulwer's friend Macaulay even compares *Lucretia* to "some fine Martyrdoms which I have seen in Italy": "The effect resembles that of Poussin's 'Massacre of the Innocents' in the Lucca Collection, or of Salvator's 'Prometheus' in the Corsini Palace. It is real suffering to look, and yet we cannot avert our eyes."[11]

Despite Macaulay's assessment, though, the trouble with *Night and Morning* and *Lucretia* may be that they do not go quite far enough in the direction of bolder aesthetic treatments of evil and cruelty. Their lurid sensationalism and occasional bombast may imply less an honest willingness to confront the horrifying facts than a desire to shock with what Bulwer emphasizes are perversities. He comes close, in the case of Lucretia herself, to conveying the terrifying sense of abandonment and anguish that motivates the retaliatory cruelties, but here too he may remain the judgmental moralist. In 1853 he would even alter the ending of *Lucretia* to bring it into closer accord with the deceptive principles of poetic justice. The concern for social inequities too may sometimes leave the reader with the impression that evil is not so much an imponderable cosmic mystery as a matter for post-revolutionary politicians and educators to remedy.

Where the novels about modern crime tend to fail, the best historical novels tend to succeed. Macaulay's assertion that "it is real suffering to look, and yet we cannot avert our eyes" may also apply more nearly to the treatments of the suffering and evil of the past. For while the historical novels do not, any more than *Lucretia*, imply an unabashed enjoyment of evil, they do suggest a gaze fixed with greater calm and more tragic resignation upon the pervasive reality of evil. They go somewhat more definitely beyond the moral vision—and, for that matter, the aesthetic vision—as they see evil everywhere and still affirm the rightness of what is or has been. As in the thinking of Carlyle too, the true ideal is not always what men have imagined; it must rather be recognized in its identity with realities.

The conviction of the rightness of the facts emerges first in connection with Bulwer's theory of his task as historical romancer. He indicates in the dedicatory epistles and prefaces to *Rienzi*, *The Last of the Barons*, and *Harold* that he has remained scrupulously faithful to his sources. Whereas Scott had permitted his fancy to take somewhat cavalier liberties with the known facts and had "employed history to aid romance," he has sought "to employ romance in the aid of history." In his study of historical fiction, A. T. Sheppard indeed criticizes Bulwer for "too close and detailed an attention to history."[12]

Of course Bulwer has made many guesses and even invented many facts and characters. In explaining his interest in historical subjects to Macready, however, he conceives of his task as one of re-creation rather than invention: "The creative Faculty, which is one with the true ideal, does not invent—it only re-creates." His method seems to resemble that outlined by Browning in Book 1 of *The Ring and the Book*. After having saturated himself in all the available evidence, he has called into play the element of "Romance" or "Fiction." This has enabled him to discern the truths among the contradictions and to discover the truths about which the documents do not speak: "Here, then, where History leaves us in the dark—where our curiosity is the most excited, Fiction gropes amidst the ancient chronicles, and seeks to detect and to guess the truth. And then, Fiction, accustomed to deal with the human heart, seizes upon the paramount importance of a Fact." Although the imaginatively detected truths refer most often to the experiences of men's inner lives, Bulwer occasionally discovers a more objective, if unrecorded fact too. He is particularly delighted, for example, with his realization that Edward IV must have attempted early in 1470 to seduce Lady Anne Nevile. Only such a hidden fact would explain so many otherwise inexplicable events. In the end, then, he has come up not just with a personal version of history but with the actual truth of the past. He has invented, according to his theory, what must after all have happened.[13]

Possessed of a vital, underlying coherence, his fiction is even truer than the "vast mass of neglected chronicles and antiquarian dissertations" with which he has begun. For he has naturally tried in planning his novels to subordinate all details of local color and other superficial elements to his allegorical sense of deeper truths— the ideas behind history. The dedicatory epistle to *Barons* thus suggests that the historical novels belong, like all his best works, to the "Intellectual" rather than the "Familiar" school. And although some modern readers have associated that "Intellectual" quality with political relevance to the hungry forties, a more abstract awareness of time and eternity surely provides the main unifying principle of these works.[14] (*Pompeii*, which lacks the intellectual content of the others, is an exception.)

History is the tragic, but coherent process whereby the free desires of various individuals and classes for what could be must always give way to that which is. The individual must sacrifice himself so that the idea he has conceived can come to visible fruition as the harvest of ensuing centuries. In considering the pattern, it will be convenient to discuss first the idea of freedom that so appeals to Bulwer's political heroes and next the quality of the necessity that must triumph. Then as history permits "some oversight of the Whole," in Carlyle's terms, of "the general sum of human Action," a certain desperate hopefulness finally emerges. The grim power of historical necessity may yet prove to be serving the ultimate cause of freedom. "Our Life," to appropriate the formulation of Diogenes Teufelsdröckh, "is compassed round with Necessity; yet is the meaning of Life itself no other than Freedom."[15]

The idea of freedom seems to exist in its primary state as an internal, individual awareness. Bulwer refers in *Rienzi* to "that Holy of Holies in our own souls, wherein we know and feel how much our nature is capable of the self-existence of a God!" (R 2:3). Like Boethius anyone may be free in the darkest dungeon, and the ineffectual Henry VI in *Barons* even finds himself freer during his captivity in the Tower than after his restoration to the throne:

"the kingdom a man makes out of his own mind," he tells a retainer, "is the only one that it delighteth man to govern! Behold, he is lord over its springs and movements; its wheels revolve and stop at his bidding" (B 3:5).

Yet to reveal its full meaning, the idea of freedom must influence events beyond the fastness of the private self-existence, and its secondary ramifications in these novels are public and revolutionary. One free mind, as Rienzi observes in connection with the extraordinary power of Petrarch, seems by its nature to effect the liberation of other minds and at an ever quickening tempo: "throughout the whole world a great revolution has begun. The barbaric darkness of centuries has been broken; the KNOWLEDGE which made men as demigods in the past time has been called from her urn; a Power, subtler than brute force and mightier than armed men, is at work" (R 1:5). In time, the subtle power of the freed intellect must also convert itself into a very tangible, physical sort of energy. Bulwer's daring inventor Adam Warner foresees in *Barons* a scientific revolution that will free men from labor and "divide the Old World from the New." While his counterpart in the story, Henry VI, delights in ruling the springs, movements, and wheels of his private mind, Warner has imagined and keeps trying to perfect an actual steam engine—"a great Promethean THING" that will "make Matter the gigantic slave of Mind" (B 1:7).

The free individual becomes most like Prometheus—or like God himself—when he kindles in other minds the passion for political liberty: "he, indeed, who first arouses in the bondsman the sense and soul of freedom, comes as near as is permitted to man, nearer than the philosophers, nearer even than the poet, to the great creative attribute of God!" (R 1:10). To create "the sense and soul of freedom" in a whole people is to create a nation, for the awareness of a common heritage of liberty constitutes the very essence of a national or racial identity. Thus Rienzi invokes dim memories of ancient liberty to arouse his followers from the slumbers of "the long night of Rome" (R 4:3). So too Harold appeals to the love of "freedom," which the Normans themselves have recognized as the dominant "passion" of the Saxons: "no saints in the calendar," Harold assures his people in his last speech, "[are] so holy as the freemen who fight for their hearths and their altars" (H 9:3; 12:6). As he has envisaged the ideal state and has printed its motto "PEACE" on his coins, he also seems to Bulwer to prophesy the ultimate triumph of the England that needs, in specific contrast to Normandy, no walled fortresses.

Although the Normans do, of course, defeat the Saxons, the divine memory of freedom survives as a revolutionary principle among the commons of England. Even the Earl of Warwick, who is not especially sympathetic to popular liberties, observes in *Barons* the continuing force of the idea: "Ye know well that ever in England, but especially since the reign of Edward III, strange, wild notions of some kind of liberty other than that we enjoy, have floated loose through the land. Among the commons, a half-conscious recollection that the nobles are a different race from themselves feeds a secret rancour and mislike, which, at any fair occasion for riot, shows itself bitter and ruthless—as in the outbreak of Cade and others" (B 7:2).[16] The outbreaks still indicate—their seeming ruthlessness notwithstanding—that the work of the ideal may yet go forward to its culmination. Once conceived in the freedom of the individual imagination, that divine dream may one day become a reality. As all nations and races recover their freedom, "Matter" will become in the most important sense "the gigantic slave of Mind."

But the apotheosis of freedom remains a far distant event in all these novels, which seek to show, indeed, why the grand idea must keep sustaining defeats. To achieve the divine purpose, a binding and seemingly evil principle must, paradoxically, keep tending to prevail. This principle, as I wish to analyze it, operates first through external physical force, secondly through subtler psychological pressures, and thirdly, and more bafflingly, through the kind of necessity associated with the zeitgeist.

Rienzi deals particularly with the first version of the binding principle. As typified by the squabbling patricians and the bandit Walter de Montreal, the force of arms and sheer physical strength seem to defy the enlightened ideas of the hero at every turn—most obviously perhaps when Rienzi captures Montreal: "as these two men, each so celebrated, so proud, able, and ambitious, stood, front to front, it was literally as if the rival spirits of force and intellect, order and strife, of the falchion and the fasces—the antagonist Principles by which empires are ruled and empires overthrown—had met together, incarnate and opposed" (R 10:3). Rienzi appears to win, since he has succeeded, according to Bulwer's sources, in reforming Rome simply through "the energy and effect of [his] single mind" (R 4:1), and he also proceeds to execute Montreal. Yet he has unfortunately lost in the competition to gain the respect of the people for his ideas. Because the "dastard and degenerate race," as he finally describes them, continue to fear and admire the force of arms, he must fall—specifically through the agency of Montreal's avenging son. His instruments and materials have been unworthy, in their very materiality, of the artist of the ideal and have defeated him: "And with such tools," he cries in disgust, "the living race of Europe and misjudging posterity will deem that the workman is to shape out the Ideal and the Perfect!" (R 9:4).

The other novels similarly dramatize confrontations between material force and free ideas—with a most interesting moral ambiguity when Warwick as representative of the "Race of Iron" and "Age of Force" suppresses the popular rising under Robin of Redesdale (B 12:6). Still it is not so much the arms themselves that threaten free and enlightened ideas as the fact that the people respect arms more highly than they respect ideas. Although the many physical clashes of opposing forces are quite bloody, the more important battlefields may remain within the minds of the men who wield the weapons. The cleverer enemies of freedom thus seek to undermine habits of independent thought rather than to exert direct physical force. Edward IV and more especially that "splendid dissimulator" the future Richard III rely, for example, upon fraudulent promises and seductive smiles to change the minds and allegiances of their enemies.

The subtlest of these invisible arms or psychological threats, which operate as a second version of the binding principle, may be the force of superstition. This weapon is also the more difficult to counteract because its effectiveness derives mainly from the innate vulnerability of the victim and only incidentally from the skill of an enemy who may craftily wield it. *Harold*, in particular, demonstrates how susceptibility to bondage makes a superstitious culture its own worst enemy. Creating a constant atmosphere of imprecise foreboding, the novel keeps characterizing the people as chronically disposed to forget their freedom and to submit to spectres: "Amidst these disasters," runs a typical passage, referring to the last months of Edward the Confessor, "the King's health was fast decaying; his mind seemed bewildered and distraught; dark ravings of evil portent that had escaped from his lips in his mystic reveries and visions, had spread abroad, bandied with all natural exaggerations, from lip to lip. The country was in one state of gloomy and vague apprehension" (H 10:2).

Anxious and indecisive, King Edward has lain "enthralled" and dying by degrees through most of the novel. Embodying all that is least noble and most superstitious in his subjects, he has neglected the defenses of the kingdom and devoted his revenues to the obsessive collection of relics. (To a lesser extent, relics also fascinate Henry VI in *Barons*.) He acquires "the thumb of St. Jude" in the course of the story and "daily expect[s] the tooth of St. Remigius"; to house these relics as well as his own, he is completing Westminster Abbey. "Like the kings of Egypt," he has effectively devoted all the resources of life to the construction of a great tomb, and England seems to have dedicated itself with him to death. "The Bones of the Dead"—the title of Book 9—are, in fact, the most significant and omnipresent symbol in the whole work. Far mightier in the fears of the Saxons than the weapons of living men, "the bones of the dead . . . and . . . their fleshless arms" must evidently prevail (H 11:6). So Harold recognizes, though relatively free of superstition himself, how terrifyingly his oath in Normandy has "ensnared" him and his cause:

As when man descends from the gilded sepulchre to the loathsome charnel, so at the lifting of that cloth, all the dread ghastliness of Death was revealed. There, from abbey and from church, from cyst and from shrine, had been collected all the relics of human nothingness in which superstition adored the mementos of saints divine; they lay, pell mell and huddled, skeleton and mummy—the dry dark skin, the white gleaming bones of the dead, mockingly cased in gold, and decked with rubies; there, grim fingers protruded through the hideous chaos, and pointed towards the living man ensnared; there, the skull grinned scoff under the holy mitre;—and suddenly rushed back, luminous and searing, upon Harold's memory, the dream long forgotten, or but dimly remembered in the healthful business of life—the gibe and the wirble of the dead men's bones. (H 9:7)

While associated with Christianity, the superstitions of the times still possess pagan overtones. The Danish Hilda continues to worship the Norse gods and fears "the wrath [of] Lok and Rana." The foreboding of the whole country may have more of the mood of the Ragnarok about it than of pious Christian horror arising from the papal excommunication of Harold. The prophecy of the "Sanguelac" that has so preoccupied King Edward and which is fulfilled in the Battle of Hastings suggests a pagan despair before the inevitable violence, bleakness, and brevity of life. Man's bondage may even seem to derive principally in *Harold* from the awful hopelessness of the mortal condition, and the novel reminds one in this respect of Arnold's *Sohrab and Rustum*. Although he has dreamed so nobly of peace, freedom, and justice, Harold is condemned to perpetual battles with the Welsh, the Norwegians, and finally the Normans, and he might have cried like a younger Rustum: "But now in blood and battles was my youth, / And full of blood and battles is my age, / And I shall never end this life of blood."

Still, the mood of pagan despair is, in Bulwer's view, a matter of superstition rather than a recognition of some genuinely cosmic fact. A higher power, of which the pagans evidently remained unconscious, had imposed the tendency toward superstition upon men in these ages—as a means toward larger, more mysterious ends. The eternal cause of freedom struggles, then, not only against fleshly arms and fleshless arms, but thirdly and most ultimately against the inscrutable fate associated with the zeitgeist. Before what Bulwer usually terms "the spirit of the age," all races and peoples—no matter whether they despair or whether they fight for or against free ideas—find themselves equally impotent.

The hostility, if not the total meaning, of the zeitgeist emerges with especially terrible clarity when seen from the perspective of the idealist wrapped in the struggles of his age. The tragedy of Bulwer's heroes is that they are, in Hegel's term, world-historical men. As each aspires with singleness of purpose to fashion a state that will reflect the idea of freedom in his mind, he loses his free "self-existence" and becomes one with his times: "His fate," Bulwer remarks of this class of men in *Harold*, "seems taken out of his own control. . . . He has made himself, as it were, a *want* to the nation, a thing necessary to it; he has identified himself with his age, and in the wreath or the crown on his brow, the age itself seems to put forth its flower" (H 10:6). But since his own fulfillment now depends so extraordinarily upon the large forces controlling the destinies of nations, he has gained the crown at great personal cost. He possesses less freedom than the happy private man who can to some degree make his own destiny independently of the times. Inevitably, too, those large forces that have made him seem the flower of his age will later thrust him aside. As Hegel had observed, the time-spirit shows no compunction when it discards the world-historical man that has served and outlived his purpose.

The organization of Harold's story in particular emphasizes the steps whereby the world-historical man loses his freedom. Harold begins as the passionate lover of Edith, whom Hilda terms his

"Fylgia, that noiselessly blesses and saves" (H 10:13). Like the anima figure in the other novels, Edith represents the most beautiful and ideal portion of the hero. Yet his destiny forbids their marriage, and one heart-rending day both of them recognize that he must renounce her for the sake of England. Indeed he must renounce his individual soul in order to rest faithful to his identity in the larger sense: "Edith had loved thee less," she has told him, "if thou hadst not loved England more than Edith" (H 10:10).[17] Becoming then an entirely public figure, he allows his omnipresent counselor and shadow, the dark Haco, to take the place of Edith. Haco possesses an astute understanding of political expediencies, and he advises Harold with wisdom consistently and ruthlessly calculated to forward the Saxon cause. In joining himself to the vision of Haco, though, Harold not only furthers the national interest; he also surrenders to the greater forces of fate, which even the crafty Haco cannot foresee. Their union, as Haco remarks, suggests their severance from ordinary mortality and their direct submission to a sort of cosmic, demonic force: "To me is not destined the love of woman, nor the ambition of life. All I know of human affection binds me to Harold; all I know of human ambition is to share in his fate. This love is strong as hate, and terrible as doom—it is jealous, it admits no rival. As the shell and the sea-weed interlaced together, we are dashed on the rushing surge; whither?—oh, whither?" (H 10:3).

The Battle of Hastings provides an answer that is tragic in a non-Aristotelian sense. As Bulwer affirms in both *Rienzi* and *Harold*, the hero has not made any discernible error; he falls not because of a tragic flaw but because of implacable historical necessity. The Colonna, Orsini, and Savelli of Rome and William of Normandy must emerge victorious in their respective centuries for the sufficient reason that they are after all closest to "the spirit of the age."

Yet the historian looking back across the sweep of time may come up with a slightly less despairing answer to Haco's "whither?—

oh, whither?" For if the zeitgeist represents the ultimate version of the principle that hopelessly binds men, it may actually become as well an indirect manifestation of the divine idea of freedom. Necessity and freedom somehow correspond to each other and can to some degree be reconciled when one analyzes the operations of the zeitgeist from a double perspective.

While it informs all three novels, the double perspective may be most clearly fundamental to the conception of *Barons*. To take first again the viewpoint of the individual idealist, the "Age" is inevitably "grim": "Awful is the duel," exclaims Bulwer as the mocking children pelt the scientist in the streets, "between MAN and THE AGE in which he lives! For the gain of posterity, Adam Warner had martyrised existence" (B 1:7). The age beats him down with special vengeance when his dependence upon the patronage of the Duchess of Bedford reduces him to the level of alchemist: "TIME had conquered the nature of a GENIUS meant to subdue time" (B 4:4). In similar fashion, the popular leader Robin of Redesdale, the gentle King Henry, the fierce Queen Margaret of Anjou, and, saddest of all, the courageous, incorruptible Warwick must all succumb to the times.[18] According to Bulwer's interesting speculations, England might just possibly have become a more prosperous and peaceful land over the next centuries if Warwick had succeeded in making the Lancastrian restoration endure. The necessary conclusion, though, is that such speculations are irrelevant to the understanding of history, for history studies what must be. The omnipotent time-spirit sweeps men's moral and philosophical concerns aside and insists upon realizing what is, in a certain sense, simply foredoomed: "Without presuming to decide which policy, upon the whole, would have been the happier for England—the one that based a despotism on the middle class, or the one that founded an aristocracy upon popular affection, it was clear to the more enlightened burgesses of the great towns, that between Edward of York and the Earl of Warwick a vast principle was at stake, and the commercial king seemed to them a more natural

ally than the feudal baron; and equally clear it is to us, now, that
the true spirit of the age fought for the false Edward, and against
the honest earl" (B 11:2).

From the second and larger perspective, then, one recognizes the
truth in "the false Edward." His reign, according to the theme first
stated in the opening chapter, has marked "an advance, in civilisation," and he now embodies the true norm: "Edward IV. [is] in
all this preeminently THE MAN OF HIS AGE—not an inch behind
it or before!" (B 4:2). By thus insisting on the necessity for a
standard, Bulwer helps to define the steady, teleological advance
that had become apparent to "the more enlightened burgesses" of
those days and even more apparent to him. Although "grim Age
. . . devours ever those before, as behind, its march," those very
devourings signalize a progress and enable men to make a blessed
sense out of history (B 12:7).

Such an assurance of progress implies the so-called Whig interpretation of history, and the novels do indeed contain occasional
phrases suggestive of the condescending smugness of Whiggism:
"that age," one reads, for example, in *Barons*, "had not the virtue of
later times, and cannot be judged by its standard" (B 6:3). Bulwer's point, however, is not to congratulate the superior virtue of
his own age, but to use the evidence of advance as an argument in
favor of the positive rightness of every particular stage along the
way. He hammers home, as a sort of relativist refrain, the everlasting necessity for accepting each age on its own terms and bowing
to its zeitgeist, even if it be embodied in the treacherous Edward.
Sustained by a faith in the teleology of history, Bulwer has in fact
made *Barons* a somewhat laconic hymn to the historical process
and to the person of its contemporary symbol. While his moral
recognition of Edward's depravity remains active, he seems content
to conclude with the acclamation that greets the victor of Barnet:
"What mattered to the crowd his falseness and his perfidy—his
licentiousness and cruelty? All vices ever vanish in success! Hur-
rah for King Edward! THE MAN OF THE AGE suited the age, had

valour for its war and cunning for its peace, and the sympathy of the age was with him!" (B 12:7).

To say that all vices vanish in success—or that might makes right—is not, admittedly, to claim that historical inevitability is slowly manifesting the divine idea of freedom. Yet Bulwer does seem to support such a theory, though he often substitutes the abstractions "justice" or "love" for the more characteristically Hegelian "freedom." He accepts the steady march of history not only because it is a fact beyond argument but even more because it is specifically under the mysterious guidance of an intelligent principle: "We are but the instruments," says Warwick in dying, "of a wiser Will" (B 12:6). While the historian sees in the voracious depradations of time a necessity beyond good and evil, the cosmic perspective will reveal a divine justice as well. "Out, then," cries Bulwer, as the story pauses momentously on the eve of Barnet,

. . . upon that vulgar craving of those who comprehend neither the vast truths of life, nor the grandeur of ideal art, and who ask from poet or narrator the poor and petty morality of "Poetical Justice"—a justice existing not in our work-day world—a justice existing not in the sombre page of history—a justice existing not in the loftier conceptions of men whose genius has grappled with the enigmas which art and poetry only can foreshadow and divine:—unknown to us in the street and the market—unknown to us on the scaffold of the patriot, or amidst the flames of the martyr—unknown to us in the Lear and the Hamlet—in the Agamemnon and the Prometheus. Millions upon millions, ages upon ages, are entered but as items in the vast account in which the recording angel sums up the unerring justice of God to man. (B 12:3)[19]

If neither poetically just nor Aristotelian in any narrowly technical sense, the tragedy of which Lear and Prometheus as well as Rienzi, Warwick, and Harold form a part is still profoundly teleological. Some passages in Bulwer's unfinished *Pausanias*, which seems in potentiality the most interesting and impressive of all his historical romances, help finally to specify the meaning of the tragedy. All thinking individuals discover that they must lose, often through no particular fault, the freedom to impose their private

visions of the good upon the life about them. They must submit to
what Pausanias considers the "Divine Principle"—"the Fate which
Zeus himself must obey." According to the wise Alcman, however,
that fate or "Necessity the All-Compelling" refers to just one aspect
of the Divine Principle, and there is a higher: "If creation proceed
from an intelligence, what we call fate is but the consequence of its
laws. . . . And there be sages who declare that Intelligence and Love
are the same." In this scheme, moreover, "the works of Evil and
Hate" are recognized as partial manifestations of Love, which continues as the fundamental motivating power of the universe:

We see its work half completed; we cry, Lo, this is misery, this is hate
—because the chaos is not yet a perfected world, and the stone block
is not yet a statue of Apollo. . . .
All things come into order from the war of contraries—the elements
fight and wrestle to produce the wild flower at our feet; from a wild
flower man hath striven and toiled to perfect the marvellous rose of the
hundred leaves. Hate is necessary for the energies of love, evil for the
activity of good; until, I say, the victory is won, until Hate and Evil
are subdued, as the sculptor subdues the stone; and then rises the divine
image serene for ever, and rests on its pedestal in the Uranian Temple.
Lift thine eyes; that temple is yonder. O Pausanias, the scultptor's work-
room is the earth. (*Pausanias* 3:1)

The sculpturing analogy that Bulwer would also apply to the
individual life (in connection with Schiller's "Das Ideal und das
Leben")[20] is here referred to the cosmic process. Or in the terms of
Adam Warner, the divine "Mind" is seeking on a universal scale
to "make Matter [its] gigantic slave." The process of enslavement
is more essentially a process of liberation because the divine mind
is free and "the divine image" it impresses upon matter will express
the idea of freedom. In all versions of the fatal binding principle,
Bulwer thus comes to recognize the instruments of liberation.

Time is similarly an instrument of eternity, for history describes
the process whereby the race slowly brings into actual form every
ramification of its infinite potentiality. Death must destroy all individuals and all generations, but "the People," in the last words

of Robin at Barnet, "are never beaten!" (B 12:6). Although Robin is, as Curtis Dahl indicates, a proto-Chartist,[21] Bulwer does not use the term "People" to refer merely to the turbulent rabble or to the lower classes. He invariably seems to associate it with the Latin *populus* and distinguishes it from the French *peuple*, which conveys, he apparently believes, the scornful overtones of *plebs*. According to one of his pet notions, there is also a vast "distinction between the grave eternal *People* & the noisy frivolous false likeness called the Public."[22] Applying *people*, then, in an ideal sense to the national or racial identity (in the manner of Herder's *das Volk*), he looks beyond individuals, classes, or generations and finds that identity in the sweep of history. Harold and his generation of Saxons had, in a sense, to be defeated in their own day so that history could march on to reveal the triumphant national identity. The individual king has gained his value not from what he has actually achieved but from his idea of the free nation—sown, as it were, on the field of Hastings and harvested over the rolling centuries:

Eight centuries have rolled away, and where is the Norman [i.e., the ashes of William] now? or where is not the Saxon? The little urn that sufficed for the mighty lord is despoiled of his very dust; but the tombless shade of the kingly freeman still guards the coasts, and rests upon the seas. In many a noiseless field, with Thoughts for Armies, your relics, O Saxon Heroes, have won back the victory from the bones of the Norman saints; and whenever, with fairer fates, Freedom opposes Force, and Justice, redeeming the old defeat, smites down the armed Frauds that would consecrate the wrong,—smile, O soul of our Saxon Harold, smile, appeased, on the Saxon's land! (H 12:9)

In his martyrdom Harold has given symbolic force to the timeless Saxon idea—just as the timeless idea of the whole human race has been briefly crystallized in the image of Zanoni's self-sacrifice. And subsequent history, as Bulwer so often implies, may then exemplify the gradual narrowing of the gap between a nation's actual character and these intimations of its ideal identity. It should be emphasized in conclusion, however, that Bulwer's view of historical progress does not completely invalidate myths of decadence. While the gap narrows between the present and a possible "far-off divine event," another gulf between the idea and the material is ever widening. The catastrophes that so spectacularly destroy each of Bulwer's last manifestations of some freedom or nobility may even seem to cut men all the more decisively off from some supreme, original value.

This is, to take a final example, the view of Sir Miles St. John in *Lucretia*. Last of a long line of baronets, Sir Miles has always maintained a life-denying loyalty to the abstract idea of his race: "as my ancestors thought, so think I. They left me the charge of their name, as the fief-rent by which I hold their lands" (L 1:1). His duty to the eternal, unevolving idea symbolized by his ancestral portraits wreaks havoc upon his living family, but he believes he thus keeps the light burning through the deepening night of time.

Yet despite his sympathy for Sir Miles, Bulwer manages to classify his attitude as mistaken, and ultimately his own view of history may seem neither progressive nor regressive. Because of his strong intuition that the same human idea underlies every single individual zeitgeist, his historical romances keep emphasizing the patterns that are constant and universal above whatever is temporary and particular in a culture. He can readily feel the vitality and the enduring validity of ancient Pompeii, for example, with "its walls fresh as if painted yesterday,—not a hue faded on the rich mosaic of its floors" (Po 5: The Last). Avrom Fleishman, who believes an historical novelist should be as alive to cultural strangeness and remoteness as to eternal verities, thus feels compelled to criticize Bulwer: "his Romans, medieval Italians, and medieval Englishmen are almost indistinguishable from each other."[23] Such a statement is exaggerated though, and it is unjust to fault Bulwer for not—as he has announced his own intentions—following the method of Scott. His desire instead to use all his painstaking historical research for the purpose of studying "the human passions . . . whose elements in all ages are the same" must remain valid.

Neither escapist flights to a remote past nor urgently timely tracts for the hungry forties, his romances are interesting primarily as documented treatments of the archetypal tragedy of man caught up in history.

While treating the tension between the eternal People and a particular public abstractly, these "Intellectual" novels suggest the logic that increasingly carries Bulwer toward engagement in the social struggles of his own generation. For the present age must always constitute the medium in which an individual actually manifests his self-sacrificing commitment to the idea of his race. In the altruistic Caxton novels Bulwer will even give up the tragic art most congenial to his private muse and recover the popular "laugh of comedy." Reconciled not only to the sweep of time in the abstract, he will also embrace, and without the mental reservations of Pelham now, "the action, the vividness, the *life* of these times."

CHAPTER VI

That Great Reality—The People

The old divisions of party politics remain; but among all divisions there is greater desire of identification with the people. . . . A vast mass of discontent exists amongst the operatives, it is true, and Chartism is but one of its symptoms; yet that that discontent is more obvious than formerly is a proof that men's eyes and men's ears are more open to acknowledge its existence—to examine and listen to its causes. Thinking persons now occupy themselves with that great reality—the People.

Preface of 1848 to *Pelham*

Victorian readers discerned in the Caxton novels the summit of Bulwer's fictional achievement, and perhaps that contemporary judgment also deserves, with some reservations, the ratification of the ages. While extraordinarily long and complicated, these works exemplify an unusual harmony between ends and means. If, as Bulwer believed, most works must remain primarily interesting for the authorial intention behind them, these often seem to achieve those intentions as well. Like *Zanoni*, in its own nearly opposite mode, they successfully create a significant sense of overall form that endows the work in its expressive wholeness with the power of a great symbol. Since *What Will He Do with It?* is, in fact, one of the two or three best works in Bulwer's entire canon, it also succeeds in far more than its wholeness and sweep: "in depth & breadth —in character, & in scenes of genuine & subtle passions" it probably is, in Bulwer's words, "the best thing I have done."[1]

As the harmony between "conception" and "execution" may suggest, Bulwer has resolved that principal tension of his own "metaphysical" history—the discrepancy between the worlds within and without. Most of his novels had of course proposed the need to

[136]

merge the cause of the individual ego with some more altruistic vision, but that theory now becomes an aspect of his actual creativity. For he has designed these novels expressly to appeal to the public of his own day. In doing so, moreover, he has not denied his own muse so much as he has discovered its identity with that "mighty inspiration," to recall his terms of 1831, "which is breathing throughout the awakened and watchful world." No longer impelled toward an "Intellectual" or unpopularly "ideal" art, he feels for the moment that he really does hold his soul in common with all men.

While sensing a unity "with that great reality—the People," he must nevertheless distinguish his own attitude from those of the warriors for popular liberties in his historical novels—a point to emphasize before dealing further with his popular aesthetics. The "mighty inspiration" he caught was no longer, as it might have been in his youth, the heady excitement of the current mass political movements. In European events of 1848 and 1849 he saw only further indications of the tragedy of heroism that devoted itself to the ideal cause of "the eternal People." Although he admired revolutionaries like Kossuth and pronounced himself "quite an enthusiast" for Garibaldi and Mazzini, he remained convinced of the uselessness of their activities: "in all Europe," he wrote of the temporary overthrow of papal rule in Rome, "I have seen nothing so heroic and with so good a cause; but, alas! so hopeless." If "the liveliest realisation of romance," it was also incongruous to find "the actual heroes of the Middle Ages in the midst of our modern civilisation."[2] His letters, his interestingly prophetic preface of 1848 to *Rienzi*, and his treatment of Italian patriotism of the previous generation in *My Novel* defended indeed a gloomily unheroic view of the Risorgimento. The Italians were neither morally nor intellectually ready to make the sacrifice necessary on behalf of a free and united Italy; the Austrians meanwhile provided a reasonably orderly and fair administration in the northern provinces.

In Britain too some of the most dangerous threats to the people came from those he considered to be idealistically doctrinaire or Utopian. "Those miserable Cobdens!" he exclaimed to Forster in 1848, "and visionary Peace Dreamers! What fools they are, and these are the men by whom England herself has been half driven to the brink of revolution." While agreeing "in theory," as he said in a Parliamentary speech of 1859, with his old friend J. S. Mill about the value of democracy, he had, in short, become a Conservative. Far more important than theories and ideals were now the practical well-being and good government of the people. His speeches on the various Reform Bills of these years constantly recurred to the question of how to secure in actuality and not merely in theory a House of Commons that would express "the common sense of the common interest."[3]

As he explains his impression of how one discerns that practical "common interest," he may come closest to defining the "great reality" on which he has based the realism of the Caxton novels. The community, whose genuine interests he and other politicians must further, still resembles, as in *England and the English*, an organism. In an important speech of 1854 at the University of Edinburgh, for example, he carefully develops an analogy between "the healthful progress of society . . . [and] . . . the natural life of man." At its most abstract, his conception envisages a "grand contest between new ideas and ancient forms" in which the health of the organism depends upon "the vital principle of civilisation"— "the unity of liberty with order."[4] Yet while the contest between the new and the ancient thereby suggests, as in the historical novels, an abstract warfare of ideas, the struggle is far from clear-cut and straightforward in practice. The wise politician may find it difficult to gain the detachment necessary for perception of the ideal outlines; his intuition must often come then to help him strike the right balance.

Bulwer elaborates the notion with respect to the qualifications of rulers most interestingly perhaps in his informal advice to Sir George Bowen, when as Colonial Secretary in 1859 he appointed him Governor of Queensland. Being "careful not to overgovern," the ruler must develop a sort of sympathetic ability to feel which attitudes are held most universally at any given moment and "appeal to those which are noblest." The "vital principle" exists in terms of whatever tendencies and traits really are most prevalently diffused throughout the social organism. The politician should thus speak as nearly as possible for "all the component parts" and allow the organism to develop at its own pace and according to its own mysterious laws. Instead of the actively "directive government" he had recommended in 1833, Bulwer now seems to indicate that the "common interest" requires close and unadventurous adherence to the zeitgeist. While the war still rages on the ideal level, a unifying recognition of overriding communal interests should always prevail in practice.[5]

On the fostering of that sense of community depends not only "the healthful progress of society" but also the health of the individual. "I often think over the wisdom of a saying of Goethe's," Bulwer observes in a characteristic statement to Lord Walpole in 1850: " 'Nothing keeps the mind more healthful than having something in common with the mass of mankind.' " In his own life the very strong desire for that something in common underlies his return to an active political career, his cooperation with Dickens in the theatrical ventures, and his increasingly serious interest in farming. And most importantly, as I have suggested, it informs the new awareness of his literary audience. Rather than appealing for the sympathy of the reader ideally like himself, he now seeks to show his own affinity for the mass of ordinary people. "Say to yourself," he writes in giving literary advice to his son, " 'Broad effects, opinions, humours, feelings, thoughts that every man in Oxford St. knows.' " The advice to the artist is of a piece with his advice to the governor of Queensland.[6]

In the Caxton novels too, then, he has wanted "to create that kind of interest which secures popularity": even "independent of its merely literary merits," he remarks of My Novel, "a work of this kind must be of an essentially *popular* nature." Yet one can scarcely separate the popular from the literary elements because Bulwer's conception of his audience may actually have given the novels their very aesthetic coherence. That audience was first of all the readership of *Blackwood's Magazine*, whose conservative bias and prudish sensibilities might, as Bulwer incidentally feared, rather easily take offense. While constantly asking the advice of the editors of *Maga* about such matters, though, he seems to have avoided making any serious concessions to the tastes of that particular body of readers. For he was designing his novels to please the whole social organism, and in his wish to make his art the mirror of its communal wholeness, he may have found his ultimate, aesthetic principle of organization. A novel like *What Will He Do with It?* thus requires, as a typical letter to *Blackwood's* explains, its length as well as certain elements that might in themselves appear objectionable: "If you see any part of the Crane & Losely substance that is the least coarse or dangerous, mark it rigidly—or if you see how to abridge it, tell me. My idea generally is that a work of this size requires a certain proportion of the lower & darker sides of life—as a needful [illegible] interest to the better & higher—And thus the Crane portion, which looks long by itself may when the whole is completed, add to the furniture and amplitude of a whole view of life."[7]

The "whole view of life" seems to include those two basic elements—"the lower & darker" as opposed to "the better & higher." The terms that Mr. Caxton introduces in *My Novel* may, however, provide a more interesting description of the duality and come closer to suggesting Bulwer's implicit aesthetic theory: "A full and comprehensive survey of the '*Quicquid agunt homines*' . . . will embrace the two views of existence—the integral and the fractional" (MN 6:1). To suggest first of all the darker or fractional view, the novel will convey its images of evil and bleakness and fragmentation. But more significantly, the complications of its plot will tend to imply a whole world in which "the designs of the Omniscient" remain obscure (C 18:8). (With some exaggeration, Ernest Baker has remarked of this aspect of the Caxton novels that Bulwer sets the reader "doing cat's-cradles": one must "conjecture from the data ... how the author can possibly find a way out of the imbroglio.") [8] From the integral viewpoint, on the other hand, all the fragments become aspects of an all-informing unity, and the reader may after all sense the workings of providence in the affairs of men. The trick for the author, then, is to reconcile an adherence to his "original conception & design" with an abandonment of himself, as it were, to the complexities of life. If he accomplishes this feat, he may even come to present his "whole view" with a success that will surprise himself:

I doubt whether any reader [of *What Will He Do with It?*] could devine how the story will end, till he comes to the last chapter. —From the original conception & design I have not varied at all—but I have arrived at it, thro' ways more various than I contemplated—And I have been enabled to achieve it without that sacrifice of life which I had thought might be essential—I hold it a principle in true Art, because a vital element in *durable* popularity which true art must always study that the soul of a very long fiction should be pleasing. I have an impression of happiness. Short and condensed tales may be deeply tragic but no reader likes to make an intimate acquaintance with characters in all those little details of feeling & then see them killed off at the end. [9]

For a while Bulwer came to set great store by his theory that a novel ought to adhere to the popular convention of the happy ending. His "whole view" is an essentially comic one, however, not only by virtue of the happy ending—and the many obviously comical situations—but also because the very fictional "soul ... [is] ... pleasing." By soul he refers to what he had called the "latent coherence" or "the sentiment of the work," and in the Caxton novels the fundamental sentiment is precisely that which should "cement" society: "my endeavor ... is to strengthen the Old English cordial feeling—& bind together those classes which the Manchester School are always trying to seperate [*sic*] & the French School would dip into the fusing pit altogether."[10] As it breathes through the work, that unifying sense of cordiality operates as a sort of representation within the microcosm of "the vital principle of civilisation"—"the unity of liberty with order." (The bulk of these novels, of which Bulwer was very apologetically conscious, admittedly makes them rather large for microcosms!)

Like the Comic Spirit of George Meredith, the cordial feeling or the vital principle may function as a civilizing awareness that is more humanist than divine. As in Meredith too, the principle simultaneously combines a love, laughter, and criticism that seeks with ever more insistence to humanize the aging egoist-misanthrope-idealist (who has been hurt in his youth by a woman). The elder Caxtons, Harley L'Estrange, and Guy Darrell must come in their respective stories to accept the absence of an ideal order and turn their attention to the realities of this life. The quest for a whole view or a sense of providence must proceed amidst the very fragmentation and absurdities of actual human experiences rather than in the abstractions of the sweeping historical perspective.

In dramatizing the final triumph of "the common sense of the common interest," Bulwer has found a new way to symbolize the still rather "metaphysical" achievement of a sense of wholeness and identity. Or, more precisely, the region in which the social organism lives its day to day existence is new to him while the most familiar of his "regions" to others. As an analysis of the structure of the Caxton novels may show, he has indeed reconciled the categories and organizing patterns most congenial to his individual muse with the "furniture and amplitude" of the familiar Victorian materials.

On one of its most basic levels, the life of the body politic suggests a great contest between "ancient forms" and "new ideas," and the novels naturally depend on the metaphor of "the Battle of Life" (C 18:8). *The Caxtons* thus deals with the career of an old soldier and alludes frequently to actual battles while the plot of *My Novel* largely derives from one bitter parliamentary election and culminates in a second "Battle of Philippi" in the same borough. Yet if the hostility between the two sides eventually implies a meaningful pattern, the violence has also contributed to the fragmentation of life. In presenting their view of life fractional, the novels therefore seek to discredit both sides in the ideal war.

At first the war may appear too comically harmless to be taken seriously. The camp of the "ancient forms," to begin with that side, is amusingly divided against itself in *The Caxtons*. The supposed autobiographer's father, Mr. Caxton, and his Uncle Roland argue heatedly, ceaselessly, but ridiculously about the identity of a fifteenth-century ancestor; vaguely at stake, perhaps, are two traditional theories of civilization. Mr. Caxton maintains that the family descends from "the great William Caxton, the printer," and accordingly lives as a quiet classical scholar and bookworm. While working year by year on his interminable "Great Book"—"The History of Human Error"—he struggles to increase the glory and influence of the "Caxtonian world" upon the intellectual battlefields. Uncle Roland, on the other hand, claims "Sir William de Caxton, who fought and fell at Bosworth" for their forebear, and he favors literal military exploits to extend the glorious Empire. Having completed a military career himself, he has now acquired a ruined ancestral tower where he lives as a quixotic and still somewhat ferocious devotee of the code of honor.

Although the war between the Caxton brothers may remain fairly comic, one soon realizes that they do typify a serious threat to the present life of civilization. Bound, indeed, to their ideas of the past, they have a positively disastrous effect upon their sons. The brutal tendencies of Uncle Roland's philosophy have helped to ruin his son's moral sensibility, and despite his own guilt his code of honor has obliged him to disown his son. Mr. Caxton, who "is nearly as Quixotical as Roland," similarly threatens to destroy the chances of his son Pisistratus. While Roland has lived amidst fantasies of a more heroic age in his tower, Mr. Caxton has existed in his library,

complacently treating the people about him as so many books to
be perused and classified. In particular he has confused Pisistratus,
whom he consistently terms the "Anachronism," with a book, and
he has moreover neglected him for the "Great Book"—his "other
son." When the representative of unsound modern capitalism
makes an easy prey of his unworldly gullibility, half his fortune
disappears. He has little of intellectual or material worth to leave
as a patrimony to his son and must sadly confess that William
Caxton too has been a "fatal progenitor."[11]

The criticism implicitly levied at the camp of the ancients may
include a condemnation not only of any exaggerated fixation with
the past but also of the past itself. Perhaps the past now has little
more to offer than "A History of Human Error." In *What Will He
Do with It?* Bulwer thus seems, in presenting his thematically very
significant history of the House of Vipont, to be insinuating the
possible bankruptcy of much of the British heritage. He considers
the House, whose head is the Marquess of Montfort, as possessed
of "a connected unity of thought and action" through the ages and
states that it has rivalled the Established Church in its institutional
importance. Yet while a "very civil, good-natured House,—courte-
ous, generous, hospitable"—its history also points up the irrele-
vance of what may have been the nobler aspects of the British past
to the British present. It had "felt small interest in Magna Charta,"
and at subsequent moments of national crisis it has "contrived to
be a minor" and thereby avoided committing itself. During the Ref-
ormation "gorged with . . . spoil, the House of Vipont, like an
anaconda in the process of digestion, slept long." Its utterly un-
dogmatic and unheroic character has therefore enabled the House
to endure or to muddle through, growing imperceptibly wealthier,
but steadily more futile. To judge from the description of the present and, it develops, the last Marquess, the "ancient forms" have
now become quite moribund:

Before his time every Head of the House had done something for it—
even the most frivolous had contributed; one had collected the pictures;

another, the statues; a third, the medals; a fourth had amassed the famous Vipont library; while others had at least married heiresses, or augmented, through ducal lines, the splendour of the interminable cousinhood. The present Marquess was literally *nil*. . . . He looked well; he dressed well; if life were only the dumb show of a tableau, he would have been a paragon of a Marquess. But he was like the watches we give to little children, with a pretty gilt dial-plate, and no works in them. He was thoroughly inert; there was no winding him up; he could not manage his property; he could not answer his letters—very few of them could he even read through. . . . He shot, it is true, but mechanically—wondering, perhaps, why he did shoot. He attended races, because the House of Vipont kept a racing-stud. He bet on his own horses, but if they lost showed no vexation. (W 5:7)

That his "constitutional apathy" represents, albeit with obvious exaggeration, something of a national dilemma becomes particularly clear in the next chapter, entitled "The British Constitution at Home in a Family Party." The "interminable cousinhood," operating in their fictional compartment very much like the Barnacles of *Little Dorrit*, gathers round the imbecile Marquess and plots to perform its imagined hereditary duty of "saving" the nation. Only the "proud and freezing" and incredibly bored Marchioness appears to understand the absurdity of the whole family effort. Vaguely recalling Dickens' Lady Dedlock, she comes briefly to life when someone mentions the name of the man she had once loved and she accidentally cuts herself with a paper cutter.

The horror of a life encumbered by those forms and traditions inherited from the past emerges most completely and poignantly in the career of the extraordinary Guy Darrell. Possibly Bulwer's most convincing protagonist, the self-torturing Darrell is (almost), as Bulwer realized, "thoro' flesh & blood": "I can hardly fancy a Reader believing that he does not exist."[12] The point, however, is that in his extreme idealism he has sought to bind his living flesh and blood to the deathliness of the past: "As a child," he confesses to Lionel in a rare fit of candor, "before my judgment could discern how much of vain superstition may lurk in our reverence for the dead, my whole heart was engaged in a passionate dream, which my waking existence became vowed to realise." In the intensity of his devotion to his father, he has determined to live his whole life within the framework of a dream conceived originally by his father: "[My father] talked of ancestors as he thought of them; to him they were beings like the old Lares—not dead in graves, but images ever present on household hearths. Doubtless he exaggerated their worth—as their old importance. Obscure, indeed, in the annals of empire, their deeds and their power, their decline and fall. Not so thought he; they were to his eyes the moon-track in the ocean of history" (W 7:9).

Astonishingly enough, Darrell has stubbornly maintained the same commitment to those Lares and the same falsely ideal view of history even after fully admitting the degree of his "vain superstition." Now at the age of fifty-two, he still clings desperately to the oath he has sworn to his father "to rebuild the House." The oath has involved him in one destructive marriage and in subsequent, doomed searches for a woman who may be worthy to bear the offspring of the ideal Lares. In the process he has, for various complicated reasons, laid waste his own life and the lives of several others, but he must continually ratify the identity to which he had bound himself in youth. Only while the past can command the allegiance of the present and future is there any possible permanence or meaning in life.

His literally "skeletal" house—the unfinished, but mouldering Fawley Manor House—operates as Bulwer's most effective symbol for the deathly "ancient forms." Stuffed with chaotically heaped art treasures and the miscellaneous lumber of many centuries, it figures so suggestively and pervasively in the novel that Bulwer considered entitling his work "Fawley Manor House." (The consideration that such a title might seem too reminiscent of *Bleak House* probably deterred him; his letters to *Blackwood's* indicate a studious wish to avoid inviting comparisons with Dickens' novels.) At Fawley, then, Darrell has appropriately dragged out his reclusive existence ever since his wife's humiliating betrayal had stung him into giving up a legal career. When Lionel first sees him in "the lifeless picture gallery" (a more symbolic version of Sir Miles' gallery in *Lucretia*), he appears very much like an inhabitant of the past himself: "a man of imposing presence stood on the threshold—stood so still, and the carved mouldings of the doorway so shadowed, and, as it were, cased round his figure, that Lionel, on turning quickly, might have mistaken him for a portrait brought into bold relief, from its frame, by a sudden fall of light" (W 2:2).

The plot will concern Darrell's ominous efforts to draw the exuberant young Lionel, his collateral relative, into the skeletal framework of his own mad dream of the past. Like the Caxton brothers in their library and tower (and like Harley L'Estrange, who educates Helen to resemble the dead Nora in *My Novel*), Darrell therefore typifies at Fawley the threat of the dead hand to life. In the form of the House of Vipont too, the past simply paralyzes the energies of modern civilization—as if, indeed, Britain still bowed before the "fleshless arms" that had defeated Harold at Hastings. Bulwer has come a long way from the attitude of *Devereux*, according to which the present properly seeks its identity within the caves of the past.

The most apparently potent opposition to the moribund "ancient forms" emanates from the "new ideas." But since these ideas are as destructive in tendency as the forms they combat, the outlook for modern civilization may sometimes appear peculiarly grim. Bulwer associates the ideas with the Manchester School and French radicalism, and although he has sought "only to *insinuate*" what he calls his "Antisocialist or Antirevolutionary" design, his animosity naturally becomes unmistakable.[13]

Once more comical at first, the insinuated criticism begins when the maternal uncle of Pisistratus arrives and startles the Caxtons with his endlessly proliferating schemes for making money. The danger of the rather Micawberish Uncle Jack cannot be dismissed too lightly, however, for his hare-brained projects do dissipate the small fortune that the family had hitherto kept prudently invested in the three-per-cents. Unwilling to learn from experience and repent, he also seems to follow Pisistratus to Australia where his irrepressible optimism bodes no good for the future of colonial civilization.

Similarly threatening in his failure to hold to any traditional principles or loyalties is the embodiment of revolution in *The Caxtons*—Uncle Roland's disinherited son Herbert. "Never speak to me about homes and fathers!" he exclaims naturally enough, and he resists all the efforts of his cousin Pisistratus to tame him (C 8:4). A disreputable Bohemian, living nonchalantly by his wits in London, he reads French novels that strike his cousin as filled with "symbols of the Destroying Principle" and perilously subversive in their "hatred, carefully instilled of the poor against the rich" (C 10:1). As the evil demon of modern civilization, he seeks finally to destroy the purity of the figure typifying the anima. He kidnaps Fanny Trevanion, the beloved of Pisistratus, and his revolt culminates in a melodramatic chase. (Fanny is eventually given in marriage, however, neither to him nor to Pisistratus but to the much older Marquess of Castleton, who must unwillingly marry to provide heirs to his name. The "ancient forms" thus triumph in this case over the revolutionary "new ideas.")

In treating the "new ideas" in somewhat less neatly diagrammatic fashion, *My Novel* attempts to relate them to a subtler and more sinister awareness of evil. The story features not only revolutionary tracts that disturb the tranquility of the working classes but also an army of intellectuals who subscribe to the supposedly modern principle that "Knowledge is Power."[14] As it echoes throughout the novel, the principle comes to refer especially to the hard-headed recognition that all human relationships involve the enslavement of individuals to each other. The intellectuals see a vast and subtle system of jails and jailors wherever they look. Indeed they appear to see such things literally, for Bulwer pays extraordinary attention to their penetrating, roving eyes, which also enable them to recognize each other by an "almost mesmerical . . . *rapport*" (MN 9:3). Beginning with the initial mock-heroic episodes around the village stocks, the novel thus develops a pervasive symbolism of both physical and mental subjugation.

Far from inspiring them to free men from the stifling forms of the past, the vision of tyranny leads the intellectuals to determine to become the jailors themselves. His special affinity for ruthless autocracy even causes the Conte di Peschiera to betray his Lombardian compatriots to the Austrians. Yet when they most appear to be cynically shoring up the cause of the old, established forms, they are also the most anarchically subversive in their utter freedom from all larger loyalties. Randal Leslie, the daring intellectual virtuoso, thus pretends to be working toward the reconciliation of Squire Hazeldean and his son while he is in reality alienating them subtly and totally from each other. And as the very genius of capitalism, the immensely rich Baron Levy has similarly developed the undermining of the old agricultural-aristocratic social order into a fine art. With methodical patience and suave charm, he wins the friendship of elder sons, eases them into debt, and forces them to encumber their reversionary expectations with post-obits. Nothing so crushes the fathers in the novel as to discover that their sons have been gambling on their life-spans. Levy's end, though, appropriately punishes him: falling obsessively and jealously in love with a seductive dancer, he must imprison her in various remote country houses. Since all his energies go toward thwarting her supposed communications with other men, the jailor becomes the real prisoner.

Beyond the vision of the vast prison, the "new ideas" are also reducing civilization to a sort of jungle. Or as Guy Darrell implies when he forbids Lionel to fish in his lake at Fawley, the society succumbing to the anarchy of laissez faire resembles the carnage under the water: "I regard my lake as a politic community, under the protection of the law, and leave its denizens to devour each other, as Europeans, fishes, and other cold-blooded creatures wisely do, in order to check the overgrowth of population. To fatten one pike it takes a great many minnows. Naturally I support the vested rights of pike. I have been a lawyer" (W 2:4).

Revealing "the lower & darker sides of life," the lengthy "Crane & Losely substance" provides one of the best examples of individuals ruthlessly exercising their "vested rights" and devouring each other. The duel between the extortioner Jasper Losely and the "grim" Arabella Crane may also parody the political struggle between the anarchy of the new and the life-destroying rigidity of the ancient. Jasper had early revolted like a more despicable Herbert Caxton against his father and has learned to live as a criminal parasite on society. While he asserts his absolute "Liberty to go to Satan in his own way," though, his spurned mistress Arabella has committed herself to his "rescue" from a certain prostitute and to his moral salvation in a very legalistic sense. To this end, she pursues him relentlessly: "Wherever he went—there went she. He might baffle the police, not her. Hunger had often forced him to accept her aid. As soon as he received it, he hid from her again, burying himself deeper and deeper in the mud, like a persecuted tench" (W 6:5). For a time the "grim Arabella Crane, in the iron-gray gown, and with the iron-gray ringlets, hatefully, awfully beneficent" succeeds in installing him in Belgium "under a surveillance akin to that designed by Mr. Bentham's reformatory Panopticon" (W 4:19). And at the very end, she gleefully controls him utterly, for he lies paralyzed by a stroke in her bedroom. As the "politic community" disintegrates apace, their sordid intrigues have once more implied the destructiveness and the sterility of both sides in the larger warfare.

Since both sides are so equally inimical to the health of society, that larger war may also take on something of a phony character. The reader may, indeed, lose consciousness of the lines of battle and see only the vast sweep of futility, for which both sides must probably share the blame. Or the question of blame may simply become irrelevant amidst what one critic has termed, with reference to this period, "the uncertainty and brokenness . . . close to the center of Bulwer's world-view."[15] Before examining how the novels discover a vital, integrating principle after all, then, it is important to observe the depiction of a fragmentation that goes almost beyond the possibility for logical comprehension and criticism.

To deal with the bleakest example, *What Will He Do with It?* conveys the impression of a world from which the integrating sense of a soul or providence has long withdrawn. Although so much of the novel involves complicated espionage and the pursuit of fugitives, a principal motif is the failure of all efforts to establish an organizing framework of intelligence. Detectives sometimes set forth after other detectives, but the fundamental discontinuities and inexplicabilities remain. Few characters succeed to the degree of Arabella (with her temporary Panopticon) and perhaps least of all the police. While confidently boasting about "a network over the three kingdoms," they fail to gather the right information or to capture the right people: "the meshes are so large," remarks the author, "that anything less than a whale must be silly indeed if it consent to be caught" (W 4:8).[16] The ubiquitous, clairvoyant cobbler Merle even becomes a sort of parody of an omniscient center of consciousness, for his crystal ball tends to remain dark about precisely the most crucial matters.

Since the story portrays so many incidents of escape, pursuit, and exhausted wandering, roads figure with particular prominence as a network that rather impedes than promotes communication. After their happy, pastoral idyl in the first book, the young Lionel and Sophy must separate, and her guardian, the Comedian Waife, makes her realize that "their paths are so different, they cannot cross each other again." She has then a terrifying vision of ever-diverging roads: "one road went this way, another that, and they on the one road were borne farther and farther away from those on the other." Some kind of baffling fact also prevents her, she understands, from ever leaving her own road: "There is a path of life, then, which I can never enter—there is a path on which I must

always, always walk, always, always, always that path—no escape!
Never to come to that other one" (W 3:14). And for most of the
novel she and Lionel do tramp literally as well as metaphorically
along different roads.

Even when the journeys bring men near each other for a season,
they fail to make significant contact. All may long, as Arabella had
once thought, "for something in common with common life," but
few know where to find it (W 4:4). Rich travellers, we are told
in a passage recalling Marx's analysis of the street-plan of Manchester, never so much as see "those labyrinths of squalid homes"
that exist in all towns just beyond "the broad thoroughfares, with
glittering shops and gas-lit causeways" (W 4:2). And if they
journey by the railroad, which figures more noticeably in this work
than in any of Bulwer's others, they may observe one more emblem
for the society without a communal consciousness: "the lifelike
iron miracle, fuming, hissing, and screeching, bore off to London
its motley convoy of human beings, each passenger's heart a mystery to the other, all bound the same road, all wedged close within
the same whirling mechanism; what a separate and distinct world
in each!" (W 4:3).

Worse than the isolation of men from each other is the alienation
of each man from himself, for almost every individual seems now
to lack a persuasion of his own meaningful integrity. "Life is a
quaint puzzle," says Darrell, as he confesses with a deceptive semblance of resignation that his ideal commitment cannot give lasting
coherence to the pieces of his fifty-two years: "Bits the most incongruous join into each other, and the scheme thus gradually becomes
symmetrical and clear; when, lo! as the infant claps his hands, and
cries, 'See, see! the puzzle is made out!' all the pieces are swept back
into the box—black box with the gilded nails" (W 2:14). The
Comedian Waife no longer even tries to keep the fragments together, and more fully and honestly than anyone alse he has accepted the implications of life fractional. "What's the good of looking back?" he asks in musing about his own discontinuity: "A

man's gone self is a dead thing. It is not I—now tramping this road, with you to lean upon—whom I see, when I would turn to look behind on that which I once was—it is another being, defunct and buried; and when I say to myself, 'that being did so and so,' it is like reading an epitaph on a tombstone" (W 3:1).

So the same roads that carry men further in space from each other are carrying each individual further in time from his own gone selves. Waife also has the impression that each self results from being temporarily "thrown together" amidst particular external circumstances; then the kaleidoscope, as it were, turns, and one is "thrown together" in a new form. Even should one meet up once more with the individuals and in the circumstances that had helped to compose a gone self, the earlier pattern would still prove to be lost forever. "Beware of parting!" the author therefore urges the traveller through life: "From the passionate farewell to the woman who has your heart in her keeping, to the cordial good-bye exchanged with pleasant companions at a watering-place, a country-house, or the close of a festive day's blithe and careless excursion—a cord, stronger or weaker, is snapped asunder in every parting, and Time's busy fingers are not practised in re-splicing broken ties. Meet again you may; will it be in the same way?—with the same sympathies?—with the same sentiments? Will the souls, hurrying on in diverse paths, unite once more as if the interval had been a dream? Rarely, rarely!" (W 1:18).

The novel propounds, indeed, something like the sad Stendhalian and Proustian theory of *cristallisation*. In the life of the nation the theory explains the astonishing capriciousness of political popularity. Chance factors suddenly crystallize about the man of the hour—and in "the mirror of the moment . . . his proportions swell—they become gigantic"—but the image dissolves as rapidly (W 6:6). In the life of the individual the phenomenon applies particularly to love affairs: "Certainly, half the peculiar charm of a person beloved," Colonel Morley tells Darrell, "must be ascribed to locality and circumstances." Once the moment with its accidental configurations and associations has passed, as Morley goes on to explain, the love may prove to have had little validity in itself (W 7:15).

In what may be, for its communication of searing psychological torture, Bulwer's most powerful scene, Lady Montfort discovers that truth for herself and comes to her own ultimate vision of life fractional. As a widow now, she seeks out Darrell, whom she had loved in her youth but had eventually rejected for the sake of the coronet proferred by the late Marquess. Walking with Darrell beside his lake in the bleakness of late autumn, she humbly wonders if the eighteen years of her disastrous marriage have not constituted a sufficient expiation for her sin. "Why can I not repair the past?" she asks: "You have not ceased to love me. Call it hate—it is love still! And now, no barrier between our lives, can I never, never again—never, now that I know I am less unworthy of you by the very anguish I feel to have so stung you—can I never again be the Caroline of old!" (W 9:1). But Darrell taunts her for her "ingenuous simplicity" and sardonically enforces, in his mocking refrain, the distinction between "the Caroline of old" and "my Lady Montfort." Disinterring their past and arguing about all its convolutions, he proves just how irreparably dead their gone selves are and leaves her baffled and sobbing at her carriage. The next day, then, she faces the dissolution of the images that had provided her desperate sense of continuity with "the Caroline of old": "When we slowly recover from the tumult and passion of some violent distress, a peculiar stillness falls upon the mind, and the atmosphere around it becomes in that stillness appallingly clear. . . . As a field the day after a battle, is the sight of our own sorrow, when we no longer have to stem its raging, but to endure the destruction it has made. Distinct before Caroline Montfort's vision stretched the waste of her misery—the Past, the Present, the Future—all seemed to blend in one single desolation. A strange thing it is how all time will converge itself, as it were, into the burning-glass of a moment!" (W 9:2).

Like a grimly ironic version of a spot of time, the awareness of eternity shows only the cosmic extent of the waste land.

The Caxton novels are nevertheless comedies that do manage at last to affirm a more benign "whole view of life." When accepted in the proper spirit, life fractional may somehow lose its bleakness; the intuition of a "vital principle" can substitute, in a sense, for a more traditional awareness of soul. In fact human life itself—as an endlessly multiplying, fractionalizing, but socializing reality—becomes the ultimate value, and each novel finally achieves its integrity as its elements coalesce to form a positive symbol for life.

Subtitled "A Family Picture," *The Caxtons* develops the domestic circle as a symbol for the "common life" in which individuals the most disparate can participate. Although all three novels, as Bulwer's letters emphasize, "apeal [*sic*] to domestic Emotions,"[17] this one does so the most obviously and—by modern tastes—the most relentlessly. Much of the intrigue concerns efforts to arouse dormant familial instincts in the rebellious Herbert and to persuade Uncle Roland to take a warmer interest in his son than in his theories of honor. As if to prove at the end his own recognition of his identity with his family, Pisistratus even marries his cousin Blanche, Herbert's sister. For the conditions of life have not, of course, permitted him to unite himself to Fanny, who had typified an unattainably ideal individuality. On the last page then, the story is rounded off with its final "Family Picture": having opened with the birth of one emblematic child, it closes with the family gathered about the cradle of the next generation.

The picture of the ongoing generations also owes its force to the Australian episodes which have applied its symbolic resolution of continuity and change to the dynamic identity of British civilization. In emigrating from the parental country to repair the family fortunes in the bush, Pisistratus and the tamed Herbert have carried with them a "philosophy of colonising"—apparently taken from Samuel Sidney's *Australian Hand-Book*. They must attempt to transplant something of the British soul to Australia so that the colonial offspring will not grow up to be "a strange motley chaos of struggling democracy, an uncouth livid giant, at which the Frankenstein may well tremble" (C 12:6).[18] Any valid identity depends upon the maintenance of certain continuities. Yet almost more important, as Coral Lansbury suggests, is the need to purify British civilization of the accumulated traditions and stultifying accretions of the centuries.[19] Although it does not evince quite the hostility of the later novels to the past, *The Caxtons* clearly implies that the colonial offspring should not look merely to the mother country for an identity. Australia should seek rather to redeem the British past, and the parent will thereby gain as much from the child as the child has gained from the parent: Australia is "destined, perchance, from the sins and sorrows of a civilisation struggling with its own elements of decay, to renew the youth of the world, and transmit the great soul of England through the cycles of Infinite Change!" (C 18:1).[20]

Since that soul is not a static, ideal entity, each generation must recover or renew its consciousness of soul in its own youth and vitality. (In 1858 Bulwer would similarly indicate that he was appealing in his works to the "Reader . . . [as] a being in whom youth is renewed through all cycles.") [21] The sons must discover their essential value in the process that continually re-creates life from decay and in the awareness that they share in that process with those about them. So Pisistratus and Herbert do not gain their saving sense of the "something in common" from their continuation of the ancient fight between William Caxton and Sir William de Caxton. Instead, they and their band merge their energies—including the once demonic, anti-social instincts of the former communist among them—in the common struggle against the wilderness. And back in England Mr. Caxton comes to define the values which men should work together to defend not as "new ideas" or "ancient forms" but as the real interests of living families: "I think we had better keep up enough of the bellicose spirit not to think it a sin if we are called upon to fight for our pestles and mortars, our three-per-cents, goods, chattels, and liberties" (C 18:8).

In those supreme domestic values all men may find their interests converging, and when fought on behalf of them, the Battle of Life becomes an instance not of life fractional but of life integral: " 't is in war," says Mr. Caxton, "that the knot of fellowship is closest drawn; 't is in war that mutual succour is most given—mutual danger run, and common affection most exerted and employed; for heroism and philanthropy are almost one and the same!" (C 18:8). Or in another term that acquires great prominence in the novel, "compassion" is the principal fruit of the common struggle. Although Bulwer sought in a later footnote to relate the struggle to the actual Crimean War, it would also appear that men generally discover their compassionate fellowship in less literally military ventures. Uncle Roland and Mr. Caxton have thus gained their sometimes surprising compassion in an old rivalry for the hand of a Lady Ellinor (the mother of Fanny) who has rejected them both. In his "Great Book" Mr. Caxton has also gone on to evince a humanist compassion for the whole race; the work implies something of a triumph for the true Comic Spirit: "It was . . . the moral history of mankind, told with truth and earnestness, yet with an arch, unmalignant smile. Sometimes indeed, the smile drew tears. But in all true humour lies its germ, pathos" (C 4:2).

Pisistratus himself naturally cultivates that compassionate smile more for the living family of man than for man through the sweep of history. For him especially, the idea of the family refers less to the common, inherited surname than to the more palpable reality of the domestic instincts and the actual love among family members. He has a vision in fact of London that implies the apotheosis of civilization in terms of the daily domestic lives of all its families. Surveying the creations of men from on high—in the tour de force of his "Chapter on Housetops"—he finds that the chimneys imply countless domestic hearths. "Imagination steps in," and as was not the case for Dickens in the view from Todgers's, his position enables him to see into the essence of each household. Soaring to its climax, his fantasy then represents the modern ordeal in the form of the fire that has resisted the civilizing containment of the hearth and has gutted one home. He re-lives "the beautiful horror," and from his "compassionate, inquisitive" perspective discerns elements of grandeur in the opposition between the human family and the wild forces of evil. When the fire engines arrive to struggle against "the red, crawling serpent," the suspense grows unbearable, but "how sublime is the war!" At last, as if to assure the survival of the domestic ideal, the mother and child are saved. "O Art!" he concludes, "study life from the roof-tops!" (C 14:2).

Fearing the "Chapter on Housetops" might seem too "Episodical," Bulwer advised *Blackwood's* that it could be omitted: "I am not satisfied with the execution," he explained, "tho' the ide[a is] good and new."[22] In fact, "the idea" may not be entirely "new" (consider, for example, Ruskin's "A Chapter on Chimneys" published some ten years previously),[23] but the chapter is in any case a good one. Like the Mt. Snowdon episode in *The Prelude*, it provides an effective image for the discovery of a principle of unity amidst seeming diversity, which will later permit the autobiographer to begin in earnest upon his artistic vocation.[24] As the ambitious author of *My Novel*, the autobiographer of *The Caxtons* will thus proceed to deal with even more complicated materials and to offer an even broader overview of modern civilization. So strong, moreover, remains his faith in an underlying principle of coherence that his panoramic novel (subtitled "Varieties in English Life") will dare to abandon the rather too neatly superimposed metaphor of the domestic hearth. Instead of the single family—with its dissensions as well as its essential unity—the complex work of art itself will become the chief symbol for the endlessly diverse but elusively coherent civilization of the nineteenth century.

But before observing how the "Varieties" escape any ready domestication, it is important to emphasize the degree to which the single family still attempts to impose its values on all of life. The

Caxtons continue indeed to provide the technical framework for *My Novel*. "It is a mere affectation," remarks Mr. Caxton in the discursive chapter introducing the second book, "to suppose that a book can come into the world without an author. Every child has a father." To avoid the "affectation," the novel keeps us resolutely aware of its paternity; each of the twelve books begins with a chapter containing criticism by Pisistratus or his family of the progressing story. The relationship between these introductory chapters and the "life" of the story itself thus parallels the symbolically and structurally important relationship between the fathers and sons of *The Caxtons*.

Although most of the family circle simply urge on their hobby horses (and may be ignored), Mr. Caxton speaks in the introductory chapters on behalf of Bulwer's traditional, ideal views of art and the artist. Any creation—whether the fictional offspring, the literal son, or the earth itself—serves primarily, in his estimation, to exhibit something of the identity of its "father." A novel thus takes its essential "tinge" from "some colouring matter within" the novelist while all physical life achieves its value insofar as it points toward the divine Creator. Often finding evidence for his theories in the story, he comes in his "profoundly metaphysical" discussion of Book 6 to refer the major fictional actions to certain myths of the soul's progress. In all that happens here, he believes, some original, divine scheme should be discernible.

Pisistratus, on the other hand, entertains a less ideal vision of life and defends his novel as if he were defending the claims of actuality against art. So far is he from imposing any integrating order upon his materials that he appears in no hurry even to decide which characters will constitute his heroes and heroines. His family puzzle about this throughout the leisurely action of the first several books. When it strikes him in Book 3 that his novel may require an identifying principle in the form of a title, he permits it to be called *My Novel* in somewhat the same accidental fashion of his own christening. The possessive adjective has no special significance, for he steadfastly refuses to take any aesthetic or moral responsibility for the developments in his action or characterization. "I guard myself from saying anything in praise or disfavour," he remarks typically: "I am but describing the man as he was, and as a man like him would inevitably be under the influences in which he lived" (MN 10:14).

Yet as the notion of inevitability implies, he does slowly become conscious of a sense of destiny that endows his world with some order beyond its fragmentation. Although he fears at times that his abdication of responsibility may have destroyed all possibility for art, life itself does finally reassure him with its own subtle principle of significance. He has felt, he tells his family, a "Providence" quite apart from his own intentions, and so it is well that he has not applied the pet, artificial theories of his relatives: "I can no more alter the fate allotted to each of the personages whom you honour with your interest than I can change your own; like you, they must go where events lead them, urged on by their own characters and the agencies of others. Providence so pervadingly governs the universe, that you cannot strike it even out of a book. The author may beget a character, but the moment the character comes into action, it escapes from his hands—plays its own part, and fulfils its own inevitable doom" (MN 12:1).

While the acceptance of fragmentation has thus led once more to the sense of teleology, the quality of the latter remains less clear than in *The Caxtons*. Surely Mr. Caxton's divine myth does not adequately explain all the events of the story. The ideal vision of Leonard Fairfield, who composes the book within a book within a book, is similarly but one fragment in the expansive vision of Pisistratus. (With the help of Boethius and the influences emanating from his mother's grave, Leonard has supposedly escaped the social prison and "the jostle of Oxford Street.")

The idea of life as an epic more comic than divine may come nearer the mark: "this history, rightly considered," Pisistratus has stated in Book 8, "is a kind of humble familiar Epic, or . . . a long

Serio-Comedy, upon the Varieties of English Life in this our century, set in movement by the intelligences most prevalent" (MN 8:1). More specifically, he has envisaged the epic as a great struggle between the adherents of "head"—with their "Knowledge is Power" slogan—and the adherents of "heart." That the sentimental party of heart may tend to triumph over the intellectuals further implies the providential quality of the epic organizing principle. Parson Dale, whose deeply touched feelings inspire him to dress the wound of a donkey in the opening chapter, may claim validly in his sermonic set piece that sympathy is the fundamental principle of human life.[25] Or as Harley L'Estrange assures the unillusioned Marchesa, "good and generous emotions" rather than the force of tyranny constitute the social cement: "Never believe the world is base; if it were so no society could hold together for a day" (MN 10:8). Still, sympathy needs some counter-balancing—the homoeopathic Dr. Morgan must even keep dosing himself with caustic to counteract the dangerous prevalance of feelings in his constitution. Although compassion may tend to redeem the human lot, it is not quite synonymous—any more than is knowledge—with the power that "so pervadingly governs the universe" and motivates all the jostle in Oxford Street.

Pisastratus can never quite specify what lies behind "most of the interests or passions that agitate mankind"; in depicting them, he has not created an orderly symbol in the usual sense. Instead, as Mr. Caxton finally concludes, he has created a "mirror": making no pronouncements and evincing no predominant qualities in itself, his novel possesses a capacity to reflect any human being whatsoever. What all men share, then, may be the fact that they possess visible bodies that a mirror will reflect. Or men somehow share the fact of their variety. As Hopkins' "Pied Beauty" unites all life through its shared quality of *pied*ness, the novel implies a providential element simply in the universality of life fractional. "True to the Varieties of Life," *My Novel* has become "Every Man's Novel," and Pisistratus dismisses it at the end to "go forth to the world."

Like its characters the book has come "into action" and so "escapes from [its author's] hands—plays its own part, and fulfills its own inevitable doom."

The culminating scene of the novel proper—wherein Egerton has died in the discovery of his son—has similarly suggested that fathers must retire from the scene once they have transmitted life to their sons. Life must simply be permitted to continue forward on its own terms whether or not it shows the "tinge" of its author's identity. Following its own mysterious laws and multiplying irrepressibly and indefinitely, life itself becomes greater than any single or familial identity. The vital principle that may unite all men involves not much more than its sheer vitality.

In *What Will He Do with It?*, to come to Bulwer's supreme, comic affirmation of life, the supposed author Pisistratus has dissolved himself even more completely in his vision of humanity. Whereas *My Novel* has depended for much of its point on those discursive Caxtonian chapters (though Bulwer considered suppressing them when he published the serialized work in book form), the last Caxton novel asserts its paternity only on its title page. Yet in its greater symbolic submission to life fractional, this last novel also manages even more successfully than the earlier ones to define what Bulwer now takes to be the providential principle in life.

"Providence mysteriously acts on the whole world," according to one of the *Caxtoniana* essays, through its immanence in that utterly mysterious creature, the "genius."[26] Whenever men come in contact with a human being who possesses genius, they may intuit divinity, for each individual genius incarnates the eternal, divine principle. Indeed, even without direct contact with a genius, men may sense the divine presence because everything of value in the whole civilized endeavor suggests something of the genius who inspired it. Mr. Caxton has perhaps adumbrated the theory most succinctly in a passage that appears in *My Novel* but that applies more interestingly to *What Will He Do with It?*:

Often lost sight of itself, [the genius's] very absence is a silent contrast to the agencies present. Merged and vanished for a while amidst the Practical World, yet we ourselves feel all the while that it is *there*; is at work amidst the workings around it. This practical world that effaces it, rose out of some genius that has gone before; and so each man of genius, though we never come across him, as his operations proceed, in places remote from our thoroughfares, is yet influencing the practical world that ignores him, forever and ever. That is GENIUS! We can't describe it in books—we can only hint and suggest it, by the accessories which we artfully heap about it. (MN 6:1)

Bulwer has, however, introduced a genius into the last Caxton novel: "William Waife was a man of genius, taking pains to appear an ordinary mortal" (W 4:8). Like the stories of disguised gods and saints, his career seems designed to indicate that divinity may lurk even amidst the most degraded conditions of mortality. We see him initially as a figure of shuffling, nondescript poverty and senility; his supposed granddaughter Sophy, "The Phenomenon," cares for him as they wander about with an acting troupe. (The configuration reminds one of Dickens' Little Nell and her grandfather as well as of Fanny and old Simon in *Night and Morning*.) Bearing scars that he claims, significantly, are due to a railway accident, he may also exaggerate his infirmities to win sympathy and alms.

Yet his mildly repulsive traits have issued from what Darrell will call "a self-immolation that seemed almost above humanity" (W 11:4). He had once permitted himself to be arrested, tried, and transported for a crime committed by his son Jasper Losely. Then returning illegally from his transportation to care for Sophy, he has submitted to the life of pathetic vagrancy, shifts, and disguises for her sake. For what he deems her good too, he will eventually "consummate his self-abnegation": he leaves her amidst guardians in a better sphere of life, and so that she can serenely forget him, he refuses even to write her. A figure of extreme pathos, he tramps down the road alone to his next adventures—cooperating in the process that rubs out all traces of men's gone selves.

Because his perpetual self-abnegation makes him no one, he is also potentially everyone, and in that possible paradox is supposed to lie his miraculous genius as an actor. Often termed simply the Comedian, he resembles in himself the "serio-comic," "epic" mirror of "Every Man's Novel." The author refers to "the epic side of Mr. Waife's character" and even compares his extraordinary talent to the skill of Proteus and Ulysses (W 3:9). Since one can scarcely say, moreover, when he is acting and when he is not, his life has become nearly indistinguishable from his epic art, and his ordinary mortality from his genius. The action keeps hinting that he lives his roles onstage—they come closest to expressing whatever the truth of his emotional life may be—while he acts his most fantastically successful roles offstage.

The episode at Gatesboro' offers one of the most absorbing instances of heroism amidst degradation and of art merged with life. Although entering town on foot, Waife "purloin[s] the respectable appearance of a passenger by the train" and "artfully" manages to insinuate that he may be good game himself for confidence men: "flymen, omnibus drivers, cads and porters marked him for their own" (W 3:9). His crafty imposture serves eventually, however, to bring out the best rather than the worst in men. As a Mr. Chapman, he graciously "agrees" to give a lecture to the factory operatives at the new Athenaeum. The "lecture" evolves into a brilliant enactment of pathetic roles that appeal to the generous emotions, including the role of superannuated soldier, and culminates unexpectedly:

While the audience was in the full depth of its emotion, generous tears in many an eye, Waife seized his moment, dropped the actor, and stepped forth to the front as the man; simple, quiet, earnest man,— artless man!

"This is no mimic scene, ladies and gentlemen. It is a tale in real life that stands out before you. I am here to appeal to those hearts that are not vainly open to human sorrows. I plead for what I have represented. True, that man who needs your aid is not of that soldiery which devastated Europe. But he has fought in battles as severe, and been left by fortune to as stern a desolation." (W 3:12)

If most heroic in that moment of enacting himself, he nevertheless remains the impostor too. The audience contribute their money under the impression that this most "genuine" of all his roles is to be taken allegorically rather than literally; he must be appealing on behalf of some noble philanthropic cause. "Probably," they reflect, as one readily detects a reference to the theatrical ventures of Dickens and Bulwer, "the stranger was an author himself—a great and affluent author. Had not great and affluent authors—men who are the boast of our time and land—acted, yea, on a common stage, and acted inimitably, too, on behalf of some lettered brother or literary object?" (W 3:13). And in a sense their persuasion of the nobility of his cause is justified. He has enabled them to discover a totally unexpected generosity in themselves and has given them a sublime impression of man's continuing heroism amidst the desolation of modern life. In that sublimity the imposture may be obliterated, and so the Comedian continues on his way—not quite honest, but somehow ennobling all who come in contact with him.

Guy Darrell provides the ultimate test of his ability to humanize his audience, and the relationship between the two seeming opposites becomes the main structural principle of the complicated plotting. Darrell, the supreme idealist who wishes to rest eternally faithful to his Lares and to the identity chosen in childhood, must recognize his better self in the Comedian, who has no identity. Or in less metaphysical terms, Darrell must agree to permit Lionel, the heir of Fawley Manor House, to marry Sophy, "the Phenomenon."

The story envisages the psychological process as a military campaign—another instance of the Battle of Life perhaps—in which Darrell must endure constant sieges at Fawley. Waife's son Jasper even breaks his way literally into the Manor House, but of course the citadel does not fall before the power of armed fraud. (As a confidence man, Jasper possesses only the ignoble aspects of his father's skill at imposture.) Darrell strengthens his defenses; still he must perceive, once the Comedian himself has entered Fawley, that his fortress is doomed: "Forlorn in that Citadel of Pride— closed round and invested with Sorrows—and the last hopes that had fled to the fortress, slain in defence of its outworks" (W 12:2). After others have mounted indecisive psychological assaults, the popular London preacher George Morley presses the final attack. (Since Waife had given him the elocution lessons that had cured his stuttering and permitted his clerical vocation, Morley considers himself Waife's creature.) He reads Darrell an impassioned sermon on the text that not the Darrell Lares but "Mankind [is] his family," and then the fortress collapses. Darrell confesses the inhumanity of his idealism. He will permit the young lovers to marry and pull down his emblematic house: "not a stone [shall] stand on stone! The ploughshare shall pass over their sites!" (W 12:4).

Yet the point is not to destroy but to humanize, and this Waife seems to accomplish as he stays on at Fawley and reads Shakespeare to Darrell—with extraordinary effect. Fawley will remain standing then in order to become a home rather than a monument to the dead. In the bewilderments of the final pages, it appears further that not only the young lovers but the misanthrope himself will wed: Darrell and Lady Montfort can unite on the basis of what they are now. As the Comedian retreats to the sidelines, the story ends in the approved—and admittedly somewhat artificial—tradition of romantic comedy.

Although the final revolution of the kaleidoscope, which leaves the complicated pieces in a pretty pattern, seems false, the story has successfully implied the operations of providence in the affairs of men. It is not, to be sure, a transcendent Providence: despite the religious orthodoxy of George Morley, the novel does not persuasively hint at "Mysteries" like those which had guided the destinies of Ernest Maltravers. Instead, providence works in conjunction with the life force; it is the vital principle that assures the defeat of all men's proud efforts to build bastions against ongoing life. So Darrell discerns in retrospect the providential quality of all his adversities: while appearing to blast his existence, they have been forcing him all along toward the blessed decision to pull down his metaphorical Manor House.

Beyond its association with the cause of life, providence also operates in each of the Caxton novels as the compassion or "cordial feeling" that unites men in the recognition of their common humanity. And here especially, perhaps, *What Will He Do with It?* succeeds. Whereas the compassion of the Caxton family may seem too domestic and bourgeois and the idea of the vast serio-comic epic too abstract, Waife does appear capable of symbolizing the archetypal man and focusing an essential humanizing awareness.

His experience identifies suffering as the quality most fundamental to the universal human condition. He has gained the "soul" he would not otherwise have possessed, says Morley, through his endurance of the long, undeserved ordeal that has been his life. Battered and often alone, he has had to wander through the most desolate parts of the modern waste land, but still he has courageously buried gone selves and pressed indomitably forward. Passing through scenes of degradation, enigmatically tainted, and frequently falling short of an ideal virtue, he can yet plead earnestly and honestly for whatever he and whatever modern man is. A hard-tested comic resilience sustains his faith in the process of living and in the value of man. To live is to suffer, he seems to say, and yet to suffer is to grow more conscious not only of the sins and follies but also of the beauty and generosity of humanity. In the growth that comes through suffering, then, even more than in their shared domestic instincts or shared physical life, men may recover their fundamental sense of community and soul. As if from the opposite direction, Waife has approached Zanoni's recognition of the worth of ordinary mortality. And as in Zanoni's immolation, so in the less spectacular but equally epic proportions of Waife's self-abnegating life and art, every man may discern his apotheosis and his soul.

In his conception of the never-ending reality of the mortal condition, Bulwer has found an intimation of permanence that may even imply, somewhat paradoxically, that only mortality is immortal. Abstract ideas, like individual identities, families, and houses must exhaust themselves and pass, but mortality keeps reconstituting itself and revitalizing the ordinary humane values that are so nearly inextricable from the cycles of life. While Bulwer's epics of the modern community still use the terms traditional to his quests for individual identity, they do not, therefore, locate the soul in the same regions of apocalyptic fulfillment. The human soul exists not as an idea that leads men restlessly beyond their present life and not even as the private property of each individual but rather in its diffusion throughout the living community of men.

Persuaded that the divine principle inheres within ordinary mortality, Bulwer has dared in this phase to create an art too that does not seek to point to something far beyond itself. Save in a few minor motifs, the Caxton novels do not seem to develop images or patterns designed to hint at the inexpressible idea within the mind of the author. Like the Comedian who supposedly is all the "Varieties in Life" he enacts, he has tried to live solely in his sympathy for his creatures. Or like the father who sends his own life forth in his son, he has dared to permit his creation to supersede the creator. The best part of his being is the humanity which must live on within the context of the created, material realm—and which depends like the selfless Caxtonian mirror upon the flesh and blood of its living readers for its vitality.

The submission of the idea to its material expression does not, however, last beyond this phase, and even in the Caxton novels the altruistic, authorial self-sacrifice contains an egoistic component that should be noticed in conclusion. By merging himself in his whole view of the life of his age, Bulwer has wanted not to dissipate himself but to make of that vast spectacle a grand symbol for himself. His "intense conviction" of his own "integral, earnest, original unity" has enabled him perhaps to sense and to emphasize a corresponding integrity in all of mortal life. He has therefore hoped, as the passage on "the author's temperament" in *What Will He Do with It?* suggests, to "stand out to distant ages a representative of the age that rather lived in him than he in it."

Soon he would revert to a less disguised preoccupation with the cause of the intensely individual ego. As the prospect of an immortality throughout the ages and regions of mortality then ceased to attract him, he would create less grandly popular and more characteristically hieratic symbols for the "something within." Still, the period in which he explored that part of his destiny held in common with "that great reality—the People"—may have constituted one of the most daring and successful phases of his creativity.

CHAPTER VII

Back to the Regions of Pure Forms

Aber in den heitern Regionen,
Wo die reinen Formen wohnen,
Rauscht des Jammers trüber Sturm nicht mehr.
                    Schiller, "Das Ideal und das Leben"

Of Bulwer's four last novels, *The Parisians* most resembles the Caxton series in conception. Aspiring once more to embody a "whole view" of modern life, it makes of the urban epitome of civilization another grand symbol for the vitality that renews itself in the cycles of change. The story opens in 1869 and presents the modern Paris as the conscious creation of the complacent Second Empire—an elaborate emblem of the supposedly enduring imperial identity. Tracing then the disintegration of that identity, the story tries to imply an underlying continuity while the diffuse elements of Parisian society reconstitute themselves in the bewildering transformations up to May 1871. Bulwer has thus sought, as a passage discussing the work of a less mature novelist within the story intimates, again to sympathize with the general life rather than to express some private awareness. Whereas the work of the "very young writer . . . will colour itself from the views of some truth in his innermost self," Bulwer may believe he has reached the "later stage of experience and art": "the writer escapes from the influence of his individual personality, and lives in existences that take no colourings from his own. Genius usually must pass through the subjective process before it gains the objective. Even a Shakespeare represents himself in the Sonnets before no trace of himself is visible in a Falstaff or a Lear" (Pa 6:4).

The not quite completed *Parisians* fails, however, to execute many aspects of its original conception, and it is not finally persuasive as another objective or dramatic celebration of "Varieties in Life." As a group, moreover, the last novels seem to challenge the assumption that the objective mode is the more mature (and possibly superior) one. Conversations in *Kenelm Chillingly*, for example, similarly define "the difference between dramatic poetry and lyrical" but imply a preference for the works of the lyric poet, who "does not put himself into other existences" (KC 6:17). The dramatic artist, evidently like Waife of *What Will He Do with It?*, "throws himself entirely out of his existence" and seems particularly and ominously to relish the "quite strange" existences of "very wicked men."

According to an essay of 1863, Bulwer had even begun to value Shakespeare himself less for the drama in which "no trace of himself is visible" than for "the many passages and sentences in which, without dramatic necessity, and not always with dramatic fitness and effect, the great psychologist utters his own cherished thoughts through the lips of his imaginary creations." A persona also maintains in another of the *Caxtoniana* essays (which really belong to this last period) that instead of passing from a lyric to a more dramatic phase, Shakespeare has perhaps learned to combine aspects of the two: "though the Drama is, of all compositions, that in which the author can least obtrude on us his personality, yet . . . of all dramatists Shakespeare the most frequently presents to us his own."[1] The notion, which Bulwer found especially applicable to *The Tempest*, is possibly open to dispute, but it helps at least to describe a final development in Bulwer's art. Apart from the social-political elements of *The Parisians*, his own last novels tend to emphasize the integral quality of an individual existence rather than the dramatic, Caxtonian vision of life fractional.

Bulwer's principal concern, in fact, may be again to isolate and protect from life fractional what a character in *The Parisians* calls the "genius that is inborn, a pervading something which distinguishes our very identity" (Pa 3:2). This "something"—compared in earlier periods to an inheritance or an imaginative dream of beauty that might ideally ennoble life here—is now chiefly the soul that will live hereafter. The historical and Caxton novels had, of course, envisioned some enduring hereafter too. But whereas they had represented it as the transmission of a vital principle through the endlessly spinning "Cycles of Infinite Change," Bulwer now refers the afterlife primarily to "some regions wholly remote from earth."[2] Quoting one of his favorite passages from Schiller again, he also allows Kenelm Chillingly to associate the "dream of a heaven" with "den heitern Regionen/ Wo die reinen Formen wohnen" (KC 6:13).[3] Awareness of the soul, therefore, tends no longer to reconcile the aspirant after immortality to his mortality. In its latest phase, Bulwer's idealism seems once more to alienate the idealist from the concerns of agora.

The alienation may derive not only from new intimations of immortality but also from revulsion against the modern civilization that had inspired Bulwer's popular, dramatic, and essentially comic art. In 1861 he had begun a more intensive study of what he sometimes called, with the capital letters, the "New Ideas," and to a large extent he designed the novels to discredit them. Since these terrifying new ideas appeared to be carrying the day now against the "ancient forms," he also rejected the Caxtonian assumption that the artist could do no better than surrender to life and celebrate the progressive triumph of some immanent and healthy vital principle. That principle began to manifest at least two distinctly threatening ramifications, which may conveniently be associated with Marxist and Darwinian interpretations of civilized history and the physical universe.

Communism began to make Bulwer aware of the apparent danger in his idea that men's instinct to sympathize and their "common sense of the common interest" should provide the continuing basis for civilized life and art. Sympathy could become, observes the essay on "The Sympathetic Temperament" in *Caxtoniana*, as easily a power for evil as for good. In the political arena, a perilous sort of sympathy seemed especially to predominate in revolutionary times. The chief attribute of Robespierre, for example, may have been "the impressionability of his nervous temperament [which] compelled him to sympathise." Like Bulwer's Edward IV and other successful politicians, "he identified himself with his country" and sympathized with whatever happened, however deplorably, to "become the spirit of the time." Paradoxically, then, Bulwer's persona in the essay views Robespierre as "a man whose sins against his kind are to be imputed to the liveliness of his sympathies."[4] And so in Britain as well—where events might already be tending toward democracy and worse—any political manifestation of a lively sympathy with the masses must arouse Bulwer's anxiety. Although politically inactive after his elevation to the peerage in 1866, he privately dreaded the consequences of Disraeli's Reform Bill of 1867 and of Gladstone's supposed secret negotiations with the first International.[5]

Horror of the underlying socialist tendencies of the times is particularly prominent in *The Parisians* of course. Much of the story concerns the establishment and growing power of an anti-imperialist journal called *Le Sens Commun*. As more and more factions come to believe that their interest converges in the attempts to bring down the Empire, Bulwer's plotting suggests the inevitable disintegration of all possibilities for orderly government. The communal principle, which Bulwer had once thought to lie at the basis of civilization, will triumph with a vengeance in the Commune and so appear to bring civilization to a halt.

Bulwer had hoped, to be sure, that he could indicate some providential purpose even in the Commune—as in the Reign of Terror with which *Zanoni* had culminated. Some aspect of a soul of civilization must survive, purified by the ordeal, to show that "even in epochs when reason is most misled and conscience most perverted, there runs visible, though fine and threadlike, the chain of destiny,

[173]

which has its roots in the throne of an All-wise and an All-good."
It was difficult, however, to find the evidence for such a chain when
a "whole society . . . unite[d] for the joyless hour . . . in the abju-
ration of soul and the denial of God" (Pa 12: The Last). Before
the spectacle Bulwer experienced a sort of failure of nerve that prevented him, despite constant efforts during the last twelve months
of his life, from finishing the novel. For reasons he would not fully
divulge to *Blackwood's*, he decided not to carry his story into the
period of the Commune, as originally planned. Even so, he could
not quite finish the novel. "The poetry of modern civilisation,"
which he had discovered when "searching for new regions in . . .
art" back in 1845, had now faded. Instead, he told *Blackwood's*,
The Parisians simply offered "general views of the restlessness that
pervades the modern social system" and little of the conviction of
the historical novels that civilization was always tending toward
some divine culmination.

While perceiving Marxist implications in man's basic, communal instinct, Bulwer also feared that his vital principle might turn
out to be identical with an equally unwelcome scientific law of life.
In his opinion Darwin and science generally were slowly discover-
ing the actuality of a cosmic first principle and at the same time
proving its materialist, anti-ideal quality. As the novels present
Bulwer's notion of a basic life force in ever more "scientific" terms,
they therefore express his growing uneasiness about it.

In the Darwinian context too, the vital first principle worked as
a form of sympathy. But before tracing some of its operations in
the novels, it should be noted that sympathy now manifested itself
in two seemingly opposed but, in Bulwer's thinking, related ways.
On the one hand it was a self-denying, negative capability (sympathy in the more usual sense of the term); on the other it was a
positively assertive volitional force. An analogy with the two poles
of magnetism may help to explain the opposing manifestations, for
Bulwer's physics tended to envisage all phenomena in terms of at-

tractions and repulsions.[6] Or it may be more accurate to say that the same cosmic energy operated on the metaphysical level as sympathy (uniting kindred spirits and ideas) and on the physical level as volition (prompting encounters among material forms).

Lucilla's father in *Godolphin*, to review some of Bulwer's treatments of these principles in fiction, had offered an idealistic interpretation of the cosmos. In good Romantic fashion he had identified sympathy not only with "the first principle . . . of all virtue," but also with animal magnetism and the physical first principle. So the force that held the supposedly material world together would enable men to evolve hereafter not in Darwinian terms but away from the planet altogether in the direction of the angels: "this sympathy, refined and extended, will make, I imagine, our powers—our very being, in a future state. Our sympathy being only, then, with what is immortal, we shall partake necessarily of that nature which attracts us; and the body no longer clogging the intenseness of our desires, we shall be able by a wish to transport ourselves wheresoever we please—from star to star, from glory to glory, charioted and winged by our wishes" (G 30).

Increasingly, though, Bulwer's many seekers after ultimate, first principles had tended, like Eugene Aram and like Adam Warner in *Barons*, to come up with less ideal explanations for the energy behind all elements of life. While not always using the term sympathy, they had implicitly defined a quasi-material version of sympathy in their talk of fluids and electricity. Mejnour, the representative of Science in *Zanoni*, for example, had "professed to find a link between all intellectual beings in the existence of a certain all-pervading and invisible fluid resembling electricity, yet distinct from the known operations of that mysterious agency—a fluid that connected thought to thought with the rapidity and precision of the modern telegraph, and the influence of this influence, according to Mejnour, extended to the remotest past—that is to say, whenever and wheresoever man had thought. Thus, if the doctrine were true, all human knowledge became attainable through a medium established between the brain of the individual inquirer and all the farthest and obscurest regions in the universe of ideas" (Z 4:5).

Such a theory threatens to subject the energies of "the universe of ideas" to the physics of will instead of encouraging man to surrender in sympathy to the metaphysical attraction of the ideas. Indeed Bulwer's short ghost story of 1857, "The Haunted and the Haunters," implies a whole cosmos in which a physical force called Will has asserted itself against divine Idea and become the first principle behind all events and phenomena. The protagonist encounters a strangely palpable and almost visible power, which turns out—in the briefer and more familiar revised version of the story—to be the volitional energy of some apparently long-dead man. This terrible man of the past has so trained and developed his will that it can operate as an active, malignant principle even beyond the bounds of his life-span. Whether Bulwer is here hinting at animal magnetism and Balzacian odic fluids or at something like Schopenhauer's impersonal, cosmic Will, the universe has in any case been reduced to a battleground of opposing wills. In the general struggle for survival, greater wills are forever magnetizing and appropriating to themselves the energies of lesser wills. The will that thereby concentrates and focuses its force most completely can magnetize Mejnour's "all-pervading and invisible fluid" and so impose itself throughout space and time.[7]

In *A Strange Story* Bulwer tries to give a more convincingly biological, if not yet really Darwinian form to his understanding of the first principle of existence. The protagonist Dr. Fenwick has written a treatise called "The Vital Principle; its Waste and Supply" and is working on a bolder "Inquiry into Organic Life." The vital principle is typified, however, in the character Margrave, whose "sympathy with Nature was . . . from the joyous sense of Nature's lavish vitality" (SS 61). Unfortunately, in Bulwer's estimation at least, sympathy with that vitality now has nothing whatever to do with any "universe of ideas." Since ideas threaten to raise lofty considerations that challenge the supreme value of the will to survive, Margrave's sympathy for life has even caused him to destroy the ideal element, the "soul," in himself. So he has perfected his frightening, amoral will and has survived as a beautiful specimen of animal vitality and the fittest of the fit well beyond the normal life-span of man.

The Coming Race—which Bulwer told Forster fictionalized "the Darwinian proposition that a coming race is destined to supplant our races"[8]—seeks to portray sympathy, volition, and vitality as still more purely organic and measurable quantities. The most important "organic peculiarity in the coming race" is its intensified "power of volition," which is related to an especially delicate "cerebral organisation." The brains of the new species, the narrator observes, have also become "by hereditary culture, much more ductile and more readily capable of acquiring knowledge than mine." Neurological developments too have endowed these individuals with the "sympathies" required for scientific research. While "their finer nervous organisation renders the female professors eminently keen," the entire race now possesses a prominent nerve in the hand that enables them to transmit volitional energy through a special wand.

Margrave too had possessed such a wand, and he had also sought out another tool—an elixir that may be Mejnour's "invisible fluid" made visible—to help in the business of survival.[9] In *The Coming Race* these and other more sophisticated technological tools have become the property of the whole community, and so this race has survived while others have become extinct. Here again, though, Bulwer carefully emphasizes that survival has resulted from a practical, biological superiority, in which the "universe of ideas" has played no part. Far from depending upon the lofty inspiration of their great abstract, theoretical thinkers, all the progress goes back to the "organic . . . power of volition," which enables them to achieve what "our mere science could not attain." Since all progress has resulted from the will to survive, Bulwer may have described, as Leo J. Henkin suggests, a more Lamarckian than Darwinian process.[10] Technology, in any case, is seen as a significant extension of a biological adaptation and practically a matter of biology and genetics itself: "Learn [the narrator is told] that the connection between the will and the agencies of that fluid which has been subjected to the control of the Vril-ya was never established by the first discoverers, never achieved by a single generation; it has gone on increasing, like other properties of race, in proportion as it has been uniformly transmitted from parent to child, so that at last, it has become an instinct; and an infant An of our race, wills to fly as intuitively and unconsciously as he wills to walk. He thus plies his invented or artificial wings with as much safety as a bird plies those with which it is born" (CR 20).

The scientific temperament, which above all other biological attributes enables the species to adapt and survive, unweaves the rainbow and reduces both the Idea and the imponderable Will to a wholly material, measurable, and controllable agency. In "the all-permeating fluid which [the coming race] denominate vril," Bulwer has therefore represented the ultimate physical version of his universal first principle. It combines in a single substance the properties of Dalibard's poison (in *Lucretia*) and Margrave's life-giving elixir: "It can destroy like the flash of lightning; yet, differently applied, it can replenish or invigorate life, . . . enabling the physical organisation to re-establish the due equilibrium of its natural powers, and thereby to cure itself" (CR 9).

Admittedly, an element of fantasy in the portrayal of vril leads one to wonder if Bulwer has really intended, after all, to convey a vision of scientific materialism. His conception of vril has thus been referred less often to the reputable theories of Victorian science than to pseudo-scientific notions like those of Balzac (especially in *Louis Lambert*), Hugo, and other French amateurs of the occult. Etymologically related to the Latin *virile*, vril has also seemed in the speculations of C. Nelson Stewart to owe something to the so-called Eliphas Lévi, who had come to London in 1854 with his theories about Astral Light. As R. L. Wolff has furthermore discovered, Bulwer actually witnessed some of Lévi's extraordinary occult demonstrations in 1861, when the latter visited him both in London and Knebworth while *A Strange Story* was appearing serially. Wolff nevertheless concludes, though, that vril does not derive simply from pseudo-scientific and occult traditions: "only a man extremely well-read in the sciences could have . . . gone on to make the connection between matter and energy." And Bulwer's correspondence with Forster on the subject of "the one great fluid pervading all nature" indicates that he was indeed most eager to suggest a genuinely scientific principle "cleared from mysticism or mesmerism."[11] His narrator therefore relates vril to such respectable phenomena as those of electricity and appeals to Faraday: "I should call it electricity, except that it comprehends . . . magnetism, galvanism, &c. . . . In vril they have arrived at the unity in natural energetic agencies, . . . which Faraday thus intimates under the more cautious term of correlation: 'I have long held an opinion,' says that illustrious experimentalist, 'almost amounting to a conviction, . . . that the various forms under which the forces of matter are made manifest have one common origin; or, in other words, are so directly related and mutually dependent, that they are convertible, as it were, into one another, and possess equivalents of power in their action'" (CR 7).

As several recent critics have noticed, vril operates throughout the novel in ways that strikingly anticipate nuclear energy. The harnessing of so potent a force has also given rise to a social and political structure that prefigures those of many more recent utopian satires.[12] For Bulwer the most salient feature of the society is that like the biological organization of its members and like the composition of its physical environment, a single principle underlies all its workings. The "compassion," which in the narrator's frequent term motivates all social behavior, obviously corresponds to the sympathetic and volitional energies associated with the physics of vril. Indeed the "compassion" that holds the civilization together is nearly identical with the vril that informs the cosmos, for in the language of this rational species the terms for "civilisation" and "civilised nations" are simply variants of the term "vril." The same physical laws thus regulate the sciences, politics, arts, and every other domain of the lives of the coming race—a development that the narrator's race "above ground" considers only theoretically possible:

The government of the tribe of Vril-ya I am treating of . . . was based upon a principle . . . that the object of all systems of philosophical thought tends to the attainment of unity, or the ascent through all intervening labyrinths to the simplicity of a single first cause or principle. . . . This singular community elected therefore a single supreme magistrate. . . . There being no apprehensions of war, there were no armies to maintain; being no government of force, there was no police to appoint and direct. What we call crime was utterly unknown to the Vril-ya. . . . Obedience to the rule adopted by the community has become as much an instinct as if it were implanted by nature. . . . Owing to the absence of competition, and the limit placed on population, it is difficult for a family to fall into distress; there are no hazardous speculations, no emulators striving for superior wealth and rank. . . . For all the members of the community considered themselves as brothers of one affectionate and united family. (CR 9)

Suggesting the triumph of the Caxtonian domestic ideal, the Marxist outcome has actually destroyed all ideals. "The materialising principle," to coin another Bulwerism, has destroyed ideals along with all other possible hostilities. Although each individual can thereby live in perfect domestic unity with his society and his physical environment, the notion of an individual identity has ceased to mean anything. An atmosphere of unpunctuated blandness has settled over the technological utopia. Since the Vril-ya avoid all controversy and anxiety and define their chief desire as "a life of serene tranquility," their literature and art lacks interest and definition.[13] Among many marvelous gadgets are those filling the air with soothing music and perfumes, while distinctions of day and night are obliterated and the climate remains perpetually

"equable, warm as . . . an Italian summer." This comfortable same-
ness begins to bore the narrator, and the uniform courtesy of his
highly urbane hosts comes even to appall him. Their compassion,
he realizes, is potentially deadly, for they must destroy whatever
threatens like himself to reinfect their stable welfare state with
egoism, dissatisfaction, biological inferiority—or idealism.

For Bulwer as for George Meredith, then, Darwinian and socialist theories reinforced each other: the physical survival of the
race demanded civilized altruism. Egoisms must subject themselves to the general will—to a wider, sympathetic consciousness of
the common interest and the cosmic facts. While Meredith continued to enjoy the unfolding process, however, Bulwer foresaw
in horror that it was leading not to the dialectical triumph of the
beautifully humane Comic Spirit but to a soul-destroying materialism. Dreading lest Darwin and Marx should indeed have history
on their side, he ceased to affirm the fundamental value of their
supposed first principles—the will to live and the instinct to sympathize with the community.

Begun in 1869, *Kenelm Chillingly* is Bulwer's most sustained
and poignant expression of disaffection from the life force. When
he comes of age, Kenelm reviews the pessimistic implications of the
new Darwinian and socialist ideas in his strange speech to his
father's tenants and concludes: "when I drink to your good healths,
you must feel that in reality I wish you an early deliverance from
the ills to which flesh is exposed" (KC 1:12). Men should not wish
to live—this young Hamlet also anticipates Hardy's Jude Fawley—
because the cosmic first principle has become a Nemesis, hostile to
the welfare of the present race: "We are living in an age in which
the process of unsettlement is going blindly at work, as if impelled
by a Nemesis as blind as itself. New ideas come beating in surf and
surge against those which former reasoners had considered as fixed
banks and breakwaters; and the new ideas are so mutable, so
fickle, that those which were considered novel ten years ago are
deemed obsolete to-day, and the new ones of to-day will in their

turn be obsolete to-morrow. And in a sort of fatalism, you see statesmen yielding way to these successive mockeries of experiment" (KC 4:9).

The soliloquies and episodes of Kenelm's own career as "dispassionate . . . looker-on" serve chiefly to expose as "shams" the various "motives" which constitute the alluring disguises of the treacherous Nemesis. "I have been doing my best to acquire a motive power," he remarks about halfway through the story, "and I have not succeeded. I see nothing that I care to strive for, nothing that I care to gain. The very times in which we live are to me as to Hamlet,— out of joint; and I am not born like Hamlet to set them right" (KC 4:2).

The term "motive power," suggesting the individual's sense of a first principle in himself, refers to an essay of that name "by a living author"—in fact, one of the *Caxtoniana* pieces. The essay also tells the story of a man without volition. Sir Percival Tracey possesses all the talents requisite for great literary or political accomplishments except the one most needful to any human achievement—"concentration of purpose," "concentration of motive," "energy concentered on one definite point, and disciplined to strain toward it by patient habit." He lacks, that is, precisely the power the Vril-ya possess to such an intense degree. Although the narrator wishes to condemn him for his lassitude, the disturbing point of the story is that Sir Percival may be right. The harried narrator, an active Member of Parliament, begins to recognize some of the absurdity of his own existence and hastily leaves the country seat of his friend: "I . . . have never visited the Castle of Indolence since those golden days. In truth I resisted a frequent and a haunting desire to do so. I felt that a second and a longer sojourn in that serene but relaxing atmosphere might unnerve me for the work which I had imposed on myself, and sought to persuade my tempted conscience was an inexorable duty."[14] So too does Kenelm Chillingly, old before his time, see through such duties, and "where honour can only be saved by flight," he seems to echo the Scholar Gypsy in his wish to "run away from the age" in quest of the *heitern Regionen* (KC 4:9).

To Bulwer the problem seemed especially acute not only because a man was trapped in the present age but also because he could no longer even appeal in his art to the sympathies of endless future ages. The artist was thus losing one of the main driving motives of his creativity. Bulwer had wanted to embody in his art "his grandest human bequest, his memory and his name" and to convey this bequest to the "Reader . . . in whom youth is renewed through all cycles."[15] As the founder of a spiritual Caxton family, he had hoped to gain an immortality similar to that which the "great soul of England" would achieve through its colonial offspring. In this vein, then, he had written in 1860 to the man he had once appointed Governor of Queensland and had used a metaphor that would soon recur to express a changed attitude: "It is indeed a grand thing to have been the Œkist, the founder of the social state of so mighty a segment of the globe as Queensland, and is, perhaps, more sure of fame a thousand years hence than anything that we can do in the old world. It is carving your name on the rind of a young tree, to be found with large letters as the trunk expands."[16]

At least partly as a result of the growing impact of *The Origin of Species*, however, Bulwer began by 1862 to question the desirability of carving one's name on anything. Sir Percival takes some guests in the *Caxtoniana* essay to a curious cave where they find on the walls the names of visitors of an earlier generation. The instinct behind such carving is the one "which makes genius desire to write its name on the 'flammantia mœnia mundi,'" and the narrator adds his name to those already on the wall. But Sir Percival refuses to carve his: "I have no motive strong enough to induce me to take the trouble." Men of mature intelligence outlive, as the essay on "Posthumous Reputation" emphasizes too, the desire characteristic of youth for an immortality of fame: "And if, on the other side of the grave, we allow ourselves to suppose that a departed spirit could be made aware of the renown which it has left on this—

could learn that, centuries or cycles after it had quitted the poor painful little school, the name it had carved on its old worm-eaten desk was still visible, and pointed out to new-comers by the head boys with respect—we can scarcely conceive that this long-departed spirit would feel any very sensible joy."[17] Indeed if the terrible coming race were then supplanting the human schoolboys, the spirit must shudder to have his memory and his name pass into such custody.

The existence of the last novels nevertheless proves that some impulse continued to move Bulwer, if not his Sir Percival, to artistic creation. When the intense will to survive in some form through the cycles of history and the intense desire for the sympathy of the everlasting Reader had supposedly abated, he had become conscious of a higher motive. This motive referred, as the passage just quoted suggests, to an immortality "on the other side of the grave" —in a realm that existed independently of the physical laws regulating survival and progress here. While social and natural scientists were dangerously threatening the "universe of ideas," they had still not succeeded, so far as the artist was concerned, in their efforts to materialize the immortal soul: "science," according to Kenelm, "turns all that is already gifted with soul into matter," but perhaps it was still possible for "Art [to gift] with soul all matter that it contemplates" (KC 1:14).

Because of the growing split between them, science and art (or science and "culture," which Kenelm observes is "the word in fashion nowadays") could not argue the issue on the same grounds. In turning away from the evidences of science and back to the truths of art, Bulwer nonetheless tried to give some degree of empirical validity to the latter. He discerned in literature, for example, an objective principle of authority; for him as for Arnold the great works of the ages testified unanimously to the same timeless and even heroic truth about man. The testimony to man's soul constituted indeed the "chief quality" of great literature and was the reason for its endurance. Clearly, then, the modern artist too should remain faithful to this principle of permanence, the true "popular element," and should not be found "pandering to popular codes" and fads.[18] Art must continue to reassure mankind that the soul survived and, in the words of a discursive passage in *The Parisians*, reveal to us all "that which was already within us, . . . what in our souls was latent" (Pa 4:1).

As they try in despite of the "New Ideas" to prove the latent soul, Bulwer's last novels offer chiefly "the heat of inward evidence." Beyond its scientific, political, aesthetic, and philosophical implications, the problem becomes a psychological one, and each of the novels—even *The Coming Race*—is in fundamental respects another of Bulwer's "metaphysical" allegories. The soul that the protagonists must discover is, in the definition of the essay on "Posthumous Reputation," "the personal integral Ego, conscious of identity" which will "survive and [be] borne to a higher state of development." Suggesting a "first principle" of identity that emerges as the ideal counterpart to vril, the soul must remain more an intuited than visible presence on earth. Although a woman naturally symbolizes the soul in each novel, Bulwer seems generally unwilling to permit the male protagonist to live through this life in actual unity with his ideal counterpart. Each protagonist appears to define his most basic identity then, not in terms of the soul he now possesses but in connection with his intimations of the soul he will possess in the "higher state of development."

Since the protagonists must recognize the soul as an unearthly quality, their quests involve the stripping away of all the earthly portions of the personality. This negative process seems to define at least three such nonessential or earthly levels of identity—the physical animal, the civilized member of a family and a society, and the private intelligence. I would like to discuss the presentation of these three negative aspects of identity in *A Strange Story*, *The Parisians*, and *Kenelm Chillingly* before considering the more positive intimations of the soul in all four novels.

Even more clearly than the other late novels, *A Strange Story* was designed, as Bulwer's letters to Dickens indicate and as Professor Fradin emphasizes, to be "read as an allegory of conflicting forces within the human personality."[19] Dr. Allen Fenwick, whose autobiography this purports to be, represents the private intelligence, and he confesses at the outset that "intellectual pride" has been "the main characteristic of my moral organisation." Throughout the period of his story he is also working on a great scientific and philosophical treatise that identifies the human animal as primarily a creature of intellect: "I defined the properties and meted the limits of natural laws, which I would not admit that a Deity himself could alter. I clamped and soldered dogma to dogma in the links of my tinkered logic, till out from my page, to my own complacent eye, grew Intellectual Man, as the pure formation of his material senses; mind, or what is called soul, born from and nurtured by them alone; through them to act, and to perish with the machine they moved" (SS 20). The strange events of his life force him to recognize, however, the unsuspected strength and somewhat horrifying implications of man's physical and social natures too. As these threaten to overwhelm him with a vision of absurdity, he will eventually intuit the need for an immortal soul to save him from the materialism that would "resolve my own living identity, the one conscious indivisible ME, into a bundle of memories derived from the senses which had *bubbled* and duped my experience" (SS 72).

From the perspective of the unintellectual animal, the chief purposes of life are to gratify instincts and, regardless of the lives of others, to postpone one's own death. The beautifully formed, radiantly healthy, and irresistibly joyous Margrave appears as a stranger in the town of L—— to enforce this truth among its "too tamed and civilised" inhabitants. As Fradin has suggested, he embodies not only man's obvious animal instincts but also the mysterious and anarchic energies of the unconscious. One evening at a reception on the fashionable Hill, for example, his singing of a wild song to his own tumultuous piano accompaniment seems to release a hitherto unsuspected demonic energy in all his auditors:

All were spell-bound; even Mrs. Poyntz paused from her knitting, as the Fates paused from their web at the lyre of Orpheus. To this breathless delight, however, soon succeeded a general desire for movement. To my amazement, I beheld these formal matrons and sober fathers of families forming themselves into a dance, turbulent as a children's ball at Christmas. And when, suddenly desisting from his music, Margrave started up, caught the skeleton hand of lean Miss Brabazon, and whirled her into the centre of the dance, I could have fancied myself at a witch's sabbat. My eye turned in scandalized alarm towards Mrs. Poyntz. . . . For the first time, no doubt, in her life, she was overcome, deposed, dethroned. (SS 26)

Against Fenwick, in particular, Margrave will bring to bear the full force of the demonic energy that helps him in the struggle for survival. Through occult phenomena associated with his animal magnetism, he gets Fenwick imprisoned on a charge of murder—a crime that Margrave had actually forced someone else to commit. Even worse is the dominion that he gains (in the tradition of Bulwer's demon-shadows) over the pure Lilian, Fenwick's fiancée and the type of the anima. Although Margrave only wishes to exploit her spirituality in the occult researches that will extend his physical life, the allegory emphasizes that the body is trying to destroy the soul and uses sexual imagery to imply the destruction. Lilian has a warning vision of "a vast serpent" (the nightmare as a whole strongly resembles that in *Falkland*); then she finds she cannot resist when Margrave extends his strange wand towards her. In a trance she leaves home and journeys for three days to his hiding place, and that is the end of Lilian so far as the scandalized town is concerned.

Whereas Margrave represents the unrestrained animal, Mrs. Poyntz, the social "Queen of the Hill" and type of civilization, indicates how far man has advanced beyond the state of nature. Recognizing higher satisfactions than those of the animal and higher energies than those of demonism, man has evolved "*the something*, without which men never could found cities, frame laws, bind together, beautify, exalt the elements of this world" (SS 32). Mrs. Poyntz suggests especially the binding impulse behind civilization. She is obsessively "at work on the everlasting knitting, her firm fingers linking mesh into mesh," whenever Fenwick sees her, and her power—"I am the WORLD!" she once sternly cries—depends upon her obedience to law: "I cannot destroy the social laws that I myself have set." Fenwick is particularly horrified to discover the degree to which her laws have bound him, for it appears in retrospect that she has arranged nearly all the important events of his career in L——: "And I," he reflects, "was my self-conceit less egregious and less readily duped than that of yon gilded popinjay's [he refers to the dandy she has captured for her son-in-law]! How skilfully this woman had knitted me into her work with the noiseless turn of her white hands! and yet, forsooth, I must vaunt the superior scope of my intellect, and plumb all the fountains of Nature—I, who could not fathom the little pool of this female schemer's mind!" (SS 57).

The power of this fascinatingly complex and rather convincing woman has also depended, as Fradin notices, upon her civilized repression of sexual instincts. Her supposedly "familiar yet harmless intimacy" with Fenwick becomes an increasingly ambiguous relationship, until the interesting scene in which she nearly recognizes and confesses the reasons for her jealousy of Lilian. But her sexuality remains unconfessed, and as the type of repression, she poses a threat to Lilian—and Fenwick's soul—that is as grave as that posed by the demonism of Margrave. Partly from jealousy and partly in obedience to her code, she overrules Fenwick's pleas and upholds Lilian's banishment from society. Lilian accordingly goes mad, and Fenwick cannot consummate his marriage to her. Yet Mrs. Poyntz never repents. While preparing to move with her daughter and son-in-law to London, she insists that only by repressing the animal and cultivating the civilized self can an individual learn to tolerate the absurdity of life: "It will amuse me [she tells Fenwick] to learn if I can maintain in a capital the authority I have won in a country town; if not, I can but return to my small principality. Wherever I live I must sway, not serve. If I succeed —as I ought, for in Jane's beauty and Ashleigh's fortune I have materials for the woof of ambition, wanting which here, I fall asleep over my knitting—if I succeed, there will be enough to occupy the rest of my life. . . . Allen Fenwick, do as I do. Be world with the world, and it will only be in moments of spleen and chagrin that you will sigh to think that the heart may be void when the mind is full. Confess you envy me while you listen" (SS 67).

Rejecting her logic, Fenwick attempts to fill the void by returning to his treatise—to the various chapters and arguments of which the story has frequently referred. As it has "soldered dogma to dogma," the treatise has become to him, the "Intellectual Man," even more than the "meshes" of her knitting have been to the "Queen of the Hill": "the work was I myself!" he once exclaims: "here, at least, was a monument of my rational, thoughtful ME— of my individualised identity in multiform creation. And my mind, in the noon of its force, would shed its light on the earth when my form was resolved to its elements" (SS 74).

Whereas he had formerly been the prisoner and dupe of Margrave and Mrs. Poyntz, he has thus become the dupe of his treatise. In accord with the insights of Bulwer's essay, he comes to realize the meaninglessness of posthumous reputation. All that he values belongs to this material existence, and when he meets up with Margrave again many years later, he is shattered to discover how perfectly Margrave understands and approves the philosophy fundamental to this treatise: "But why such a waste of argument," asks Margrave, "to prove a fact so simple? In man, as in brute, life once lost is lost forever; and that is why life is so precious to man" (SS 76). That simple fact sums up the truth for the physical, social, and intellectual aspects of the personality. The man who believes one of those selves constitutes his essence is probably doomed, then, to a sort of despair in the face of death. Fenwick admits that he has simply built a tomb for himself, like the great mausoleum of the murdered Sir Philip Derval, which has also figured as an important motif in the story: "on the theorems of Condillac I had built up a system of thought designed to immure the swathed form of material philosophy from all rays and sounds of a world not material, as the walls of some blind mausoleum shut out, from the mummy within, the whisper of winds, and the gleaming of stars" (SS 72). Along with Margrave and Mrs. Poyntz he has contributed to the process that kills man's soul.

While a much more diffuse work than *A Strange Story*, *The Parisians* also develops a coherent strain of sepulchral imagery to indicate a desperate longing for life amidst the awareness of a bondage to materialism and death. The theme is stated in the opening pages when Alain de Rochebriant, a young, poor, and fiercely legitimist Breton noble arrives for the first time in Paris. Bringing with him a mournful and exaggerated loyalty to his dead ancestors, he stays "in that museum of mummies, the Faubourg St. Germain." From this vantage point, the remainder of imperial Paris appears deceptively filled with a vitality that can never be his: "It is what is new in Paris that strikes and enthrals me. Here I see the life of France, and I belong to her tombs!" (Pa 1:1).

The convulsions of 1870 and 1871 will soon imply an even more striking allegory of death and the longing for rebirth: "A new social system is struggling from the dissolving elements of the old one," claims Rameau, an atheist and communist, "as, in the fables of priestcraft, the soul frees itself from the body which has become ripe for the grave" (Pa 11:15). Yet the soul of a new society never quite frees itself. The sentiment of a universal, but unfulfilled yearning for life and freedom remains because, as Vane explains in response to some feminist notions, the social discontent derives from a still unsolved problem confronting the individual psyche:

Do you suppose that, in this whirl and dance of the atoms which compose the rolling ball of the civilised world, it is only women that are made restless and uneasy? Do you not see amid the masses congregated in the wealthiest cities of the world, writhings and struggles against the received order of things? In this sentiment of discontent there is a certain truthfulness, because it is an element of human nature; and how best to deal with it is a problem yet unsolved. . . . Ascend from the working classes to all others in which civilised culture prevails, and you will find that same restless feeling—the fluttering of untried wings against the bars between wider space and their longings. (Pa 2:7)

The bars that restrain longing individuals and classes seem to a large extent those of the cash nexus. Under the Empire the Bourse has become "the heart of Paris." Like the "science" that turns "soul" into "matter," capitalism has created a market for the voices of opera singers and is busily transforming everything else it touches into gold. The great capitalist "knocks off a million as a poet does an ode,—by the force of inspiration"—and has practically replaced the artist and intellectual: "Philosophy, Eloquence, audacious Romance: all Literature now is swallowed up in the sublime epic of *Agiotage*, and," adds Vane of one of the most brilliant financiers, "Duplessis is the poet of the Empire" (Pa 1:4). Duplessis even buys up the supposedly incorruptible Alain and gives the unwitting young marquis, ancestral tombs and all, to his daughter. (The reader ironically welcomes this development because it prevents the not terribly bright Alain from needlessly ruining himself in his excessive devotion to the past.)

A Strange Story had focused the meanings of the enveloping materialism primarily through the increasingly sensitive consciousness of Fenwick, as he had struggeld to relate his experiences to his scientific epic. The awareness of the bars and the longing to fly beyond them is now spread throughout society, but it belongs in particular to several individuals who possess a more or less artistic temperament. Containing long extracts from the correspondence and the journals of Isaura Cicogna, the principal artist, the novel is even to a large extent a *Künstlerroman*. Isaura and the two men in her life imply the three levels of the now specifically artistic personality, which aspires to a worthier epic vision than that of *Agiotage*.

On the lowest level (and so corresponding to Margrave) the narcissistic poet Gustave Rameau edits the anti-imperialist periodical *Le Sens Commun* and tries with his shrill poetry to rouse the rabble to break their "bonds." Gaining his "inspiration" from absinthe, he appears in his life and his poetry to equate freedom with undisciplined sensuality and self-indulgence. On the middle level, the English statesman Graham Vane, whose oratory supposedly makes him a great artist, attempts to communicate a more conservative and civilized vision of the disciplined freedom inherited from the past. Like Mrs. Poyntz, however, he unfortunately upholds traditional prejudices as well as freedoms, and, most disastrously for the heroine, "he held in fastidious regard the proprieties and conventions by which the dignity of woman is fenced around." The sublime Isaura, finally, represents the highest level of the artistic personality. A young Italian opera singer, she elicits the noblest responses of all in the breasts of her auditors. As the liberated, modern, intellectual woman, she also attempts through a novel called *The Artist's Daughter*—in progress, like Fenwick's treatise, for most of the story—to articulate some high intuition of freedom. But although the imagery of the story constantly associates her with winged creatures (her surname, of course, means stork), she remains aware that she lives still in a "cage" or in the "chrysalis."

None of these politically oriented artists can fulfill himself or enable his audience to escape the Arnoldian "brazen prison." Rameau ends as the pitiful slave of his habits and must recognize too that certain political interests have bought and duped him. Vane, who is in fact a new and less successful version of Bulwer's Guy Darrell, has embraced too uncritically a concept of duty that obliges him to carry out an absurd, inherited "mission." So he finds himself figuratively entombed—bound by "the swathes and trammels which had kept him galled and miserable with the sense of captivity, and

from which some wizard spell that took strength from his own superstition had forbidden to struggle" (Pa 10:7).

Isaura becomes a prisoner in an even more awful sense. She had
at first believed with her mentor, Madame de Grantmesnil, that her
divine "mission" (ever a prominent word in the novel) had required
her to obey only the laws of her art—"and in being faithful to your
art, be true to yourself." Like so many of Bulwer's artists, however,
she comes to suspect that only through a fuller engagement in the
human condition can she be truly free. It also appears heartbreak-
ingly impossible, in Bulwer's portrayal of the social situation, for
the nobly aspiring woman to pass unscarred and uncompromised
through life unless she has a husband beside her. When Vane cannot in his conventionality marry an opera singer or an authoress,
Isaura awakens one day to see herself inexorably "bound" to Rameau, whom she had been trying to redeem. Her "peculiar star"
merges "into the cluster of all these commonplace girls," and like
Eliot's Dorothea Brooke she must acknowledge that the acceptance
of her "duty" has destroyed her value in the world. Her journal
wonderingly contrasts the theory behind her action with its fatal
results:

Moral aspiration has the same goal as the artistic,—the attainment to
the calm delight wherein the pain of effort disappears in the content
of achievement. Thus in life, as in art, it is through discipline that we
arrive at freedom, and duty only completes itself when all motives, all
actions, are attuned into one harmonious whole, and it is not striven for
as duty, but enjoyed as happiness. . . .
   And yet now, in the duty that life imposes on me, to fulfil which I
strain every power vouchsafed to my nature, and seek to crush down
every impulse that rebels, where is the promised calm, where any approach to the content of achievement? Contemplating the way before
me, the Beautiful even of Art has vanished. I see but cloud and desert.
(Pa 11:16)

Her wings still beating against the bars, Isaura fails to find in
herself the principle that would heal the self-division and reconcile
her to the bondage. At the same time the Prussian siege is imprison-

ing Paris, and the politicians are vainly arguing about the theories that will enable the whole society to heal and revitalize itself. Although the siege will end and France will gain a new constitution, however, the individual may never escape the awareness of restlessness and fragmentation amidst "the whirl and dance of the atoms."

Throughout most of *Kenelm Chillingly* too, the underlying principle of identity eludes the wandering protagonist. The problem, which had been associated in the earlier novels with the literary efforts of the scientist and the socially engaged artist, now becomes the dilemma of a youth who desires only psychological health. Kenelm aspires neither to create works that will live after him nor to emerge as a great benefactor of the race. Holding instead to the moral precept that "a good man does good by living," his bondage results from an inability like Isaura's to fulfill the primary precondition of that precept: "But, for that, he must be a harmony and not a discord" (KC 3:20). The impression of a radical discordance among the elements of his personality provides indeed the chief impetus for his escapist career.

Even more obviously than the other protagonists, Kenelm follows the negative path and in the search for truth denies all aspects of himself and his world that can be denied. At the age of eight he asks, as the young Bulwer had actually done, "Mamma, are you not sometimes overpowered by the sense of your own identity?" He is already at war with the overpowering identity that he suspects his family and their world of foisting upon him. They educate him according to a "system" carefully designed to fill him "brimful of new ideas" and so to give him an advantage in the struggle for preeminence among his contemporaries. Yet he loses, as I have already indicated, the will to live in the contemporary world, for the notions taught "in the Academe of New Ideas" keep striking him as false and hollow. His observation of some spiders, for instance, suggests the absurdity of the proletarian International! In order to discover a more valuable and convincing sanction than those presently offered him, he decides upon achieving his majority to drop out of his world and to flee the oppressive Chillingly selfhood. Above all, perhaps, he wishes to escape the boredom of his existence: " 'It is,' soliloquised Kenelm Chillingly, 'a strange yearning I have long felt, to get out of myself—to get, as it were, into another man's skin—and have a little variety of thought and emotion. One's self is always the same self; and that is why I yawn so often. . . . Myself is Kenelm Chillingly, son and heir to a rich gentleman. But a fellow with a knapsack on his back, sleeping at wayside inns, is not at all like Kenelm Chillingly—especially if he is very short of money, and may come to want a dinner. Perhaps that sort of fellow may take a livelier view of things. . . . Courage, Myself,—you and I can but try' " (KC 1:15).

From this point until the most decisive episode of his career, he wanders in and out of three different worlds seeking vaguely the right "sort of fellow." While again suggesting the three levels of the personality as in the earlier works, these worlds also imply the past, present, and future in the idealist's version of an evolutionary process that leads man toward the angels. Kenelm's favorite guidebook is, in fact, a defense of celibacy called "Approach to the Angels," and his progress in self-denial recalls the Tennysonian process of "mov[ing] upward, working out the beast."

Setting forth "like Amadis of Gaul, like Don Quixote" and many others, he enters first the realm of the rural peasantry, and here all his principal adventures have sexual overtones. He finds it easy enough to resist the temptation of the "youth" who turns out to be a girl in disguise, for he has long known that every woman is "a sham,—a sham from the moment she is told to be pretty-behaved, conceal her sentiments, and look fibs when she does not speak them." But when he observes how the sexual instinct has aroused the not-so-latent demonism of the jealous Tom Bowles, he concludes that "man must never relax his flight from the women." After an heroic fight with Tom, he manages to exorcise the "demon" and the "perilous stuff"—an exorcism that applies symbolically to the old man in himself as well as in Tom: "You see, Tom, we have both of us something in our old selves which we must work off. You will work off your something by repose, and I must work off mine, if I can, by moving about. So I am on my travels. May we both have new selves better than the old selves when we again shake hands" (KC 3:13).

Recalling the repressive, civilized worlds of Mrs. Poyntz and Graham Vane, the second realm is that of the seemingly inescapable Chillingly identity. Even during his adventures among the peasantry, the shrewd farmers had tended to pierce his incognito and to recognize the gentleman beneath the farm hand. His actions, too, had always been those of the bringer of civilization: Squire Travers had specifically thanked him after the fight with Tom "for having done a public service in putting down the brute force which has long tyrannised over the neighbourhood." Yet while he cannot help but act as a civilizing influence wherever he goes, each return to the hypocritical world of gentlemen further depresses him with its enslaving laws: "Everywhere, in this hateful, civilised life, one runs one's head against a system. A system, Mr. Travers, is man's servile imitation of the blind tyranny of what in our ignorance we call 'Natural Laws,'—a mechanical something through which the world is ruled by the cruelty of General Principles, to the utter disregard of individual welfare" (KC 3:4). So he resists the cruel, artificial laws that would force him into a proper marriage with Cecilia Travers or into politics with his cousin Chillingly Gordon, in whom "the Chillingly race culminates . . . and becomes Chillinglyest." Unable to share any of the "motives" of the "real" world—"from the normal pursuits of whose inhabitants he felt so estranged"—he even decides that all of this "real life is a phantasmal sham." He trusts that the false "class of gentlemen was about to be superseded by some finer development of species," while he, in any case, will exorcise this degrading phantom as he had exorcised the other old man.

He appears to enter the third realm whenever in the woods or by the streams he encounters the Wandering Minstrel—one of the

most obviously allegorical figures in the story. As a "lawless vaga-
bond" who had received his education in Germany, the minstrel
obeys only the idealising principle in his poetry and his drawings.
His ideal images, like that of "the child on the sunlit hill, high
above the abodes of men, tossing her flower-ball heavenward," also
come to haunt Kenelm. Yet the imagination, which Kenelm appears
to associate with the disturbing amorality of "the Æsthetics of
Goethe," cannot actually save a man any more than could indulgence of the "old self" or the "Chillinglyest" self. Instead of finally
helping to free Kenelm, the minstrel seems to enable him to recognize the cosmic extent of his discordance and alienation from himself. "I set out on my travels," Kenelm confesses to him, "to escape
from shams, and begin to discover that I am a sham *par excellence*."
While the minstrel composes a melancholy lyric on the theme of his
boundless discontent, Kenelm applies to himself, in his characteristically satiric vein, "a horrible, phantasmal crotchet of Goethe's,
that originally we were all monads":

My monad, meant for another region in space, has been dropped into
this, where it can never be at home, never amalgamate with other
monads, nor comprehend why they are in such a perpetual fidget. I
declare I know no more why the minds of human beings should be so
restlessly agitated about things which, as most of them own, give more
pain than pleasure, than I understand why that swarm of gnats, which
has such a very short time to live, does not give itself a moment's repose.
. . . And yet, perhaps, in another planet my monad would have frisked
and jumped and danced and seesawed with congenial monads as con-
tentedly and as sillily as do the monads of men and gnats in this alien
Vale of Tears. (KC 2:16)

No matter how far he progresses in self-denial or in exorcism of
phantasmal shams, he can never, in the cosmic perspective, approach much closer to the angels. Indeed he must ironically question the value of the whole endeavor when he journeys to Oxford
to call on the Reverend Decimus Roach, the author of "Approach
to the Angels." Like the pilgrimage of Jude Fawley to the hymn-

writer, the experience ends in disillusionment, for Roach has since conveniently repudiated the arguments of his treatise. Kenelm cannot reconcile himself so easily as Roach, however, to the limitations and shams of reality. He had once told Cecilia that true happiness could issue only from "the lasting harmony between our inclinations and our objects; and without that harmony we are a discord to ourselves, we are incompletions, we are failures." He remains himself a failure, alienated from "that something afar! that something afar! never to be reached on this earth—never, never!" (KC 3:19).

Kenelm and the other protagonists do, however, discover some underlying principle of identity. At first the development may appear as something of a *deus ex machina* in the structure of each novel. Arbitrarily, stubbornly, and even perversely disregarding the logic of his own psychological and other evidence, Bulwer insists at last upon the existence of the soul. And yet, as I have indicated, the heat of inward evidence does provide a certain justification for the dénouement of each story. A summary of Bulwer's discovery and interpretation of this evidence in his own life may help clarify the logic of his protagonists' development and suggest in conclusion the symbolist overtones of these anti-materialist novels.

To take first his seemingly perverse side, Bulwer once more set his affections on the *heitern Regionen* safely above the ravages of Marx and Darwin and refused to give the "New Ideas" in religion even a chance. It was "best not to puzzle one's head" about the intricacies of theological disputes: "Christ says nothing about the cultivation of the intellect—Christ coming to announce a future world, and not to expatiate upon all that can civilise this one." He therefore entreated his son in their correspondence upon religious matters in 1861 and 1862 just "to hold fast to the conviction of soul and hereafter, and the connecting link between[,] which is found in habitual prayer." Regardless of the evidences of the new Biblical scholarship, he had decided that man simply needed such convictions to live: "Browning's Bishop is right in his way. But what he says as a cynic I say as a gentleman and an artist. I have not read the works you name about St. Paul, nor wish to do so. Scriptural criticisms I avoid on system. I have not read Strauss and probably never shall, nor 'Essays and Reviews,' &c."[20]

While avoiding modern scriptural criticism, however, he was studying "an immense variety of physiological and metaphysical works" of the past (he mentions Anaxagoras, St. Augustine, Erigena, and Descartes) in order to find "philosophical proof of soul and another life." His favorite proof, as he outlines it in letters and in discursive passages of *A Strange Story* and *The Coming Race*, seems a sort of disguised reaffirmation of the discredited argument from innate ideas. Bulwer admits with Locke and Condillac that ideas of "Deity, Soul, Hereafter" are not necessarily innate, but he finds it fascinating that man's *tabula rasa* possesses an innate capacity to form such abstract ideas. Alone among the species man can even form ideas that weaken the will to survive here. The fact of such a capacity implies the necessity for an afterlife, because "truthful" nature uniformly reveals that "for each desire"—including those frustrated by circumstances—"a counterpart object" at least exists. Referring to the Kantian term "receptivity" and to Sir William Hamilton's "passive power," he concludes that in man's "*inherent capacity* to receive ideas" of the soul and hereafter "lies the certain proof of soul!"[21] (On the basis of the uniformity of natural laws, Bulwer has paradoxically, if not perversely, proved man's exemption from one of the most universal of natural laws. The argument, in any case, again recalls Browning's "imperfection means perfection hid," which Arnold's Empedocles seems to challenge so bitterly: "Fools! That in man's brief term / He cannot all things view, / Affords no ground to affirm / That there are gods who do; / Nor does being weary prove that he has where to rest.")

But whatever the possible philosophical deficiencies, Bulwer's "proof" implies an interesting definition of the soul and explains why the soul necessarily eludes detection in any search for the positive aspects of the human personality. Always female of course, the inherent soul is a negative capacity—an emptiness that has resulted from the absence of a corresponding fulness. The apparent void may thus be described as the potentiality for fulness, and Bulwer's metaphors very frequently identify the soul during its earthly career as a potentiality. What is only potential here seems, moreover, to refer to what already exists as an actuality within the dimensions of some radically different universe. Like anti-matter and matter, the potential soul of this life and the actual soul of the hereafter somehow define each other.

To some extent Bulwer's metaphors for the soul and the interpretation he places upon Kant's "receptivity" remind one of Paterian attitudes. For Pater too would come to reject the conception of identity associated with the myth of earthly life as a vale of active soul-making. Not allowing any of his experiences permanently to affect or make him, Marius the Epicurean thus maintains "the tablet of the mind white and smooth" and defines himself in terms of his blankness or his eternally virgin potentiality. This carefully guarded negative capacity will permit him to receive the "beatific vision"—if it should ever come—and to the end "a kind of candid discontent" supplies him with what Bulwer would term his "motive power": "the unclouded and receptive soul quitting the world finally, with the same fresh wonder with which it had entered the world still unimpaired, and going on its blind way at last with the consciousness of some profound enigma in things, as but a pledge of something further to come." Such pledges of the "something further to come" are perhaps less reassuring to Pater, however, than they are to Bulwer (and to Browning). And the extreme empiricism of Pater prevents him from abandoning, as Bulwer does entirely, one of the Goethean-Carlylean precepts that is so basic to nineteenth-century representations of *Bildung*: "*America is here and now*," Marius has been given to understand; at every given moment, the realm of fulfillment must be "*here or nowhere*."[22]

Denying the value of the empirical here and now, Bulwer carries his platonic faith in the immortality of the soul to the extreme of seeming to overlook the orthodox Christian doctrine of the resurrection of the body. Indeed he prizes all that makes him dissatisfied with the body—not in order to prepare like Marius for new sensations but to remind himself of the utter inadequacy of all physical being. He rejoices in his world-weariness, his discordance, and his conviction of a fundamental "incongruity": "The sublime discontent of earth," according to Haroun of Aleppo in *A Strange Story*, "is the peculiar attribute of soul" (SS 39).[23] The discontent is sublime, again, because it implies the possibility for contentment elsewhere, and Bulwer can thus redefine the negative "attribute of soul" in a more hopeful terms as "the impulse to pray" to heaven. Now the most important and undeniably innate of human instincts, the impulse to pray has supplanted for him the will to survive.

At this stage in Bulwer's thinking, the "capacity of prayer" also seems to have replaced the Imagination as the most godlike of human powers and the agency whereby man perceives truth. Treating prayer as another negative capacity, Bulwer preferred not to importune for specific favors but to express in his prayers a calmly grateful reliance upon God. Prayer thus became the vehicle that above all others enabled him to transform pain into a foretaste of heavenly joy and the recognition of emptiness into an awareness of the promised soul. In a letter to his son, for example, he described the almost palpable quality of the reassurance prayer had afforded him during a recent "dark lonely night." After mentioning his exhausted wakefulness due to intense suffering from lumbago and his painful efforts to inch himself into a more comfortable position, the letter continues: "With great slowness and caution I at last contrived this. The sense of relief was instantaneous and I felt I could then have a chance of sleep. With that relief there came a sudden joy, and in the sudden joy I thanked God! The moment I had so thanked God there settled upon me a train of thoughts, lulling, soothing, a sense of security, a gratitude to think that in that dark lonely night there was an ear I could address. I felt my soul! Now

I would not have given up that capacity of prayer, tho' called forth by such a trifle, for millions."[24]

A man may be most himself—most in touch, that is, with the missing principle of his identity—at those moments in which he calmly and fearlessly anticipates the dissolution of his physical being. As in the Cave of Quietude of Keats, the instant of trustful, passive contentment follows suddenly, unexpectedly, but with apparent inevitability upon the climactic intensity of loneliness, yearning, and anguish. It seems plausible in the novels too, therefore, that the weary process of self-denial and the growing sense of alienation, fragmentation, or emptiness should finally lead the protagonists to the affirmation of soul. Beyond the three earthly levels of the personality and beyond the aching desire for the "something afar! never to be reached on this earth" lies the profoundly serene intuition that one must awaken from this life to the presence of that something.

Returning to the intimations of soul and hereafter in the novels, then, it is interesting to observe how the protagonists become conscious of a sort of anti-universe. In *The Parisians*, to start with the simplest example, the symbolic image of one of Isaura's favorite songs comes to fascinate Vane. The song concerns a Neapolitan fisher who spies an apparent nymph below the surface of the bay and seeks in vain to capture her in his nets; she is actually a girl standing on the rocks above him. Although the song warns of the dangers of nympholepsy, it also suggests that the soul may be perceived in this life as a vacant reflection of the beauty existing positively in another sphere. Vane in particular seems to possess such a vacancy, for he lacks "the woman-part of [man's] nature which Goethe ascribes to the highest genius." The art of Isaura begins to reveal it to him. Her singing moves him to tears as he intuits the "something unexpressed," and in its *Anders-streben* her novel too tries to hint at "the archetypal form of Graham Vane . . . idealised, beautified, transfigured." Unfortunately, he fails to recognize "therein the reflection of himself."

The protagonists in the other novels must actually journey down into the shadowy depths of the underworld. The American narrator of *The Coming Race*, for instance, passes the "monstrous reptile" (another Dweller of the Threshold) and descends to the vast realm that seems in many respects the parodic antithesis of this one. Most significantly perhaps, he observes a reversal of some sexual characteristics. The females have achieved superiority over the males in size, in intelligence, and in the volitional power enabling them to yield the vril rods; during courtship they also pursue the males. The young Zee, who becomes so amorously attached to the narrator thus suggests, admittedly in somewhat travestied form, the positive aspect of the soul that exists only as a negative capacity in this life. When he kisses her in farewell and returns across the threshold to his own world, she remains in his memory as an angel whom he may possibly meet again after death. Meanwhile he lives on earth with the awareness of a missing element—"disappointed, as most men are, in matters connected with household love and domestic life."

The underworld is not itself, however, the anti-universe. It represents instead the psychic depths beyond the threshold of the ordinary consciousness wherein the hero begins to intuit, like the symbolist poets, the ideal counterpart to this universe. The Vril-ya, who possess a far more advanced and sublime religious faith than that of mankind, thus discourse about the celestial regions they expect to attain after death.

The pattern of a psychic journey to the underworld may emerge most clearly in *A Strange Story*, which is one of the Bulwer novels that seems most directly to have influenced Villiers de L'Isle-Adam.[25] In despairing recognition of the void, Fenwick travels with his bride (who had gone mad at Windermere) across dark seas— for the story mentions only the nights at sea—to the underworld. There, in Australia literally, he finds himself far indeed from "the light which gave 'glory to the grass and splendour to the flower.' " He has entered the "blind mausoleum" of his own "material philosophy," and so the Australian bush generally appears more barren

[203]

and deathly to him than it had to Pisistratus Caxton. At one point a storm even drives him into a deep cave "strewed with strange bones, some amongst them the fossilised relics of races destroyed by the Deluge."

A final desperate determination to break out of the tomb sustains him during the ordeal of brewing the magical elixir that may restore Lilian to health and reason. He wills to pass "the boundary which divides his allotted and normal mortality from the regions and races . . . that are hostile." But his will is not quite strong enough, and he does not escape the bounds of mortality until the frustration of all human hopes forces him to discover still more deeply within himself the negative capacity for prayer. Beyond the weak and fading Lilian of the underworld, he then perceives the potentially divine creature who belongs to the realms already foreseen in her own rapt visions. So in the darkness and the void he at last feels his immortal soul:

Know thyself! Is that maxim wise? If so, know thy soul. But never yet did man come to the thorough conviction of soul but what he acknowledged the sovereign necessity of prayer. In my awe, in my rapture, all my thoughts seemed enlarged and illumed and exalted. I prayed—all my soul seemed one prayer. All my past, with its pride and presumption and folly, grew distinct as the form of a penitent, kneeling for pardon before setting forth on the pilgrimage vowed to a shrine. And, sure now, in the deeps of a soul first revealed to myself, that the Dead do not die forever, my human love soared beyond its brief trial of terror and sorrow. Daring not to ask from Heaven's wisdom that Lilian, for my sake, might not yet pass away from the earth, I prayed . . . my Maker . . . so to guide my steps that they might rejoin her at last, and, in rejoining, regain forever! (SS 89)

Once Fenwick has attained such an apprehension, it ceases to matter, allegorically speaking, whether Lilian actually recovers. Bulwer had originally planned, in fact, for her to die, and although he later relented on this point, the love between Lilian and Fenwick here on earth is chiefly significant as a symbol and earnest of their reunion hereafter. (*The Parisians*, in which Vane does eventually marry the consumptive and apparently doomed Isaura, emphasizes the same allegorical truth.) Fenwick thus gives up his dependence upon empirical facts and renounces his scientific treatise; in the *Strange Story* he composes instead, he communicates the symbolist's vision of the universe and defines not the "Intellectual Man" but the true "indivisible ME."

In *Kenelm Chillingly* the hero's pilgrimage progresses a step further than the initial feeling of soul, for Kenelm seems more completely than his predecessors to journey beyond the underworld and to approach the celestial regions. The psychic journey is once more an essentially watery one: "I have a strange love for rivulets and all running waters," Kenelm tells Lily, "and in my foot wanderings I find myself magnetically attracted towards them." The waters lead him in this case to Moleswich, where he arrives as an eccentric angler—in fact, as the apotheosis of a series of fishermen with curiously mythic overtones in Bulwer's late novels.[26]

Moleswich is, to be sure, a prosaic English village, and Kenelm and Lily talk in somewhat prosaic Arnoldian language of the soul as "the best self." (He also reverses the Goethean maxim that had figured in *Eugene Aram* and discusses the "something in every man's heart" that "would make us love him" if we could see it.) Yet the conversations with Lily also become ecstatic, and when Kenelm recognizes her as his own "best" or "innermost self, so . . . immeasurably higher than one's every-day self," he is no longer thinking in Arnoldian terms. Moleswich becomes then a symbol for regions of the soul—Lily actually collects and lovingly tames butterflies—and Kenelm feels he has wholly escaped the bounds of mortality: "Our own souls are so boundless that the more we explore them, the more we shall find worlds spreading upon worlds into infinities; and among the worlds is Fairyland. . . . Am I not in Fairyland now?" Indeed one of the nicknames of the strangely ethereal Lily is Fairy, and the Moleswich idyl contains numerous references to specific fairy tales as well as to Bulwer's favorite story of Egeria. Suspected in an earlier episode of being "a prince in disguise," Kenelm is now associated with a certain prince from fairyland; the figure possesses humps that will, despite their seeming ugliness, develop into wings. He will at last be able to approach the angels.

Although the episode represents Bulwer's most extended attempt in these novels to symbolize the atmosphere of the other universe, Moleswich is, of course, only a symbol. Kenelm must eventually lose Lily in whom he has found the "sympathy with his own strange innermost self which a man will never feel more than once in his life." So he too must settle down to a life apart from his soul. He returns symbolically across Westminster Bridge at the end to wait for a reunion in Heaven.[27]

One other interesting, if not surprising aspect of Bulwer's efforts to represent intimations of a platonic immortality deserves emphasis. Like Wordsworth and many others, he evidently imagined the soul largely in connection with certain recollections of childhood and youth. The particular settings he uses to symbolize the life beyond death thus tend to suggest returns, in the phrase from *In Memoriam*, to "the eternal landscape of the past." Throughout *The Parisians*, for example, Isaura keeps recalling with nostalgia her "charmed . . . childhood" in Sorrento where she had first read Tasso and had discovered the whole spiritual dimension of the universe. At the end of the novel, Rameau breaks their engagement, and "as a bird that escapes from the cage and warbles to the heaven it regains," she returns joyously to Sorrento with Vane. (Vane's predecessor, Guy Darrell of *What Will He Do with It?*, had also meditated spending his last days reading Horace in the ageless serenity of Sorrento.) In *A Strange Story* Fenwick fondly remembers an eternal landscape that is even more nearly Wordsworthian, for he has grown up in the Lake District. Returning to the shores of Windermere with Lilian just before their marriage, he hopes to recover his innocence. He rows out into the lake that his prose apostrophizes so lyrically and casts the diabolical wand wrested from Margrave into the depths.

The Lake District also constituted a haunting eternal landscape for Bulwer himself. In 1824, it will be recalled, he had toured the region on foot during his pilgrimage to the grave of his early love, and he returned in 1859 to find the district as enchanting as ever: "I have not been here since I was a boy," he wrote from Keswick: "Since then I have seen much of beautiful scenery abroad; but I never saw any which surpassed what enchants the eye in these hills and Waters."[28] Yet even beyond that scenery, the country along the Brent near Ealing may have haunted Bulwer's recollections. There he had passed the happiest days of his existence during that idyllic love affair, and that is the setting to which he has given the name of Moleswich in *Kenelm Chillingly*. Indeed the long episode of Kenelm's love for the ethereal Lily reproduces almost the precise details of the young Edward Bulwer's tragic love for the girl at Ealing. Robert Lytton indicates the degree to which Bulwer has returned in his last novel, completed a couple weeks before his death, to the crucial, defining event of his life:

My Father read the manuscript of *Kenelm* to my wife and myself, and at particular parts of it he could not restrain his tears. Throughout the day (it was New Year's Eve—the eve of the year of his own death) on which he finished the chapter describing Kenelm's sufferings above the grave of "Lily," he was profoundly dejected, listless, broken; and in his face there was the worn look of a man who has just passed through the last paroxysm of a passionate grief. We did not then know to what the incidents referred, and we wondered that the creations of his fancy should exercise such power over him. They were not the creations of fancy, but the memories of fifty years past.[29]

The affair at Ealing had retained its full tragic value. "Nothing we ever gain in after life," Bulwer had told Forster in 1867, "compensates for the loss of youth"; and the loss of Lily's "sympathy with his own strange innermost self" had been the most irreparable of all. Yet the memory of everything that had disappeared with Lily did at least remain, and in that bitter memory was now the chief assurance of his soul. So against the efforts of time and modern civilization to destroy the individual soul, Bulwer tried in his last novels to reassert the validity of the regions where the pure forms of youth still lived.

Despite the fascination with the soul and despite the vision of this life as a realm of loss and vacancy, Bulwer did not recommend asceticism or cultivate a death wish. The last novels pay at least lip service to the proposition that reconciliation to reality is desirable, and Bulwer told Lady Sherborne that he did not share the characteristics of her "religious temperament": "The Creator has set bounds to this yearning of the soul while on earth," and he did not long with the saints "to absorb himself in divinity itself." His interest in worldly affairs remained, in fact, keen. Although "despair[ing] of fellow-feeling with an age which says Pope is no poet and Rossetti is a great one," he followed the careers of younger writers carefully. He read critically and appreciatively, for example, each new novel by George Eliot. The young Swinburne also found him an especially sympathetic and helpful counselor in 1866 during the scandal surrounding the efforts to publish the first series of *Poems and Ballads*. (Bulwer must have recalled his own troubles with *Lucretia*.) And Matthew Arnold too commented in 1869 on Bulwer's generous "humanity" towards everyone—including his tenants, who appeared to adore him.[30]

Bulwer remained, however, on the sidelines. In 1863 he refused the provisional offer of the throne of Greece, which might once have sorely tempted his ambitious nature. He spoke of himself characteristically as land "lying fallow" or a vessel lying in port "to take in coals" for another voyage. He had not yet reached a terminal phase, requiring extirpation of all concern for the affairs of this life, but he had withdrawn from full, hectic involvement. He still felt split, one gathers, between the here and the hereafter—as earlier between the worlds without and within—and he hoped that prayer could serve, like the Imagination of former days, as at least a partial reconciling agent. His references to a certain literary and political figure of the Old Testament are worth observing in this context.

Even when the mortal and immortal aspects of his personality appeared most opposed, David had shown how prayer enabled them validly to coexist:

It is difficult to conceive a more erring mortal, and yet I understand why he is called after God's own heart. He has established so fully the link between himself as the naughty, affectionate child and the Divine Creator as the indulgent Father, to whom he comes in every difficulty, utters his every joy and his every sorrow, and never allows his greatest sin to intercept his communion with the All-perfect. Did we find such a man now in life, the Public would call him a hypocrite and impostor. But to my mind, he is presented to us as an example of the efficacy of prayer. His life is one encouragement to pray, no matter how unworthy we make ourselves of an approach to God, if regarded only as the Judge and not as the Father.[31]

Described in this way, the career of David may still exhibit a degree of schizophrenia, but in the understanding forgiveness of God the "erring mortal" is lost in the "affectionate child." The idea of returning to the dependent position of the child seems increasingly to have appealed to Bulwer: "let us be satisfied," he remarks later in the same letter to Lady Sherborne, the closest friend of his last years, "that we do love God, if we thus approach Him, like David, with supreme confidence in His fatherly regard for us, rejoicing in His smile and not overawed at the thought of His power." Such a confidence in the father also underlies the conclusion of *Kenelm Chillingly*, for the understated, but deeply tender reconciliation of Kenelm and Sir Peter is one of the most moving things about the novel. In portraying that reconciliation, Bulwer has evidently been referring on the "metaphysical" level—whether consciously or unconsciously—to the approach of death. He has noted on a stray paper from exactly the same period that "the act of dying reminds [him] of the traveller who has long been absent from his father's home and is recalled to it more suddenly than he anticipated or wished for": "as nearer and nearer he comes to the sacred precincts, farther and farther fade away his regrets for the things left behind uncompleted. Softer and softer sinks into his soul the tender remembrance that none ever so loved as the father whom he has so often forgotten. It is to a father's judgment that he is to render the account of his wanderings—it is to a father's home that he returns."[32]

The irascible General Bulwer, who rather ignored and disliked his youngest son and who died when the son was four, hardly resembles the archetypal father of this description. One can understand, though, the relief of the idealist who has come to the end of the long ordeal of this sphere, in which everyone seems perforce to repeat the career of the prodigal son in exile. Although he has not been able fully to maintain or to communicate his awareness of the "something within," he has at least guarded intact a basic loyalty to his divine heritage. Even when forced like so many Victorians to face what David Copperfield had called the "unhappy loss or want of something," he has eventually managed to turn that consciousness too into an intimation of immortality. So he can return hopefully to the serene regions in which all the contradiction and tension of life apart from the pure forms is resolved.

CHAPTER VIII

The Timeless Achievement
of the Quest

Yet it is pity we had lost tidings of our souls: —actually we
shall have to go in quest of them again, or worse in all ways
will befal!

Carlyle, *Past and Present*

According to a characteristically Victorian attitude that Bulwer's
story "The Haunted and the Haunters" associates with Macaulay,
the wise and healthy man always accepts the common-sense values
and realities of "practical life." In his sane, practical vision, every-
day realities seem to be of a piece with all realities, and the em-
pirically adduced laws governing all known and familiar aspects
of life are assumed to govern the unfamiliar too. Research beyond
the present frontiers of knowledge must therefore serve to domesti-
cate, in a sense, the entire universe, placing all mysterious phenomena within the respectable framework of the usual and the
natural: "the supernatural," asserts Bulwer's protagonist, "is the
impossible, and . . . what is called supernatural is only a something
in the laws of Nature of which we have been hitherto ignorant." Or
as Robert Louis Stevenson points out with respect to Utterson—
his "lover of the sane and customary sides of life" in *Dr. Jekyll and
Mr. Hyde*—"the fanciful was the immodest" and must consequently
be defined out of existence (along with everything else that could
bring a blush to the cheek of the young person).

Whether Victorian art as a whole enforces Macaulay's and Utterson's healthy appreciation for the ordinary may remain a debatable point. On the one hand, Victorian artists probably seem in
most specific instances to be discrediting the Macaulays, Uttersons,

and Podsnaps of this world. Yet critics like Mario Praz, on the other hand, have discerned in the Victorian novel a virtual celebration of the truth and beauty of the ordinary. And while deploring the fact, Bulwer seems to have agreed with this now possibly outmoded school of interpretation. His own relentless attacks upon the reigning myth of realism may even have helped—paradoxically—to establish an impression of the strength of the myth. To understand his fiction, one needs in any case to take some account of the great stronghold of "conventional morality" wherein "Novelist after Novelist had entrenched himself."

Among the defenders of the conventional frontiers—to recall briefly some traditional impressions about Victorian realism—are generally ranked Thackeray, who was once unfairly dubbed "The Apostle of Mediocrity," and Trollope, in whose work Bradford A. Booth has discerned "the apotheosis of normality." George Eliot too became an eloquent propagandist on behalf of Bulwer's "Regions of Custom and Prescription"—if not precisely on behalf of conventional morality. Never one to hope for a miraculous intervention or an heroic escape from the boundaries of custom and environmental determinism, she began by discerning even the "sacred" and "sublime" aspects of "commonplace people" and urged the reader of *Amos Barton* "to see some of the poetry and the pathos, the tragedy and the comedy, lying in the experience of a human soul that looks out through dull gray eyes, and that speaks in a voice of quite ordinary tones."[1]

Associated by Bulwer, Praz, and many others with Dutch painting, this vision of ordinary, commonplace reality is capable of conveying—as it has often seemed—all the grandeur that Booth's term "apotheosis" implies. Zanoni himself can thus urge the artist who has failed in a higher quest to "feel what beauty and holiness dwell in the Customary." Yet such a beautiful and holy vision can never persuade us of its absolute truth, for it must always establish its own validity in terms of a dialectical relationship with its opposite. Thackeray hints, for example, at the deadly, threatening elements that lurk below the surface of "Vanity Fair." And most Victorian domestic novels may similarly hint at what Gordon Ray has called "the menace that underlies everyday life" or what the preferred author of the pious Miss Clack in *The Moonstone* has called "The Serpent at Home."[2] Bulwer's own apparent celebration in *The Caxtons* of conventional domesticity thus recognizes—as in the imaginary, serpentine fire of the "Chapter on Housetops"—perils that threaten the very realities of the family with dissolution. By constantly arousing fear of some unspeakable, lurking menace, this kind of Victorian art also increases the blessed value of the refuge it offers. And so while the extraordinary Victorian underworld becomes ever vaster and uglier, that powerful cultural myth of the solidity, truth, holiness, and beauty of ordinary reality is sustained.

Just as a secret symbiosis may have united the believers in the myth with their Nemesis, so the enemies of realism may also have had a strange need for the myth they were attacking. In fact Bulwer's attitude toward the supposed everyday verities of Oxford Street sometimes seems enormously complex. In *Falkland* his protagonist had discovered his all-important counterpart in a denizen of those regions of mediocrity and conventionality and frequently thereafter Bulwer had pondered the aspect of himself that related him to commonplace humanity. He even studied the language spoken in Oxford Street and felt for a time that his own particular vision required validation in the form of a translation into that language. Yet a fear that the translation would falsify his message evidently preoccupied him as well. In the "commonplace medium" (as *Middlemarch* terms it) his unique "genius" must evaporate; under the "tyranny of every-day life" he would simply be "absorb[ed]." So a Nemesis worse than any Dweller of the Threshold may have come to haunt him in a form like that of Peer Gynt's Button-Moulder, who would deny all remarkable visions, unsupported by facts, and who would melt all individuals down into the mediocre blandness of the mass.

Both in his fascination with the conventional regions and in his revulsion against them, Bulwer seems, as I have suggested, to confess their prestige and to sustain their mystique. That Hegelian logic, which informs the age through and through, has forced the idealist to help create the antithetical myth of realism. Once that point is recognized, though, it may nevertheless appear that Bulwer's attacks upon the myth of realism are nearly the least ambiguous and most forthright in all of Victorian fiction. For he seems always to have known that the Button-Moulder was only a figment of the modern imagination and that only the conspiracy of silence kept men from mutually confessing the fraudulence of the commonplace Victorian verities. From the explicitness of *Lucretia*, which Macaulay himself so oddly appreciated, to the subtlety of the Caxton series, his efforts to expose the conspiracy are thus remarkably uninhibited. While he can honestly admit whatever virtues there may be in the ordinary vision of things, his insistence upon its purely arbitrary, conventional, and fictional quality is weakened very rarely, after all, by any sneaking yearning to believe. He constantly views the supposed realities of his own century from the perspective of eternal truth.

Although his career must be seen, then, as a reaction against the enemy of contemporary realism, it also transcends its own age and does not need to be defined entirely with respect to that particular zeitgeist. Occasionally even indifferent to the facts of his own age, he appears to be prosecuting the quest of the romantics for some mode of ideal awareness. He knows visible phenomena to be the mere outward manifestations of shadowy energies and figures existing in the regions beyond. His fiction, accordingly, does not usually seek to portray truth by surrendering—like the mirror at the end of *My Novel*—to a mimetic rendition of things as they appear. Far indeed from apotheosizing reality, his art imposes an a priori conception upon its materials and so furthers the divine cause; it tries to restore the material to harmony with the original Idea. Or, as may sometimes appear, Bulwer gives up on reality and deals simply with those ideal "apparitions" in as pure a form as possible.

The most spectacular of Bulwer's researches "beyond that range of conventional morality" are probably those into the territory of the occult. Here, the persuasive Robert Lee Wolff has concluded, Bulwer may have established his principal claim to a place of eminence among his contemporaries: "Taken altogether, the record of Bulwer's active interest in the supernatural and his literary use of occult themes is probably unique among English writers of the period. Some few others dabbled in mesmerism, like Dickens himself, or went in for mysticism like George MacDonald. But, so far as I know, no other English writer embarked on such active investigation as Bulwer or displayed such an open mind and such commitment in this field."[3]

Indeed the fascination with the supernatural and the extraordinary pervades all Bulwer's novels and romances. His protagonists are always trying metaphorically, when not literally, to contact the ghosts of the past or to find those mysterious communications from the regions of the dead. And with equal fervor they may seek the ghosts of the future, just as Bulwer himself was so anxiously attempting to communicate with an endless posterity. If only, his novels seem to say, one could share for a moment the serenely timeless, detached vision of a Zanoni or a Mejnour over the "UNIVERSAL HUMAN LOT"! Then one might almost be reconciled to the subsequently engulfing immediacy of the ordinary and the temporal.

Bulwer bases his hope of transcendence, of course, not so much upon his experience of the specifically occult and visionary as upon his awareness of those psychological archetypes that survive eternally superior to time. As I have tried to demonstrate, it is by charting the territory of psychological myths—and not simply by dealing with the occult—that his entire oeuvre achieves its significance. His great strength, as Dickens too seems to have recognized in a letter of 1861, lay in his ability to elucidate "those strange psychological

mysteries in ourselves, of which we are all more or less conscious."
In pursuing these mysteries, Bulwer evolved what Dickens went on
to term his distinctive and "curious weapons in the armoury of
fiction."[4]

These weapons were especially well fitted to press the attack upon the tyranny of everyday realism. For as Bulwer had discovered
and allegorically suggested at least as early as *Pompeii*, the prevailing sense of stable realities was even more vulnerable to ignored
or repressed psychological energies than it was to revolutionary
political threats. (Typifying demonic, psychic energies, Vesuvius
thus proves, in my interpretation, to be far more destructive than the
impending revolt of Pompeian slaves.) More directly perhaps than
Dickens, Wilkie Collins, and the other novelists who discerned the
same menace, Bulwer went on to brave the dangers and to release
the forces of the psychic regions that might also offer man an eventual salvation.

Within these new regions Bulwer discovered many sorts of
archetypal figures. Since the individual novels also define them and
dramatize configurations and relationships among them in many
different ways, they may appear to merge unstably into each other.
Yet from a study of all the novels a certain fundamental pattern
seems nevertheless to emerge, and I would like to specify its nature
again in conclusion. Indicative of the levels of man's physical being,
the pattern appears to include three principal figures, which can,
as Bulwer finally understands, enter into an almost harmonious
connection with each other. Still the pattern remains tragically incomplete because Bulwer cannot, somehow, fit a certain essential
and elusive fourth figure into a satisfactory relationship with the
other three.

The most dangerously powerful figure and the one that the ex-
plorer may encounter first appears in his most archetypal guise as
the Dweller of the Threshold. Associated in our own minds probably with the *id*, this figure seems to have embodied for Bulwer several kinds of partially related, partially contradictory energies.

Most simply—as the representations beginning with Falkland (in some of his aspects) and continuing through Tom Bowles in *Kenelm Chillingly* imply—he evinces the fierce energy of sexuality. Secondly, he is sometimes related, as in the case of Bulwer's terribly malignant criminals, to the radical evil that seems so mysteriously moved to destroy all virtue. And finally, Bulwer appears to discern in many of his manifestations an amoral life force or survival instinct. He incarnates in this context the frightening "WILL" or the principle of "vril" which drives each individual toward ruthless self-gratification in the struggle for life. This element is, as Bulwer confesses in his implicit comparison of himself with the future Richard III of *Barons*, one of the chief components of the ambition to which he has owed so much of his own success.

After the frank Byronism of *Falkland*, Bulwer felt some compulsion to discredit these demonic figures or to dramatize the process of their domestication. Yet it may also be a sign of the honesty of his art that he continued to assert the necessity for the demonic and in *Lucretia*, for example, to reaffirm its possible beauty as well. In *A Strange Story*, furthermore, he dared to speculate in the manner of Nietzsche about the possibility that the amoral Will would enable some members of the race to become sublimely beautiful supermen. Bulwer's Margrave prefigures Wilde's Dorian Gray too, for he has successfully divorced himself from the soul and so escaped the supposed consequences of original sin. A perfectly beautiful animal, untroubled by ethical consciousness, he discovers that the laws decreeing that sin must bear its penalty and that man must age and die are only the illusions of priestcraft. His will to live (and the elixir to which this has led him) may enable him to survive forever. Man thus becomes terribly free in a cosmos that does not sustain the laws and repressive ordering principles of the moral imagination.

Bulwer's second typical figure shares many of the demonic attributes of the first. In fact these two are often combined into a single entity (as in the cases of both Falkland and Margrave perhaps) or seen as corresponding sides of the same fundamental evil (as in the symbiotic juxtaposition of the Dweller of the Threshold and Mejnour). Still it seems useful to distinguish the two and to observe in this second figure the less anarchic energies of a rational egoism. To this class belong, most memorably, such crafty opportunists as Lord Vincent in *Pelham*, the Abbé Montreuil in *Devereux*, Lumley Ferrers (who has his wild symbiotic counterpart in Cesarini) in *Maltravers* and *Alice*, and both Randal Leslie and Baron Levy in *My Novel*. These figures perceive in the amoral intellect the chief glory of man, and that intellect prompts them to discipline their chaotic instincts so that they can attain the more exquisite gratifications.

In this sometimes ascetic figure too Bulwer's honesty often compels him to recognize a validity and necessity, for from this aspect of man derives the Faustian will to know that has prompted all the advances of science. While eminently capable of debasement, the Baconian precept, "Knowledge is Power" (which thunders throughout *My Novel*), has inspired individuals like Mejnour to attain serene power over "the farthest and obscurest regions in the universe of ideas." Mejnour has thus become the very type of the "SCIENCE that contemplates." As more humanly manifested in the guise of Allen Fenwick, the physician of *A Strange Story*, this science frees man from terrors and brings him incalculable blessings.

The third typical figure represents more ethical and social values and is almost invariably female. Since her romantic passion tends to be muted and associated with a nearly maternal tenderness, she generally tames the hero's sexuality while also luring him from Faustian and other egoistic or misanthropic indulgences. The most fascinating embodiments of this civilizing and law-giving figure are probably Lady Roseville in *Pelham*, Constance in *Godolphin*, Lady Montfort in *What Will He Do with It?*, Mrs. Poyntz in *A Strange Story*, and Lady Glenalvon in *Kenelm Chillingly*.

Even more signally, though, this feminine energy triumphs in the entire society of the Vril-ya. As *The Coming Race* portrays that civilization in which the women have become the stronger sex, it has carried scientific research to the ultimate and thereby learned to harness the hitherto anarchic energy of vril. The achievement typifies the harmonious fusion at last of all three forces: the basely demonic, the aloofly rational, and the higher energy that creates and cements a moral order. It is perhaps the full acknowledgment of the three that has permitted them to reinforce each other, and the social result may symbolize the analogous possibility for integrating the individual id, ego, and super-ego.

Yet Bulwer did not ultimately define salvation as a Freudian integration of the human personality, or as a Marxist conclusion to the class struggle, or as a Meredithian reconciliation of man with the natural environment. Man does not really achieve salvation in *The Coming Race* because the all-important element of soul is still missing from the pattern of integration: to attain their perfection, the Vril-ya have, it will be recalled, largely suppressed the individualizing principle and have come curiously to resemble the soulless Margrave. Indeed what the three elements in the integration share most fundamentally may be a certain hostility to Bulwer's fourth typical figure, the anima. For even those attractive female incarnations of civilizing morality seem on occasion to reinforce the danger which the demonic and egoistic masculine figures pose for the innocent embodiments of the soul. Although Lady Roseville and Lady Montfort, for example, characteristically assume the role of protectress of the innocent maiden, there are some curious hints that they may corrupt their protégées. The older women also become to varying degrees the rivals of the younger, and, as is the case with the worldly Constance and Mrs. Poyntz, their actions may indirectly hasten the fall of the innocent young female into madness. The integration of what Bulwer considered the three aspects of man's physical being may therefore amount to an unholy alliance. As in traditional pacts with the devil, the immortal soul is sacrificed for the sake of success and security in this life.

While exploring the subterranean domains of the Vril-ya and

other versions of his regions beyond, Bulwer therefore tends to wield in two ways his "curious weapons" for attacking conventional morality and realism. First his works continually show that the ordinary social surfaces are far less solid than they appear because society and its individual members have not achieved even the physical self-integration of the Vril-ya. From *Falkland* and on, "the fair show" deceptively conceals a horrifying void or a chaos of un-acknowledged demonic and egoistic energies that gravely imperil the conventional sanctities and rules of the marketplace. Secondly, though, Bulwer implies that recognition and integration of those energies would not suffice to redeem the regions of custom and prescription anyway. For to achieve authenticity, both society and the individual would need to be reconciled with the exceedingly elusive element of soul.

At times Bulwer believes such a reconciliation might prove pos-sible—as in the symbolic child at the end of *Zanoni* and in the struc-ture of the Caxton novels. His experience led him most often, how-ever, to indicate that the soul could have no useful commerce with the energies motivating man's everyday existence, and he was ac-cordingly alienated from the everyday. While George Eliot and others were able to make of positivistic reality an all-determining deity that could substitute for an absent transcendent God, Bulwer could not deify that which remained soulless. His attack upon the rather tyrannical deity of realism—or materialism, as he often terms it—therefore became radical. Far from simply urging reform of Victorian realities, he wished to show that reality was fraudulent by its very nature.

The career of Bulwer may thus have helped to prepare the way for the decadents. Yet a vast difference remains, of course, between him and them. While they could manage without realities and could make do instead with artificial and fictitious identities, Bulwer had to believe in the truth of some absolute, transcendent first principle. So his longings drew him beyond the material regions that social and physical scientists were measuring and for that matter beyond the perceptions of idealists like Schopenhauer of a cosmic Will. Beyond all his other archetypal forms, he sought that identifying figure of the soul. Underlying the existence of everything that is, the very *idea* of soul existed to assure him of the indestructible uniqueness of all selfhoods.

That he could maintain this faith in the supreme value of individual identity must surely constitute the most noteworthy fact about him. For despite his supposed logical proofs, there was no empirical evidence of the soul and perhaps not much evidence of any other kind either. Still—like other Victorians with their various sorts of irrational faith—he believed and sought repeatedly to achieve the impossible: to convey the quality of the soul that must remain ineffable and imageless. In the process he made of the art of fiction a vehicle to carry on the idealist tradition of Romantic poetry and so helped not only to save the soul of man but also to save fiction to serve visions other than that of mimetic realism. In the process too, as all his individual works actually do seem to point, like so many spires, toward their single, ideal first cause, Bulwer may have provided evidence after all for the existence of "that something afar! never to be reached on this earth,—never, never!"

The Influence of Bulwer-Lytton in His Own Times

Bulwer wanted his art to possess a timeless validity, and this study has generally emphasized those aspects of his work that imply his desire to appeal to the ages. Yet since he also achieved immense popularity within the context of his own age, his particular influence upon his contemporaries and immediate successors is also a matter of interest. To assess this influence fully would require one to consider the force not only of his fiction but also of his very carefully constructed plays—especially the enormously successful and frequently revived *The Lady of Lyons* (1838) and *Money* (1840). In summarizing the evidence of his influence, I shall nevertheless remain within the area of his fiction and fictional theory, which have constituted the subject of my study. His notions about the basic duality of art—the external form as opposed to the internal soul— may also help once again to organize my discussion. For his novels demonstrated their immediate power both in the more superficial aspect of their relevance to various fads and schools and in their more fundamental adherence to his theories of ideal art.

Pelham, which changed the fashion in men's evening clothes in 1828, was Bulwer's first spectacular success, and in subsequent works by the so-called silver-fork novelists one discerns the first instances of his literary influence. Novels by his friend Lord Mulgrave and by Mrs. Catherine Gore (with whom after an initial misunderstanding he would also be on cordial terms) thus seem to have perpetuated his literary legend about fashionable life. Although he would insist on the independent, realistic accuracy especially of Mrs. Gore's observations, his own achievement had helped—along with novels by Ward and Lister—to make the fashionable world possible for art. *Pelham* had enforced, for example, the conventional impression of a pattern and a center—Almack's —around which an otherwise futile society could seem to circle. Certain stereotypes of social climbers, dandies, and bored women, he had also shown, could make effectively interacting central characters, while a point of view that combined affection with satire could provide such works with some complexity of interest.[1]

Yet despite the extreme copiousness of silver-fork production, only Bulwer's novel and Disraeli's *Vivian Grey* (the first part of which had appeared in 1826) may seem to possess any enduringly significant aesthetic value. More interestingly than in the succeeding silver-fork novels, the influence of the author of *Pelham* may consequently be sought in his diffusion of a most intriguing public legend about himself. For very much like *Childe Harold* before it, *Pelham* had conveyed the impression of an identity between protagonist and author, which the author had then taken pains for some years to validate. The Pelham image, as Bulwer so successfully adumbrated it, was that of an outrageously flippant and cynical dandy aristocrat, who nevertheless had a hidden social conscience and who was utterly dedicated to noble political and aesthetic ideals. While references to it are ubiquitous in the period, the image evidently fascinated Disraeli in particular. Frequently and quite consciously, Disraeli modelled his public deportment upon Pelham's and attributed his allegedly startling social successes to his having "Pelhamized" people. In the years from 1830 to 1837, during which he struggled so hard to get into Parliament, he also submitted to the guidance of Bulwer in person. As his constant mentor, Bulwer kindly introduced him to the right people (including the woman he would marry in 1839) and enabled him to gain the social credentials required for the launching of a political career. One can also find evidence of Bulwer's influence, of course, upon most of Disraeli's novels from *The Young Duke* (1831) and onwards.[2]

In the United States, where Bulwer's contemporary reputation was if anything even greater than in Britain, the author of *Pelham* had a notable effect upon Edgar Allan Poe. As "the most powerful influence on Poe's early prose writing," Bulwer seems to stand, in the opinion of Michael Allen, behind Poe's frequent literary use of a persona and his general elaboration of "the fictional method of self-projection." Poe naturally drew his inspiration in this regard not only from the self-propagandizing Pelham but more especially from Bulwer's shorter tales, such as "Monos and Daimonos" (1830), and from the discursive *Asmodeus at Large* series (1833). And outside his art too, Poe belongs very much to the histrionic Byronic and Bulwerian tradition of the dandy who "walk[s] the paths of life," as Bulwer said, "in the garments of the stage." Emphasizing his southern gentility, Poe created his aristocratic role, which the example of Bulwer further assured him could be admirably adapted to a career of public service—in particular, as a journalist. For Bulwer had also offered Poe most striking evidence of the fact that magazine writing (which Carlyle had once termed "below street-sweeping as a trade") was now properly occupying "the first men in England." Poe dreamed for many years of editing a journal that would possess the characteristics of the *New Monthly Magazine* under Bulwer's editorship (1831–33). As described in a prospectus of 1843, Poe's journal would be resolutely independent and impartial, would endeavor to please while elevating the public taste, and, most importantly of all, would bear throughout its pages the definite, individualizing imprint of a single mind. Although successfully realized, according to Allen, in only a few numbers of *The Broadway Journal*, Bulwer's ideals thus continued to haunt Poe, even when he conceived of his career—still in the histrionic manner—as a lurid failure.[3] And when Poe died, it seemed appropriate to his literary executor to publish an obituary that compared him at length to a character in Bulwer's most recent novel, *The Caxtons*. That character, Francis Vivian, is the noble, promising dandy gone bad, and his association with Poe appeared to have sufficient justice to enable it to endure for some years in the public consciousness.[4]

Paul Clifford (1830) provided some of the first practical evidence of Bulwer's own commitment to noble political and social causes, and more definitely than *Pelham* it opened up a new field for the contemporary novel. While deriving from Godwin, its way of arguing on behalf of legal and penal reform appears to have made it the first important *Tendenzroman* in Britain. Bulwer followed it with *Eugene Aram* (1832), in which he advanced a thesis about criminal psychology and which remained throughout his lifetime one of his five or six most popular works. When other novelists hastened to imitate these works, though, they created not so much a school of novels with a thesis as a host of thrilling accounts of criminal life—the so-called Newgate novels. Among the most significant works to be referred thus to Bulwer's paternity are Ainsworth's best-selling *Rookwood* (1834) and *Jack Sheppard* (1839) as well as Dickens' *Oliver Twist* (and many portions of *Barnaby Rudge* and *Martin Chuzzlewit*).[5] Later on, as Joseph I. Fradin has argued, the influence of *Paul Clifford* is also evident in Charles Reade's more genuinely tendentious novels—especially in "the prison scenes and reform program of *It Is Never Too Late to Mend*" (1856).[6] Of incidental interest too is Reade's choice of the title "Masks and Faces" for a play he subsequently turned into a novel because Godwin had once proposed the same title to Bulwer for *Paul Clifford*.

Reade's *It Is Never Too Late to Mend* derives likewise from Bulwer's treatment of crime in *Night and Morning* (1841) and *Lucretia* (1846). Fradin finds these last two works even more important, however, as forerunners of the detective story. Once called—probably inaccurately—the "earliest detective story in the English language," *Night and Morning* introduced in the character Favart the ancestor of the subsequently stereotyped "quietly menacing, ubiquitous" detective of English fiction. This novel, which has retained its peculiar power to enthrall some readers (and which contains, incidentally, an unexpectedly naughty scene in a French boarding house), surely impressed Wilkie Collins, who has more usually received credit for the invention of the English detective story. Sheridan Le Fanu was similarly influenced by Bulwer's way of plotting his stories of crime, and Fradin has noticed some startling parallels between the plots of *Lucretia* and Le Fanu's *Uncle Silas* (1864).[7]

Still one returns to the conclusion that most of the novels following in the wake of Bulwer's criminal tales use their horrific material and the carefully contrived element of suspense towards an end that differs considerably from Bulwer's own. Whereas Bulwer subordinates everything else to his overriding desire to convey a message or establish some "metaphysical" pattern, the works of his disciples exist primarily as sensational entertainments. This fact again becomes obvious, as Fradin once more forces the point home, in connection with the supernatural fad that *Zanoni* (1842) apparently inspired. To this fad one can attribute some rather brainless works by Ainsworth and Le Fanu—as well as aspects of Collins's more satisfactory *Armadale* (1866).[8]

Despite the extraordinary number of successors to Bulwer's early novels of fashion, crime, and the supernatural, their influence may be gauged almost more interestingly, then, with respect to the opposition they aroused. For the opposition was indeed widespread. While Bret Harte, for example, would later write a parody entitled "The Dweller of the Threshold" (1865), Bulwer's supposed responsibility for silver-fork and Newgate fiction provoked immediate and violent storms of rage. Bulwer received the greatest share of the blame for all those books that were allegedly lending glamor to high and low life and inspiring young men to become either dandies or criminals. The impression that *Pelham* merited denunciation as the very archetype of silver-fork fiction even became such a commonplace that Carlyle, who had almost surely not read the novel himself, naturally felt he could repeat it in *Sartor Resartus*.[9] Although *Pelham* (very definitely) and its successors (rather less definitely) imply a satiric judgment of the society they treat, the satire often escaped notice, and the dandy novels were savagely parodied. At times, however, the parodies also betrayed a sneaking tendency to relish the snobberies of high life, and the dividing line between the celebrators and the satirists of the fashionable milieu is still a difficult one to draw. When the silver-fork genre had ceased properly to exist, its parodists continued their ambiguous and widely appreciated efforts: "the fashionable novels seem to have taken," remarks Kathleen Tillotson, "a lot of killing."[10] The efforts of the celebrators and the satirists of fashionable life finally culminated in *Vanity Fair*—whose author had been parodying the silver-fork school in general and Bulwer in particular for many years.

Thackeray had been parodying, indeed, not only Bulwer's "fashionable" poses but also—in works like "Elizabeth Brownrigge" (1832), *Catherine* (1839–40), and "George de Barnwell" (1847)—Bulwer's Newgate fiction. And because of the degree of his obsessive animosity toward Bulwer, one must actually consider Thackeray as one of the principal Victorian novelists to have been affected by Bulwer. In Bulwer's novels, he confessed in 1848 to their mutual friend Lady Blessington, "there are big words which make me furious, and a pretentious fine writing against which I can't help rebelling." Yet as Ellen Moers points out, "Thackeray's early diary testifies to the closeness with which he followed Bulwer's exclusive rise to fame, and the care with which he read *Falkland*, *The Disowned*, *Pelham*, *Devereux* and so on." In fact, he was constantly comparing himself jealously to Bulwer, and behind his revulsion lurked a guilty longing, not fully admitted until much later in life, to enjoy a youth like Pelham's. The complex fascination Bulwer's image of the dandy artist held for him must help to explain, then, his many contributions to the notoriously vicious campaign that *Fraser's* waged against Bulwer throughout the 1830's. It explains most importantly the *Yellowplush Papers* (1837), wherein Thackeray's protagonist is "an upside-down Pelham," as well as *Pendennis* (1848–50), which constitutes Thackeray's "serious imitation of and commentary on the fashionable novel as Bulwer and Disraeli had made it." In *The Newcomes* and *Philip* he would also employ projections of himself as commentators within the story and confess that he had learned the device from Bulwer.[11]

Beyond the boundaries of the novel of society—high and low—and of particular social problems, Bulwer's influence operated in less controversial ways. *Ernest Maltravers* (1837) and *Alice* (1838) remained popular and quietly helped, for example, to make the usefulness of the Goethean pattern of *Bildung* clear to subsequent novelists. Although in earlier works Carlyle, Disraeli, and Bulwer himself had already employed elements of the plotting found in *Wilhelm Meister*, these two novels in particular brought the plot into an effective focus. The three-stage plot, which Bulwer would continue to use with many variations, involves the hero's rebellion and setting forth on his quest, his chastening experiences leading to his repentance, and finally his return home to discover that the object of his quest had been there all along. The pattern underlies innumerable Victorian novels, and one suspects that Bulwer, who was always recognized as an important channel for German influences, thus had some effect on many major works by Dickens, Meredith, Trollope, Eliot, and Hardy.[12]

More easily documented, perhaps, is his influence, as Coral Lansbury has defined it, upon the novels that contributed to a certain myth about Australia. Bulwer derived from Samuel Sidney's propaganda the impression that Australia, in particular, could constitute the blessed land in which experience chastened and redeemed the hero. Hard work enabled the prodigal there to earn back the squandered patrimony, and as a new and successful man he might even hope to return to England and to harmony with himself. In a larger sense Australia was the land in which the lost soul of England—the true patrimony of Englishmen—must be recovered and nourished back to health. Given enormous popular currency in *The Caxtons* (1848–49), the Australian myth clearly influenced Dickens—for example, in his sending of Micawber (who resembles not only John Dickens but also Uncle Jack in *The Caxtons*) off to Australia. Reade's *It Is Never Too Late to Mend* likewise derives in this respect, as well as in the others I have mentioned, from Bulwer, while Henry Kingsley's Australian novel, *Geoffry Hamlyn* (1859), also owes the structure of its plot to *The Caxtons*. Since many works of literature thereafter perpetuated it, the myth came profoundly to affect the Australian consciousness of identity. It was as an author, then, rather than as Colonial Secretary that Bulwer exerted his most important influence upon Australia.[13]

Bulwer's historical romances contributed to a related popular myth that informed the national consciousness back in Britain. As "the great disseminator of Scott's impulse in the early Victorian period," Bulwer thus seems important to Avrom Fleishman at least in part because he transmitted Scott's ambiguous myth of "the Norman yoke" on to Charles Kingsley (especially in *Hereward*), Thomas Hardy, and D. H. Lawrence. Present in both *The Last of the Barons* (1843) and *Harold* (1848), the myth amounts to an awareness of the still-enduring, rural, Saxon soul of England, which centuries of rule by an alien Norman culture have never quite extirpated. Hardy, in particular, may seem to show the evidence of Bulwer's influence here and in his own brooding sense of the large historical forces that forever reduce individual man caught in time to impotence. For his historical consciousness resulted precisely from his boyhood absorption in the romances of Bulwer—along with those of Scott, Ainsworth, and G. P. R. James—and that absorption penetrated all aspects of his mature work.[14]

The historical works of Bulwer also have their more contemporary and timely relevance as comments upon political and social movements of the 1830's and 1840's, and some critics have found Bulwer influential in this respect too. Curtis Dahl believes Bulwer defined a new type of historical novel with present relevance, to which one can refer "Eliot's *Romola*, Shorthouse's *John Inglesant*, Thackeray's *Henry Esmond*, Reade's *The Cloister and the Hearth*, Morris's *The Dream of John Ball*, and . . . a large proportion of the historical poetry and drama of the age." As James C. Simmons has furthermore indicated, Bulwer's works influenced not only historical novelists but also professional historians, whose citations of Bulwer strengthened a prevailing impression that he was as significant an historian as Hume or Palgrave.[15]

In another way too the historical works carried Bulwer's influence beyond the boundaries of fiction: from *The Last Days of Pompeii* (1834) and on, they in particular inspired dramatic adaptations. Most of these adaptations are, to be sure, inconsequential, but Bulwer's *Rienzi* (1835) did become the source for Wagner's third opera. And *Harold*, for which Bulwer had done the research in the library of Tennyson d'Eyncourt, provided the chief source for Tennyson's play. (In the area of historical legend and poetry, it is also worth recalling that Tennyson believed Bulwer's epic *King Arthur* of 1848 had helped at least to prepare the public taste for his *Idylls*.)

Of the remaining fictional schools one might perhaps define a novel of domestic life for the sake of the Caxton series, which in addition to *The Caxtons* includes *My Novel* (1850–53) and *What Will He Do with It?* (1857–59). But while proving that these works carried Bulwer to the zenith of his popularity, Edwin M. Eigner has also argued that in them Bulwer seems to have been following rather than influentially leading the fashion.[16] In the case, similarly, of Bulwer's contribution to the tradition of Utopian satire, evidence of his specific influence remains somewhat elusive. His *The Coming Race* (1871) apparently did have a decided influence on George Bernard Shaw, and it is clearly relevant, at least, to the entire flurry of such satires at the end of the nineteenth and the beginning of the twentieth centuries. Yet *The Coming Race* did not, it seems, have any effect on Butler's *Erewhon* (1872). Early reviewers guessed that *Erewhon* must have been written by the author of *The Coming Race*, but Butler maintained he had not yet even read Bulwer's work and resented the ascription.[17]

Bulwer's most significant influence—to turn finally from what he considered "externals" to the "soul" of his aesthetic theory—ultimately transcended the framework of the individual schools and types of fiction. With all his prefaces, introductions, and assorted critical essays, he even became in many minds, both friendly and hostile, less the author of particular novels than the theorist and apologist for fictional "Art." His propaganda on behalf of the "metaphysical" novel may thus have implied more than just an effort to establish one fictional genre at the expense of many others. For he was seeking to define the criteria that could make novels of all sorts works not merely of entertainment but rather of high aesthetic seriousness. And although many Victorians were beginning to converge from their various quarters toward this same goal, Bulwer may deserve a special share of the credit for ensuring the success of the tendency. "After Carlyle" and—to expand Mrs. Tillotson's observation—after Bulwer, "the rift between the 'prophetic' and the merely entertaining novel widens."[18]

The specific influence of Bulwer in this tendency to treat fiction as serious art is probably detectable in much of the critical writing of the period. K. J. Fielding has noticed, for example, Bulwer's relevance to John Forster's theory of the novel, as embodied in his articles for the *Examiner*. Also readily documented is the widespread attention and respect accorded in particular to Bulwer's advocacy of "wholeness" or "unity" in fiction. Poe thus observed of *Night and Morning* that Bulwer had sacrificed everything to unity of plot, and Poe's own definition of a plot as "that in which no part can be displaced without ruin to the whole" again suggests the impact of Bulwer upon him. In worrying about how to achieve "unity" in *Vanity Fair*, Thackeray too affirmed the value of the aesthetic virtue that was linked, as Mrs. Tillotson implies, with Bulwer's name. The hostile critic W. C. Roscoe would likewise concede in 1859 the exemplary value in Bulwer's work of "the grasp of the whole design" and the way in which "he marshals all his material and concentrates his various forces on one result." But while revealing Bulwer's influence beyond the field of fiction, Matthew Arnold may provide the most interesting testimony to the force of this aspect of Bulwer's fictional theory and practice: "If I have learnt to seek in any composition for a wide sweep of interest," he wrote Bulwer in 1868, "and for a significance residing in the whole rather than in the parts, and not to give over-prominence, either in my own mind or in my work, to the elaboration of details, I have certainly had before me, in your works, an example of this mode of proceeding, and have always valued it in them."[19]

Other readers valued Bulwer's works especially for their blend of "idealized patterns of meaning" with the "appearance of reality," and it seems likely that Bulwer influenced Nathaniel Hawthorne very strongly in this area. Indeed, as John Stubbs analyzes it, Hawthorne's entire, well-developed theory of the romance appears to derive from Bulwer—although to some extent from Scott and Cooper too.[20] Professor Eigner's forthcoming book will tend, moreover, to show that Bulwer's theories underlie not only his own and Hawthorne's works but also those of Dickens, Emily Brontë, and Melville.

In some of these cases—and most clearly so in that of Emily Brontë—the affinity with Bulwer has probably not resulted from his specific influence. The relationship between Bulwer and Dickens, however, offers one of the most definite and important instances in literary history of two friends who profoundly and profitably influenced each other. Roughly like Goethe with respect to Schiller and Coleridge with respect to Wordsworth, Bulwer may generally have acted as the more intellectual and philosophical party in the relationship. In Bulwer's own opinion at least, Dickens was "no metaphysician" whereas he did understand "the practical part of authorship beyond my power."[21] So their strengths operated in happily complementary fashion not only during their collaboration to produce Bulwer's *Not So Bad As We Seem* (and their other efforts on behalf of their Guild) but in all aspects of their long literary association. Their value to each other emerges with especially interesting clarity in their correspondence of 1860–62 about Bulwer's *A Strange Story*, which Dickens was publishing in *All the Year Round*.

Limiting attention, though, to Bulwer's influence upon Dickens, one may recall that Bulwer persuaded his friend to change the ending of *Great Expectations*. And while critics formerly suspected that Bulwer must have urged basely commercial considerations, it now seems clear that he had appealed to the lofty theories which he and Dickens by then held in common. For Dickens had, in fact, subscribed for many years to Bulwer's important theories: "It is indisputable," in the opinion of H. P. Sucksmith, "that many of the principles of narrative art in Bulwer's early essay ['On Art in Fiction'] were put into practice by Dickens from 1838 and onwards with striking success." Not only did Dickens thus repeat innumerable small motifs, details of plotting, and character types from Bulwer's novels, but he also began to use some of Bulwer's grandiose, Aristotelian vocabulary in his musings about the structure of his own novels. Sucksmith finds Dickens' application of Bulwer's notions about "reversal of fortune" and "multiple catastrophe" especially illuminating in this context. It is not surprising too, then, to observe Dickens meditating upon the technical importance of "sympathy" and of "idealised effects" which Bulwer had probably discussed with him before elaborating them in the *Caxtoniana* essays of 1862–63.[22]

Even while elaborating his theories of a serenely ideal art, Bulwer had recognized the significance of the demonic element in life and art, and here one may observe a last important area of his influence. Melville and Poe surely responded to this aspect of his art,[23] but it may be that Dickens, once again, best intuited the terrible beauty in his vision of revolutionary wildness and evil. Jack Lindsay has thus linked *A Tale of Two Cities* most persuasively back to *Zanoni* and the unfinished *Edwin Drood* to *A Strange Story*, and

Fradin has added force to the linkages. The same two critics have also gone on to identify Bulwer as one of the major links between the Romantic believers in the energy of the Imagination and the symbolist and surrealist adventurers into the realms of the irrational.[24]

It is perhaps only necessary to add that whatever else may be debatable the supernatural elements in Bulwer's fiction did very definitely constitute a principal influence upon Mme. Blavatsky and her theosophists.[25] In the context, however, of Bulwer's extraordinarily pervasive influence upon the fiction, the myths, and the very conceptions of reality of his contemporaries, his contributions to theosophy may seem a distinctly minor affair.

Notes

CHAPTER I

1. 2nd Earl of Lytton, 2:27–28. (See my note regarding citations and editions which appears above on pp. xvi–xvii.)

2. "On the Want of Sympathy," *The Student*, 1:225. See also *New Monthly Magazine* 35:24, 407; 37:27, and 1st Earl of Lytton, 2:164.

3. 1st Earl of Lytton, 1:101, 107–8, 109. 2nd Earl of Lytton, 1:36.

4. 2nd Earl of Lytton, 1:61, 65. See also Busch, passim.

5. *England and the English*, pp. 280, 281.

6. *New Monthly Magazine* 29:515. "On the Increased Attention to Outward Nature in the Decline of Life," *Caxtoniana*, 1:8.

7. 1st Earl of Lytton, 1:337; 2:36. 2nd Earl of Lytton, 2:523. "On the Want of Sympathy," *The Student*, 1:221–22. Bulwer treats his affair with Lady Caroline Lamb in "De Lindsay," "Greville," and "Lionel Hastings." His long poem "O'Neill" and his prose tale "Glenallan" seem to derive primarily from Lady Caroline's *Glenarvon*.

8. Preface of 1848, *Pelham*. In 1834 Bulwer had written in the same vein to Lady Blessington: "What is self? A thing that changes every year and month. The self of last year has no sympathy with the self of the one before" (2nd Earl of Lytton, 1:458).

9. *New Monthly Magazine* 35:401.

10. *England and the English*, p. 286. *New Monthly Magazine* 31:24.

11. *England and the English*, p. 289. *New Monthly Magazine* 34:422; 35:50, 51. J. S. Mill contributed an interesting appendix to *England and the English* in which he analyzed the strengths and weaknesses of Bentham in the manner of the more famous essay of 1838.

12. *England and the English*, p. 398. It is Mill's appendix that compares Bentham's legal achievement with the work of "the greatest scientific benefactors."

13. *New Monthly Magazine* 31:24; 37:69; 38:135.

14. *New Monthly Magazine* 35:420; 29:512.

15. *New Monthly Magazine* 34:422.

16. *New Monthly Magazine* 37:69; 31:439.

17. *New Monthly Magazine* 35:407. "On the Want of Sympathy," *The Student*, 1:225.

18. *New Monthly Magazine* 34:357.

19. "On the Distinction between Active Thought and Reverie," *Caxtoniana*, 1:210, 213, 211.

20. *Monthly Chronicle* 1:42. "The Sympathetic Temperament," *Caxtoniana*, 1:297–98.

21. In his essay "On Certain Principles of Art in Works of Imagination," *Caxtoniana*, 2:145, Bulwer associates the anecdote with Correggio and concludes that "the porter, on the canvas, was lost in the saint."

22. "The Sympathetic Temperament," *Caxtoniana*, 1:297.

23. *New Monthly Magazine* 31:18.

24. *New Monthly Magazine* 29:517; 35:405, 407.

25. *Monthly Chronicle* 1:42. *New Monthly Magazine* 34:430. Matthew Arnold wrote Bulwer in 1868 to thank him for some criticisms of his *New Poems:* "If I have learnt to seek in any composition for a wide sweep of interest and for a significance residing in the whole rather than in the parts, and not to give over-prominence, either in my own mind or in my work, to the elaboration of details, I have certainly had before me, in your works, an example of this mode of proceeding, and have always valued it in them" (2nd Earl of Lytton, 2:445).

26. *Monthly Chronicle* 1:138–39.

27. *Monthly Chronicle* 1:551. "On Some Authors in whose Writings Knowledge of the World Is Eminently Displayed," *Caxtoniana*, 2:256.

28. *Monthly Chronicle* 1:139. *New Monthly Magazine* 32:252; 35:27.

29. Preface of 1835, *The Disowned*. *Monthly Chronicle* 1:47, 50. Regarding the "compound" character, see also *England and the English*, pp. 267–68, 276–77.

30. Preface of 1845, *Night and Morning*. For a more complete discussion of Bulwer's theories of the "metaphysical novel" and their relationship to the theories of other nineteenth-century novelists, one will need to consult Edwin M. Eigner's impressive, forthcoming study. Eigner considers, for example, the way in which various novelists set their archetypal characters against backgrounds of "a suitable remoteness."

31. *Monthly Chronicle* 1:149, 51. *New Monthly Magazine* 37:

146; 34:430; 38:140. With respect to the novel that leaves moral "gold" within the mind of the reader, observe too a passage from the preface of 1828 to *Pelham:* "under that which has most the semblance of levity I have often been the most diligent in my endeavours to inculcate the substances of truth. The shallowest stream, whose bed every passenger imagines he surveys, may deposit *some* golden grains on the plain through which it flows."

32. *Monthly Chronicle* 1:50.

33. *New Monthly Magazine* 33:303; 38:302. "On . . . Knowledge of the World," *Caxtoniana*, 2:256. *Kenelm Chillingly*, 4:6.

34. *New Monthly Magazine* 37:146.

35. *Monthly Chronicle* 1:50.

36. Preface of 1835, *The Disowned.*

CHAPTER II

1. 1st Earl of Lytton, 2:106. See also the discussion of novels and the "metaphysical knowledge of morals" in *Pelham*, 2:15.

2. 2nd Earl of Lytton, 1:205.

3. 2nd Earl of Lytton, 1:15. Honan, Introduction, p. viii. *England and the English*, p. 278.

4. 1st Earl of Lytton, 2:180.

5. The parenthetical references in the first section of this chapter are all to the four books into which *Falkland* is divided.

6. In a letter of 1835 to Thomas W. White, Poe mentions Bulwer's lurid metaphysical tale "Monos and Daimonos" (collected in *The Student*) as an instance of "the ludicrous heightened into the grotesque: the fearful coloured into the horrible: the witty exaggerated into the burlesque: the singular wrought out into the strange and mystical. You may say all this is bad taste. I have my doubts about it" (*The Letters of Edgar Allan Poe*, ed. J. W. Ostrom, 1 [Cambridge, Mass.: Harvard University Press, 1948]: 57–58).

7. The parenthetical references in the second section of this chapter are all to the volume and chapter numbers of *Pelham*.

8. 1st Earl of Lytton, 2:188.

9. An anarchic force like Falkland, Glanville can scarcely exist convincingly, in Bulwer's later opinion, within the framework of Pelham's fairly ordinary vision of reality (see 1st Earl of Lytton, 2:189–90). Eigner, on the other hand, suggests in his forthcoming book that *Pelham* provides one of the clearest instances of "the sequential split be-

tween realism and romance" that Bulwer quite intentionally employed in all his metaphysical novels: "*Pelham* . . . begins as a glittering example of the silver fork school of society fiction, but it ends as a Gothic detective story." The work conforms in this way to Eigner's definition of "the metaphysical novel [as] an oxymoron, in which experience is first presented in purely materialistic or positivistic terms, then contradicted and transfigured from the idealist point of view."

10. McGann, p. xviii. McGann does not, however, believe that Pelham needs to descend metaphorically to the underworld at this late stage in his development.

11. In a passage dropped after the first edition, Pelham has one further encounter with the demonic as Glanville dies: "I *felt*, as it were, within me some awful and ghostly presence . . . it was as if some preternatural and shadowy object darkened across the mirror of my soul" (3:21).

12. 2nd Earl of Lytton, 1:185. Preface of 1848, *Pelham*. In the preface of 1840 to *Ernest Maltravers*, Bulwer seems to confess at least to "half sympathising with the follies" of Pelham, and his son has indicated the degree to which he did indeed "live" in Pelham and his other protagonists (1st Earl of Lytton, 2:197).

13. The friend was Frederick Villiers, natural son of a Mr. Meynell and a Miss Hunloke, and *not*, as J. J. McGann states (p. xii), George William Frederick Villiers, later the 4th Earl of Clarendon. Bulwer would indeed have some dealings with the latter, but not until the 1860's, when Bulwer's son married Lord Clarendon's niece. Bulwer rather objected then to the Villiers family, and there is no indication in any of his chilly references to Lord Clarendon that the two of them had ever been intimate friends. (See also 2nd Earl of Lytton, 1:124–34, and Sadleir, p. 189 n.)

CHAPTER III

1. 2nd Earl of Lytton, 2:43. "Greville," published in 1st Earl of Lytton, 2:374.

2. J. W. von Goethe, *Wilhelm Meister*, trans. Thomas Carlyle, 1 (New York: Scribner's, 1899): 444.

3. Sadleir, p. 136. 2nd Earl of Lytton, 1:457.

4. Disraeli's "Mutilated Diary," quoted in W. F. Monypenny, *The Life of Benjamin Disraeli, Earl of Beaconsfield*, 1 (New York: Macmillan Co., 1910): 235.

5. Sadleir, p. 35.

6. 2nd Earl of Lytton, 1:360–61. Cazamian, pp. 81–91, and Hollingsworth, pp. 65–82, offer the most complete discussions of the social and political tendency of *Paul Clifford*.

7. Published three months after the hotly-debated Catholic Emancipation Act, *Devereux* makes a great point of the fact that its hero's Catholicism unfortunately debars him from any worthy career in England.

8. Dedicatory Epistle of 1836, *Devereux*.

9. Hollingsworth, pp. 44–47, discusses the connection between Henry Fauntleroy and Bulwer's Crauford.

10. Cazamian, too, p. 87, finds Brandon the most vigorous figure in the novel.

11. In his forthcoming book Eigner discusses the use by Bulwer, Dickens, and others of the "Madonna figure" who is "not just an embarrassing convention, but also a significant symbol . . . the most potent symbolic embodiment available to their century." See also Alexander Welsh's consideration of this "redemptive figure" in *The City of Dickens* (New York: Oxford University Press, 1971), p. 212. With respect to the Psyche motif, note also Dickens' presentation of the marriage of Bella Wilfer and John Rokesmith / Harmon (and of course Wagner's treatment of Elsa and Lohengrin).

12. In similar imagery, Diogenes Teufelsdröckh sees the universe in his negative phase as "dead and demoniacal, a charnel-house with spectres" (Thomas Carlyle, *Sartor Resartus* [New York: Scribner's, 1899], p. 150).

13. Carlyle, *Sartor Resartus*, p. 130.

14. Lady Flora happily comes with the earldom; she had been unwillingly betrothed to Clarence's late older brother, but she is now restored to Clarence as to the true earl.

15. Godwin, who read "parts of the book . . . with transport" had given Bulwer the idea for the novel and had suggested the interesting title "Masks and Faces" (1st Earl of Lytton, 2:247, 258; 2nd Earl of Lytton, 1:364).

16. Similarly likening books to their author's actual, physical body, Bulwer remarked to John Auldjo in the Dedicatory Epistle of 1836 to *Devereux*: "*you* know, and must feel, with me, that these our books are a part of us, bone of our bone and flesh of our flesh! They treasure up the thoughts which stirred us, the affections which warmed us, years ago; they are the mirrors of how much of what we were!"

CHAPTER IV

1. Preface to first edition, *Godolphin.*
2. 2nd Earl of Lytton, 1:455, 457; 2:9.
3. *Confessions of a Water-Patient*, p. 13.
4. Praz, p. 284. George Eliot also provides, of course, an especially good example of the general Victorian preference for the Dutch school —as Praz shows, p. 325, in quoting a passage from chapter XVII of *Adam Bede:* "It is for this rare precious quality of truthfulness that I delight in many Dutch paintings, which lofty-minded people despise. I find a source of delicious sympathy in these faithful pictures of a monotonous homely existence. . . . I turn, without shrinking, from cloud-borne angels, from prophets, sibyls and heroic warriors, to an old woman bending over her flower pot." Bulwer thought that Dutch painting lacked precisely the "rare precious quality of truthfulness." In his worshipful attitude toward Raphael, he was joined most notably— according to Eigner's forthcoming book—by such idealists as Hegel, Goethe, Hugo, Carlyle, Dickens, Emerson, Hawthorne, and Melville.
5. Introduction to *Zanoni.* Dedicatory Epistle to *The Last of the Barons.* References to Bulwer's ideas about Italian art in my next three paragraphs too are largely taken from these sources. In *Zanoni*, see also the dedication, chapter 9 of Book 2, and the note of 1853.
6. Ruskin observes in the well-known lecture "Traffic" in *The Crown of Wild Olive:* "Take a picture by Teniers, of sots quarrelling over their dice; it is an entirely clever picture; so clever that nothing in its kind has ever been done equal to it; but it is also an entirely base and evil picture. It is an expression of delight in the prolonged contemplation of a vile thing, and delight in that is an 'unmannered,' or 'immoral' quality. It is 'bad taste' in the profoundest sense—it is the taste of the devils. On the other hand, a picture of Titian's, or a Greek statue, or a Greek coin, or a Turner landscape, expresses delight in the perpetual contemplation of a good and perfect thing. That is an entirely moral quality—it is the taste of the angels" (*The Works of John Ruskin*, ed. Cook and Wedderburn, 18 [London: George Allen, 1905]: 436).
7. 2nd Earl of Lytton, 1:542. Goethe is also said to have reciprocated Bulwer's admiration for him; according to Howe, p. 177, he once told Müller that he considered Bulwer and Carlyle the two most promising young English literary figures of the day. I have not, however, been able to locate such remarks myself in *Goethes Unterhaltungen mit*

dem Kanzler Friedrich von Müller, ed. C. A. H. Burkhardt (Stuttgart: J. G. Gotte'schung, 1898).

8. Bornia, p. 32. Wolff, pp. 159–232, discusses quite exhaustively and fascinatingly Bulwer's skillful use in *Zanoni* of countless literary and occult sources. 2nd Earl of Lytton, 2:37, 39.

9. Sadleir, pp. 285, 280, 281. Wolff, pp. 221–24.

10. Wolff, pp. 212–13, believes it is primarily the dedication to Gibson that undercuts the moral lesson of the romance itself. In my opinion (and apparently that of Lloyd, p. 39, too), though, a fundamental ambiguity is built into the structure of the entire romance.

11. *Westminster Review* 27:171.

12. Ibid.

13. The funeral of John Vernon provides another example of style operating to conceal the reality of death: "deserted in life by all, [he] was interred with the insulting ceremonials of pomp and state. Six nobles bore his pall: long trains of carriages attended his funeral. . . . They buried him in Westminster Abbey" (G 2).

14. *Godolphin* constitutes, in part, an anatomy of Exclusivism between 1815 and 1832. Rosa, pp. 95–96, discusses this aspect of the novel and goes on to speculate on the degree to which the heroine and hero may have been modelled on Bulwer's friends Lady Blessington and Count D'Orsay (the novel is dedicated to the latter). Sadleir, p. 291, has concluded that "Constance, though the mouthpiece of many of Lady Blessington's theories, was not a portrait of Lady Blessington, nor was Godolphin himself D'Orsay." Bulwer's heroine may, I suspect, have derived some of her qualities from the beautiful Lady Cowper, whom Bulwer would describe in 1838 as "still handsome and very intelligent and interesting. She is associated with my first *beaux jours*, the early tickets for Almacks and my first fine lady love" (2nd Earl of Lytton, 2:13).

15. As Howe, pp. 153, 158, and Rosa, p. 94, have indicated, Lucilla is based on Goethe's Mignon (very clearly so when she innocently pleads with the hero to let her live with him), while Fanny Millinger is based on Goethe's Philine (a fact that Bulwer's own anonymous review of the anonymous novel also acknowledges [*New Monthly Magazine* 38:142]). The patterns of the plot—whereby Constance and Godolphin find themselves alienated from each other and drawn into the liaisons with Lord Erpingham and Lucilla respectively—may also remind one of the *Wahlverwandtschaften*, but Bulwer had ap-

parently not yet read that Goethean novel when he composed *Godolphin*.

16. Since Maltravers has not hitherto believed in the existence of the devil, his tutoring of the ignorant Alice in religious doctrines had specifically avoided this dark aspect of religion.

17. Become Lord Vargrave in his latest metamorphosis, the proud Ferrers had received a final chance to repent and had, in a scene reminiscent of *Don Giovanni*, refused.

18. Lord Saltream reinforces several thematic elements of *Godolphin* in rather interesting ways, and it is unfortunate that in 1840, when he acknowledged his authorship of the novel, Bulwer removed this character from the story. The similarity of Saltream to an actual eccentric, the late Lord Dudley, a violent opponent of the Reform Bill, was widely considered shocking. (Sadleir, p. 290, and Rosa, pp. 95–96, also seem to disapprove of Bulwer's having introduced Saltream in the first place.)

19. Wolff, p. 225, has also observed a connection between the Terror and the Dweller of the Threshold: "Once [the revolutionaries'] impatience had led them too soon to imbibe the heady elixir [of violence], the Terror, like the Dweller of the Threshold, was in their midst."

20. Goethe, *Wilhelm Meister*, 1:444.

21. The story has hinted that the reconciliation of husband and wife could probably not have endured in any case; Bulwer was speaking from his own bitter marital experience at that precise moment.

22. As the note of 1851 to *Alice* summarizes the allegorical aspect of the story: "GENIUS, . . . duly following its vocation, reunites itself to the NATURE from which Life and Art had for a while distracted it; but to Nature in a higher and more spiritual form than that under which Youth beholds it—Nature elevated and idealised."

23. Wolff, p. 167.

24. To the 1853 edition of *Zanoni*, Bulwer appended his note and—while leaving its authorship anonymous—Miss Martineau's key to the abstract meanings of the characters and the plot.

25. In her "Self-Confessional," for example, Viola mentions her frequent fits of abstraction, in which "it was so sweet to sit apart and gaze my whole being into the distant heavens. My nature is not formed for this life, happy though that life seem to others. It is its very want to have ever before it some image loftier than itself!" (Z 3:5).

26. Lindsay, pp. 364–69, presents an interesting discussion of the relationship between *Zanoni* and *A Tale of Two Cities*.

27. Bornia, pp. 34–35, lists the clues that suggest that the myste-

rious author is Clarence Glyndon grown old. Bornia believes in the actual existence of Glyndon and argues that *Zanoni* constitutes a largely true story.

28. Tillotson, pp. 150–56.

29. Frank Kermode, *Romantic Image* (London: Routledge and Kegan Paul, 1957), pp. 11–19.

CHAPTER V

1. 2nd Earl of Lytton, 2:96.

2. The phrase is that of Fradin, "The Novels of Edward Bulwer-Lytton," p. 251.

3. *Foreign Quarterly Review* 29:276.

4. Hollingsworth, pp. 182–91, discusses the career of Wainewright and its connection with *Lucretia*; on pp. 170–77 he considers the Newgate aspects of *Night and Morning*.

5. Lautz, p. 94, points out the contrast between the brothers of the older generation, Philip and Robert Beaufort, and refers the contrast to "the Jones-and-Blifil or Charles-and-Joseph-Surface tradition."

6. Preface of 1845, *Night and Morning*. See also Lindsay, pp. 196–98. Hawthorne incidentally refers to an actual encounter with Pecksniff's supposed original during his English tour of 1856, when he sought out many of Dickens' and Bulwer's familiars (*The English Notebooks: By Nathaniel Hawthorne*, ed. Randall Stewart [New York: MLA, 1941], pp. 313, 315, 349).

7. Eigner and Fradin, "Bulwer-Lytton and Dickens' Jo." The treatment in *Lucretia* of the body-snatcher and the references to life on convict ships and in Australian penal colonies must similarly have influenced Dickens' presentation of Orlick, Magwitch, and Compeyson in *Great Expectations*.

8. Hollingsworth, pp. 191–202, discusses the scandal.

9. *Pompeii*, 3:9. Serpents appear similarly in dreams in *Barons*, 8:3, and *Harold*, 4:2.

10. 2nd Earl of Lytton, 2:89, 86.

11. 2nd Earl of Lytton, 2:94, 93.

12. Preface, *Harold*. Sheppard, p. 62. Simmons too, pp. 299–305, discusses Bulwer's "imaginative" faithfulness to the historical evidence as a factor in the popularity of these romances but does not consider their implicit philosophy of history.

13. Shattuck, p. 225. Dedicatory Epistle, *Barons*.

14. Dahl, pp. 61ff., emphasizes the degree to which Bulwer has manipulated historical events in order to make them more neatly analogous to contemporary political situations. After commenting on Bulwer's erudition and the fact that he was probably the first to bring Italian history into Victorian fiction, Fleishman similarly decides, pp. 33–35, that Bulwer's best historical romances are most interesting as tendentious tracts for the times. In fact, I believe, these works may provide additional examples of the nineteenth-century ideas of time and the myths of national identity that Fleishman analyzes so fascinatingly in novels by other authors. Although Fleishman does not deal at any length with the tradition of German idealism (which is especially relevant to Bulwer), his general discussion of historical hermeneutics could usefully have been applied to Bulwer's fiction. Fleishman treats, for example, the "historical imagination" which, in reconciling all manner of opposites, is able to see the particular as an expression of the universal and the dependence of the universal upon its particular manifestations. "What makes a historical novel historical," he concludes in a statement that could refer with special force to Bulwer, "is the active presence of a concept of history as a shaping force—acting not only upon the characters in the novel but on the author and readers outside it. . . . The protagonists of such novels confront not only the forces of history in their own time, but its impact on life in any time. The universal conception of the individual's career as fate becomes symbolized not by the gods but by history" (p. 15).

15. Thomas Carlyle, "On History," *Critical and Miscellaneous Essays*, 2 (New York: Scribner's, 1899): 95; and *Sartor Resartus* (New York: Scribner's, 1899), p. 146.

16. The statement implies the so-called myth of "the Norman yoke" that informs both *Harold* and *Barons*. Fleishman, pp. 26–27, associates the myth especially with Scott and suggests that it survives in the "peculiarly English populism of Hardy and Lawrence." According to the myth England has remained the slave of alien Norman values and has never fulfilled its essentially Saxon birthright.

17. Bulwer would have followed the same pattern in his development of the story of Pausanias. In fact, Pausanias was destined to kill his beloved Cleonice, as Bulwer's son indicates in the Dedication to his publication of the unfinished romance.

18. The essay on the Reign of Terror—*Foreign Quarterly Review* 29:286—draws certain parallels between the revolutionary period in

France and the late fifteenth century in England and suggests that the virtues of Louis XVI, including "his excellent heart, his sweet and amiable nature, were as wholly lost and thrown away in the turbulence of the time, as were the virtues somewhat similar of our own Henry the Sixth in the convulsions of a civil war."

19. Cf. Mr. Caxton's solution to the historical problem of evil: "Not one great war has ever desolated the earth but has left behind it seeds that have ripened into blessings incalculable" (C 18:8).

20. "The Sympathetic Temperament," *Caxtoniana*, 1:297. See chapter 1 above, p. 14.

21. Dahl, p. 65.

22. Shattuck, p. 163. Regarding the distinction between the People and the Public, see also *England and the English*, pp. 398–99; *Ernest Maltravers*, 7:1; *Foreign Quarterly Review* 29:289, 308; and 2nd Earl of Lytton, 1:557.

23. Fleishman, p. 34.

CHAPTER VI

1. Usrey, p. 181.

2. 2nd Earl of Lytton, 2:127, 119.

3. 2nd Earl of Lytton, 2:161, 314, 315.

4. 2nd Earl of Lytton, 2:195, 194.

5. 2nd Earl of Lytton, 2:284–88. Sir George attributed "in no slight degree the success of [his] career to [his] strict adherence to the advice given in [Bulwer's] letter," and in one of his own letters from Queensland, he praised the "author of *The Caxtons*" for his accurate knowledge of the situation in Australia (Stanley Lane-Poole, ed., *Thirty Years of Colonial Government: A Selection from the Despatches and Letters of the Rt. Hon. Sir George Ferguson Bowen, G.C.M.G.*, 1 [London: Longmans, 1889]: 106–12). For some reason Coral Lansbury, pp. 80, 144, has the impression that Bulwer's performance as Colonial Secretary was "calamitous," but there is no evidence for this view, even in the source she cites—J. Rutherford, *Sir George Grey, K.C.B., 1812–1898: A Study in Colonial Government* (London: Cassell, 1961), pp. 414–26, 436–38.

6. 2nd Earl of Lytton, 2:130–31, 398. Bulwer remarks similarly in "The Sympathetic Temperament," *Caxtoniana*, 1:295: "I have always thought it well for the man whose main pursuit must be carried

on through solitary contemplation, to force himself to some active interest in common with ordinary mortals, even though it be but in the culture of a farm. He will be more reconciled to the utter want of sympathy in the process by which the germ of a thought grows up into flower within his own secret mind, if, when he goes into the marketplace, he finds and reciprocates abundant sympathy in the effect of the weather on hay and barley."

7. Usrey, pp. 155–56, 70, 171–72.

8. Baker, p. 198.

9. Usrey, pp. 179–80. Eigner, in "Bulwer-Lytton and the Changed Ending of *Great Expectations*," summarizes the arguments which Bulwer must have used to convince Dickens of the aesthetic desirability of happy endings.

10. Usrey, pp. 61–62.

11. Like the unproductive scholar Christopher Clutterbuck in *Pelham*, Mr. Caxton is based on Bulwer's studious and quixotic grandfather, Richard Warburton Lytton (2nd Earl of Lytton, 1:12–13, 68).

12. Usrey, p. 178.

13. Usrey, p. 73.

14. The aphorism was supposedly Baconian, but Bulwer observed in a letter to Blackwood: "I always suspected that Bacon could not [have] been the author of that silly aphorism Knowledge is Power & Resolved to hunt him all thro' to see if I could find it— And certainly it is not in Bacon. Thinking it might possibly have Escaped my search I then applied to Macaulay's Wonderous Memory & to a gentleman who has taken Bacon as his one study Both bear me out." In a note on this letter, however, Usrey indicates, p. 89, that Bacon used the aphorism both in *De Haeresibus* and in *Novum Organum*.

15. Fradin, "The Novels of Edward Bulwer-Lytton," p. 205.

16. Bulwer removed a portion of this passage from later editions of the novel; for the complete passage see *Blackwood's Magazine* 83:25.

17. Usrey, p. 132.

18. Using the same metaphor, Bulwer would later express his fear that the Reform Bill of 1867 had created such a monster even in the mother country: "Since [Conservatism] has chosen to be Frankenstein & create a Giant, for which I doubt if there were any necessity—it can't escape from the Giant & had better made a friend of him than an enemy" (Usrey, p. 376).

19. Lansbury, pp. 79–80, 85–86.

20. Bulwer similarly remarks in the middle of an interesting discussion of the United States at the time of the American Civil War: "Enough of pride for me, as an Englishman, to know that whatever state in that large section of the globe may best represent the dignity and progress of human thought shall have had its fathers in Englishmen, and shall utter its edicts in the English tongue. I! a prejudice against Americans as Americans!—enough answer to that charge for me and my countrymen that fathers have no natural prejudice against their children!" ("The Organ of Weight," *Caxtoniana*, 1:274–75).

21. *Blackwood's Magazine* 83:429.

22. Usrey, p. 56.

23. From a more seriously architectural viewpoint, Ruskin attempts in his "A Chapter on Chimneys"—published in 1838 in the series *The Poetry of Architecture*—to determine whether urban English chimneys are really expressive of the "comfortable . . . fireside disposition" of "carbonaceous England" with its beloved domestic icons of hobs and blazing Christmas hearths. He concludes that chimneys are handled better on the continent and that the chimneys of English cities betray chiefly the ugliness and cheerlessness of modern urban life (*The Works of John Ruskin*, ed. Cook and Wedderburn, [London: George Allen, 1903], 1:54–65).

24. Eigner carries the Wordsworthian analogy further in his forthcoming book: "Pisistratus must undergo a circuitous journey, to Australia and back, before he can be the first person narrator of *The Caxtons*, which turns out to be a prelude, a Wordsworthian 'ante-chapel' to Bulwer's 'gothic church,' the succeeding Caxton novels." As Eigner also suggests, *Zanoni* similarly tells the story of how its author has achieved the perspective that has enabled him to write his book, and to this list one could add *Devereux* and *A Strange Story* as well.

25. Parson Dale is surely based on Fielding's Parson Adams, and *My Novel* seems frequently, in fact, to confess a debt to Fielding— most noticeably in Bulwer's handling of the discursive introductory chapters, which he told Blackwood were "like Fieldings" (Usrey, p. 65). *The Caxtons* on the other hand owes many of its technical and thematic elements to Sterne, an influence that receives some interesting attention from Fradin, "The Novels of Edward Bulwer-Lytton," pp. 196–216.

26. "Motive Power," *Caxtoniana*, 2:105. See also *The Parisians*, 1:8.

CHAPTER VII

1. "Posthumous Reputation," and "Motive Power," *Caxtoniana*, 2: 187, 48.
2. "Posthumous Reputation," *Caxtoniana*, 2:199.
3. Bulwer also quotes these lines in *Zanoni*, 1:8, and *My Novel*, 10:1. In his published translation of Schiller's poetry, the passage from which these lines are taken reads:

> But in the Ideal Realm, aloof and far,
> Where the calm Art's pure dwellers are,
>   Lo, the Laocoon writhes, but does not groan.
> Here no sharp grief the high emotion knows—
> Here suffering's self is made divine, and shows
>   The brave resolve of the firm soul alone.

4. "The Sympathetic Temperament," *Caxtoniana*, 1:287.
5. Usrey, pp. 353–54, 428.
6. The essay on "The Sympathetic Temperament," *Caxtoniana*, 1: 302, explicitly likens sympathy to magnetism: "sympathy exists in all minds, as Faraday has discovered that magnetism exists in all metals; but a certain temperature is required to develop the hidden property, whether in the metal or the mind."
7. Since the fluid, represented in the story by "the saucer of crystal . . . with a clear liquid," transmits a deadly rather than precisely vital power, it may also recall the ultimate, imperceptible poison of *Lucretia*. As a man of inhuman inflexibility of purpose, whose poison is the unseen extension of mental determination, Olivier Dalibard in *Lucretia* has indeed prefigured Bulwer's later, more preternatural embodiments of will. So too, for that matter, has the "terrible boy" Richard of Gloucester with the "Power of his calm WILL" in *Barons*, 10:7. And in his *Confessions of a Water-Patient*, p. 16, Bulwer refers to his own "great belief in the power of WILL. What a man determines to do— that in ninety-nine cases out of the hundred I hold that he succeeds in doing."
8. 2nd Earl of Lytton, 2:465.
9. Wires in the wand sympathetically vibrate or expand in accord with the holder's nervous impulses and so help him to focus his volitional energies and transmit them through the atmosphere. As for the elixir of life, Margrave and Fenwick seem to distill it from the bowels

of earth and night during the concluding ordeal of mental concentration.

10. Henkin, p. 236.

11. Stewart, p. 37. Wolff, pp. 260–64 (re: Eliphas Lévi), 315–22 (re: Balzac, Hugo, etc.), 328–30 (re: vril). 2nd Earl of Lytton, 2:466, 467.

12. Lautz, p. 185, Wagner, p. 381, and Wolff, p. 328, mention the anticipation of atomic energy, and Wagner goes on to relate Bulwer's satire to works by Butler, Wells, Bennett, Wyndham Lewis, Huxley, and Orwell.

13. It is perhaps an unintentional paradox that the whole way of life of the Vril-ya depends on the intensity of their volition even though their highest desire is for an indolent serenity.

14. "Motive Power," *Caxtoniana*, 2:127.

15. *Blackwood's Magazine* 83:429.

16. Stanley L. Lane-Poole, ed., *Thirty Years of Colonial Government: A Selection from the Despatches and Letters of the Rt. Hon. Sir George Ferguson Bowen, G.C.M.G.*, 1 (London: Longmans, Green, 1889): 177.

17. "Motive Power" and "Posthumous Reputation," *Caxtoniana*, 2: 74, 75, 204–5.

18. 2nd Earl of Lytton, 2:399.

19. Fradin, " 'The Absorbing Tyranny of Every-day Life,' " p. 9. Bulwer told Dickens while the story was being serialized in Dickens' *All the Year Round:* "Margrave is the sensuous material principle of Nature"; "Fenwick is the type of the intellect that divorces itself from the spiritual"; "Lilian is the type of the spiritual divorcing itself from the intellectual" (2nd Earl of Lytton, 2:346).

20. 2nd Earl of Lytton, 2:407, 411.

21. See in particular *A Strange Story*, ch. 73, and 2nd Earl of Lytton, 2:403, 405.

22. Walter Pater, *Marius the Epicurean* (New York: New American Library, 1970), pp. 100, 283.

23. Bulwer had similarly remarked in *Rienzi* (10:8) that the "yearning for the Great Beyond attests our immortality."

24. 2nd Earl of Lytton, 2:409.

25. Fradin, " 'The Absorbing Tyranny of Every-day Life,' " pp. 15–16, discusses the evidence of Bulwer's influence upon Villiers de L'Isle-Adam.

26. Ardworth in *Lucretia* is perhaps the first of these anglers who whistle airs from Izaak Walton's songs and seem to respond more in-

tensely than most to "that unspeakable peace which Nature whispers to those attuned to her music" (L 1:1). The tradition continues with Christopher ("Gentle Kit") Cotton in Bulwer's unfinished "Lionel Hastings." Kit, who keeps playing the fiddle to console himself, is given a copy of Walton's *Angler* in the course of the story, and he is clearly an earlier version of another of Bulwer's eccentric musicians and anglers, the flute-playing Dick Fairthorne in *What Will He Do with It?* (Bulwer's son—1st Earl of Lytton, 1:175—has observed that *What Will He Do with It?* must have grown in part out of "Lionel Hastings.") The Neapolitan Fisher of Isaura's song in *The Parisians* may also be related to Bulwer's other anglers. But the most fascinating of them all is probably the mad angler, John Burley, of *My Novel*. He responds to the demonic in the "watery element" and actually reminds one very distinctly of Melville's Captain Ahab. Indeed he might seem a parody of Captain Ahab except for the fact that the portion of *My Novel* in which we learn his story appeared in *Blackwood's* in July 1851, some four months before publication of *Moby Dick*. Burley has devoted his life to efforts to catch a certain "diabolical" fish living in the Brent near Bulwer's beloved Ealing: "a PERCH—all his fins up, like the sails of a man-of-war—a monster perch—a whale of a perch!—No, never till then," says Burley, "had I known what leviathans lie hid within the deeps." Once he had hooked the perch's eye, and eight times since then he has almost caught "the mocking fiend" whom he now knows "better than [he] knew [his] own lost father." An obsession with that fish prevents him from taking lucrative positions in Jamaica or India and has ruined his life. Yet he also admits that he does not really want to capture the fish, for this would remove the single object of his existence (MN 6:8).

27. Westminster Bridge had figured with similar symbolic prominence in *My Novel*.

28. Usrey, p. 204.

29. 2nd Earl of Lytton, 2:484.

30. 2nd Earl of Lytton, 2:456, 431, 453.

31. 2nd Earl of Lytton, 2:456–57.

32. 2nd Earl of Lytton, 2:488.

CHAPTER VIII

1. Walter Frewen Lord, "The Apostle of Mediocrity," *The Nineteenth Century* 51 (1902): 396–410. Bradford A. Booth, *Anthony*

Trollope: Aspects of His Life and Art (Bloomington: Indiana University Press, 1958), p. 5. George Eliot, *Scenes of Clerical Life*, 1 (London: Hawarden Press, 1899): 59.

2. Gordon N. Ray, Introduction to *The Life of Wilkie Collins* by Nuel Pharr Davis (Urbana: University of Illinois Press, 1956), p. 5.

3. Wolff, p. 314.

4. [Letter of 12 May 1861], *The Letters of Charles Dickens*, ed. by his sister-in-law and his oldest daughter, 3 (London: Chapman and Hall, 1882): 200.

AFTERWORD

1. Rosa, pp. 74–98, provides the most complete account of Bulwer's contribution to the silver-fork tradition.

2. Moers, pp. 94–100, usefully summarizes the evidence of Bulwer's influence upon Disraeli in this period.

3. Michael Allen, *Poe and the British Magazine Tradition* (New York: Oxford University Press, 1969), pp. 32–33, 47–48, 50, 57–58, 65–66, 68–70, 78–79, 101–2, 136, 187, 195. Allen's discussion of Bulwer's effect on Poe also constitutes a good analysis of Bulwer's editorship of the *New Monthly Magazine*—an important subject which is receiving more thorough attention from Linda Bonnell Jones in a study now in preparation. With respect to the influence of both Bulwer and Disraeli on Poe, see also Alexander Hammond, "Poe's 'Lionizing' and the Design of *Tales of the Folio Club*," *Esquire* 18 (1972): 154–65.

4. Arthur Hobson Quinn, *Edgar Allan Poe: A Critical Biography* (New York: Cooper Square, 1969), pp. 646–47, 661, 676.

5. Hollingsworth, passim.

6. Fradin, "The Novels of Edward Bulwer-Lytton," p. 144.

7. Maurice Willson Disher, *Blood and Thunder: Mid-Victorian Melodrama and Its Origins* (London: Frederick Muller, 1949), p. 122. Fradin, "The Novels of Edward Bulwer-Lytton," pp. 145–46 and n. Regarding the special power of *Night and Morning* to affect certain readers, Macaulay assured Bulwer: "It moved my feelings more than anything you have written, and more than a man of forty-three, who has been much tossed about the world, is easily moved by works of the imagination." And on the same page (2:331), the 2nd Earl of Lytton records his own reactions to the novel: "I remember the breathless interest which this book excited in me when I first read it as a boy,

and the description of the discovery of the gang of coiners and the death of Ga[w]trey their leader, still remains one of the most vivid impressions which I received when first reading my grandfather's works." Escott, p. 252, asserted in 1910 that "two generations of readers have seen in *Night and Morning* one among the most interesting of Bulwer's narrative melodramas." See also Lautz, pp. 91–116.

8. Fradin, "The Novels of Edward Bulwer-Lytton," pp. 154–55 n.

9. Moers, p. 183, offers convincing arguments to show that Carlyle, who had no personal grudge against Bulwer, was most unlikely to have read *Pelham* or *The Disowned* himself.

10. Tillotson, p. 86.

11. Gordon N. Ray, ed., *The Letters and Private Papers of . . . Thackeray*, 4 vols. (Cambridge: Harvard University Press, 1945–46), 2:485, and 3:298. Moers, pp. 198–213. See also Sadleir's account of Thackeray's attacks on Bulwer, pp. 229–33, 256–58, and of the general campaign of *Fraser's* against Bulwer, pp. 226–29, 233–43.

12. Susanne Howe's work remains the most complete study of the Goethean pattern in English fiction, but her analysis does not deal adequately with novels subsequent to Bulwer's. Far more to the point in defining the pattern and theory of *Bildung*—although it mentions Bulwer only in passing—is the article by G. B. Tennyson, "The *Bildungsroman* in Nineteenth-Century English Literature," *University of Southern California Studies in Comparative Literature*, 1 (1968): 135–46.

13. Lansbury, pp. 103, 111, 120, 158, and passim. Bulwer's preface to *The Caxtons* also implies the work's relationship to the *Bildungsroman* tradition: "the interior meaning . . . is . . . that, whatever our wanderings, our happiness will always be found within a narrow compass, and amidst the objects more immediately within our reach, but that we are seldom sensible of this truth . . . till our researches have spread over a wider area."

14. Fleishman, pp. 26–27, 35–36, 180.

15. Dahl, p. 62. Simmons, pp. 304–5.

16. Eigner, "Raphael in Oxford Street," pp. 61–73.

17. Wagner, pp. 379–85. B. G. Knepper, "Shaw's Debt to *The Coming Race*," *Journal of Modern Literature* 1 (1971): 339–53.

18. Tillotson, p. 156.

19. Sucksmith, p. 118 n., reports that Professor K. J. Fielding has told him about these discoveries with respect to the nature of Bulwer's influence upon John Forster. Quinn (see n. 4 above), pp. 314–15. Tillotson, p. 240. W. C. Roscoe, "Sir E. B. Lytton, Novelist,

Philosopher, and Poet," *National Review* 7 (1859):308. 2nd Earl of Lytton, 2:445.

20. John Caldwell Stubbs, *The Pursuit of Form: A Study of Hawthorne and the Romance* (Urbana: University of Illinois Press, 1970), pp. 9–11, 20, 30–31.

21. Bulwer's two paragraphs of interesting and balanced assessment of Dickens, written on the flyleaf of a book, were printed in the brochure of the Dickens Centenary Exhibition (1970) at Knebworth House.

22. Eigner and Fradin, "Bulwer-Lytton and Dickens' Jo," pp. 98–102. Eigner, "Bulwer-Lytton and the Changed Ending of *Great Expectations*," pp. 104–8. Sucksmith, pp. 110–19, 152, 232, 252. See also Sibylla Jane Flower, "Charles Dickens and Edward Bulwer-Lytton," *Dickensian* 69 (1973): 78–79.

23. With reference to Bulwer's influence on Melville, see Leon Howard, *Herman Melville: A Biography* (Berkeley: University of California Press, 1951), p. 171. Professor Howard has told me of his increasing conviction that Melville responded to many aspects of Bulwer's art, possibly because a Pittsfield neighbor used to give him copies of Bulwer's books. Henry A. Murray considers Bulwer one of the possible "architects of Melville's early ideal self" (see Murray's Introduction to Melville's *Pierre: Or, The Ambiguities* [New York: Farrar Straus, 1949], pp. xli, lxvi).

24. Lindsay, pp. 196–98 (which also relate "the dynamic element" in *Night and Morning* to *The Old Curiosity Shop*), 364–69 (re: *Zanoni* and *A Tale of Two Cities*), and 406–9 (re: *A Strange Story* and *Edwin Drood*, to which works Wilkie Collins' *Moonstone* should presumably also be compared). See also Lindsay's Appendix on Bulwer, which virtually reprints his article, "Clairvoyance of the Normal," *Nineteenth Century* 145 (1949):26–38. Fradin, "The Novels of Edward Bulwer-Lytton," pp. 165–66, 170–73. Fradin, " 'The Absorbing Tyranny of Every-day Life,' " pp. 15–16.

25. Liljegren, passim.

Selected Bibliography

WORKS BY EDWARD BULWER, FIRST LORD LYTTON

Caxtoniana: A Series of Essays on Life, Literature, and Manners. 2 vols. Edinburgh: W. Blackwood & Son, 1863.

Confessions of A Water-Patient: In a Letter to W. Harrison Ainsworth, Esq., Editor of "The New Monthly Magazine." London: Henry Colburn, 1845.

England and the English. Edited with introduction by Standish Meacham. Chicago: University of Chicago Press, 1970.

Falkland. Edited by Herbert Van Thal. Introduction by Park Honan. London: Cassell, 1967.

Miscellaneous Prose Works. 3 vols. London: R. Bentley, 1868.
    As indicated, however, in my note on pp. xvi–xvii above, these volumes (which do not include all of Bulwer's non-fictional prose writings) are difficult to find, and my references to essays not collected in *The Student* or *Caxtoniana* are to the periodicals in which the essays were first published.

[The New Knebworth Edition of the Novels and Romances of the Right Hon. Lord Lytton]. 28 vols. London: George Routledge & Sons, 1895–98.

Pelham; or, The Adventures of a Gentleman. Edited with introduction by Jerome J. McGann. Lincoln: University of Nebraska Press, 1972.

The Poems and Ballads of Schiller, translated, With a Brief Sketch of Schiller's Life. 2 vols. Edinburgh: W. Blackwood & Son, 1844.

The Student: A Series of Papers. 2 vols. London: Saunders & Otley, 1835.

Zanoni: A Rosicrucian Tale. Preface by Paul M. Allen. Blauvelt, N.Y.: Rudolf Steiner Publications, 1971.

[255]

OTHER WORKS CONTAINING
PRIMARY MATERIAL

Lytton, Robert, 1st Earl of. *The Life, Letters, and Literary Remains of Edward Bulwer, Lord Lytton, by his Son.* 2 vols. London: Kegan Paul Tench, 1883.

Lytton, Victor Alexander, 2nd Earl of. *The Life of Edward Bulwer, First Lord Lytton, by His Grandson.* 2 vols. London: Macmillan, 1913.

Shattuck, Charles H., ed. *Bulwer and Macready: A Chronicle of the Early Victorian Theatre.* Urbana: University of Illinois Press, 1958.

Usrey, Malcolm Orthell, ed. "The Letters of Sir Edward Bulwer-Lytton to the Editors of *Blackwood's Magazine*, 1840–1873, in the National Library of Scotland." Ph.D. dissertation, Texas Technological College, 1963.

SECONDARY SOURCES

Allen, Walter. *The English Novel.* New York: E. P. Dutton, 1954.

Baker, Ernest A. *The History of the English Novel.* Vol. 7. London: H. F. and G. Witherby, 1936.

Bangs, Archie R. "Mephistophiles in England; or, The Confessions of a Prime Minister." *PMLA* 47 (1932):200–19.

    I do not, incidentally, agree with the thesis of this article, that a certain anonymous novel of 1835 should be attributed to Bulwer.

Bell, E. G. *Introduction to the Prose Romances, Plays and Comedies of Edward Bulwer, Lord Lytton.* Chicago: W. M. Hill, 1914.

Blake, Robert. "Bulwer-Lytton." *Cornhill Magazine*, no. 1077 (1973), pp. 67–76.

Bornia, Pietro. *Il Guardiano della soglia.* 2. edizione, aggiuntovi un' appendice di E. Bulwer. Napoli: n.d.

Busch, Gustav. *Bulwers Jugendliebe und Ihr Einfluss auf Sein Leben und Seine Werke.* Dresden: Druck von Albert Hille, 1899.

Carré, Jean-Marie. *Goethe en Angleterre.* Paris: Plon-Nourrit, 1920.

Cazamian, Louis. *Le Roman social en Angleterre, 1830–1850.* Paris: Société Nouvelle de Librairie et d'Edition, 1904.

Dahl, Curtis. "Bulwer-Lytton and the School of Catastrophe." *Philosophical Quarterly* 32 (1953): 428–42.

————. "Edward Bulwer-Lytton." In *Victorian Fiction: A Guide to*

Research, edited by Lionel Stevenson. Cambridge: Harvard University Press, 1966. Pp. 35–43.

———. "History on the Hustings: Bulwer-Lytton's Historical Novels of Politics." In *From Jane Austen to Joseph Conrad*, edited by Robert C. Rathburn and Martin Steinmann, Jr. Minneapolis: University of Minnesota Press, 1958. Pp. 60–71.

All references to "Dahl" in my notes are to this article.

———. "Recreators of Pompeii." *Archaeology* 9 (1956):182–91.

Eigner, Edwin M. "Bulwer-Lytton and the Changed Ending of *Great Expectations*." *Nineteenth-Century Fiction* 25 (1970): 104–8.

———. "Raphael in Oxford Street: Bulwer's Accommodation to the Realists." In *The Nineteenth-Century Writer and His Audience*, edited by Harold Orel and George J. Worth. Lawrence: University of Kansas Humanistic Studies, no. 40, 1969. Pp. 61–74.

———, and Joseph I. Fradin. "Bulwer-Lytton and Dickens' Jo." *Nineteenth-Century Fiction* 24 (1969): 98–102.

Escott, T. H. S. *Edward Bulwer, First Baron Lytton of Knebworth: A Social, Personal, and Political Monograph*. London: George Routledge & Sons, 1910.

Flower, Sibylla Jane. *Bulwer-Lytton: An Illustrated Life of the First Baron Lytton, 1803–1873*. Aylesbury: Shire Publishing, 1973.

Fradin, Joseph I. " 'The Absorbing Tyranny of Every-day Life': Bulwer-Lytton's *A Strange Story*." *Nineteenth-Century Fiction* 16 (1961): 1–16.

———. "The Novels of Edward Bulwer-Lytton." Ph.D. dissertation, Columbia University, 1956.

Fleishman, Avrom. *The English Historical Novel: Walter Scott to Virginia Woolf*. Baltimore: Johns Hopkins University Press, 1971.

Henkin, Leo J. *Darwinism in the English Novel, 1860–1910*. New York: Corporate Press, 1940.

Hollingsworth, Keith. *The Newgate Novel, 1830–1847: Bulwer, Ainsworth, Dickens, and Thackeray*. Detroit: Wayne State University Press, 1963.

Honan, Park. Introduction to *Falkland*, edited by Herbert Van Thal. London: Cassel, 1967. Pp. vii–xviii.

Howe, Susanne. *Wilhelm Meister and His English Kinsmen: Apprentices to Life*. New York: Columbia University Press, 1930.

Kelly, Richard. "The Haunted House of Bulwer-Lytton." *Studies in Short Fiction* 8 (1971): 581–87.

Lansbury, Coral. *Arcady in Australia: The Evocation of Australia in Nineteenth-Century English Literature*. Carlton: Melbourne University Press, 1970.

Lautz, Richard Eugene. "Bulwer-Lytton as Novelist." Ph.D. dissertation, University of Pennsylvania, 1967.

Liljegren, S. B. *Bulwer-Lytton's Novels and Isis Unveiled*. Cambridge: Harvard University Press, 1957.

Lindsay, Jack. *Charles Dickens: A Biographical and Critical Study*. London: Andrew Dakers, 1950.

Lloyd, Michael. "Bulwer-Lytton and the Idealising Principle." *English Miscellany* 7 (1956): 25–39.

Lytton, Victor Alexander, 2nd Earl of. *Bulwer-Lytton*. Denver: Alan Swallow, 1948.

    All references to the "2nd Earl of Lytton" in the notes are, however, to the two-volume biography of 1913, which contains a great deal of primary material and is listed above.

McGann, Jerome J. "The Dandy." *Midway*, Summer 1969, pp. 3–18.

————. Introduction to *Pelham; or, The Adventures of a Gentleman*, edited by McGann. Lincoln: University of Nebraska Press, 1972. Pp. xi–xxv. All references in the notes to "McGann" are to this essay.

Moers, Ellen. *The Dandy: Brummell to Beerbohm*. New York: Viking Press, 1960.

Praz, Mario. *The Hero in Eclipse in Victorian Fiction*. Translated by Angus Davidson. London: Oxford University Press, 1956.

Rosa, Matthew Whiting. *The Silver Fork School: Novels of Fashion Preceding "Vanity Fair."* New York: Columbia University Press, 1936.

Sadleir, Michael. *Bulwer: A Panorama: Edward and Rosina, 1803–1836*. Boston: Little, Brown, 1931.

Seeber, Hans. "Gegenutopie und Roman: Bulwer-Lyttons *The Coming Race* (1871)." *Deutsche Vierteljahrsschrift für Literaturwissenschaft und Geistesgeschichte* 45 (1971): 150–80.

Seifert, Hellmuth. *Bulwers Verhältnis zur Geschichte*. Borna-Leipzig: Grossbetrieb für Dissertationsdruck von Robert Noske, 1935.

Sheppard, Alfred Tresidder. *The Art and Practice of Historical Fiction*. London: Humphrey Toulmin, 1930.

Simmons, James C. "Bulwer and Vesuvius: The Topicality of *The Last Days of Pompeii*." *Nineteenth-Century Fiction* 24 (1969): 103–5.

————. "The Novelist as Historian: An Unexplored Tract of Victorian Historiography." *Victorian Studies* 14 (1971): 293–305.

Stevenson, Lionel. "Stepfathers of Victorianism." *Virginia Quarterly Review* 6 (1930): 251–67.

Stewart, C. Nelson. *Bulwer-Lytton as Occultist*. London: Theosophical Publishing House, 1927.

Sucksmith, Harvey Peter. *The Narrative Art of Charles Dickens: The Rhetoric of Sympathy and Irony in his Novels*. Oxford: Clarendon Press, 1970.

Taft, William Howard, IV. "Lytton as a Literary Critic." Ph.D. dissertation, Princeton University, 1942.

Tillotson, Kathleen. *Novels of the Eighteen-Forties*. Oxford: Oxford University Press 1961.

Wagner, Geoffrey. "A Forgotten Satire: Bulwer-Lytton's *The Coming Race*." *Nineteenth-Century Fiction* 19 (1965): 379–85.

Watts, Harold H. "Lytton's Theories of Prose Fiction." *PMLA* 50 (1935): 274–89.

Wolff, Robert Lee. *Strange Stories, and Other Explorations in Victorian Fiction*. Boston: Gambit, 1971.

Index

INDEX